The Official Luxology® modo® Guide

Dan Ablan

THOMSON

COURSE TECHNOLOGY

Professional ■ Technical ■ Reference

ISBN-10: 1-59863-068-7

ISBN-13: 978-1-59863-068-8

Library of Congress Catalog Card Number: 2005929817

Printed in the United States of America

07 08 09 10 11 BU 10 9 8 7 6 5 4 3 2 1

Publisher and General Manager, Thomson Course Technology PTR:
Stacy L. Hiquet

Associate Director of Marketing:
Sarah O'Donnell

Manager of Editorial Services:
Heather Talbot

Marketing Manager:
Heather Hurley

Executive Editor:
Kevin Harreld

Marketing Coordinator:
Adena Flitt

Project Editor/Copy Editor:
Cathleen D. Snyder

Technical Reviewer:
Greg Leuenberger

PTR Editorial Services Coordinator:
Erin Johnson

Interior Layout:
Shawn Morningstar

Cover Designer:
Mike Tanamachi

DVD-ROM Producer:
Brandon Penticuff

Indexer:
Katherine Stimson

Proofreader:
Gene Redding

THOMSON

COURSE TECHNOLOGY

Professional ■ Technical ■ Reference

Thomson Course Technology PTR, a division of Thomson Learning Inc.
25 Thomson Place ■ Boston, MA 02210 ■ http://www.courseptr.com

For Maria and Amelia

Foreword

I have known Dan Ablan for many years, and I am pleased to recommend this book to anyone who is interested in learning 3D or the modo software in particular. Dan is a meticulous writer who has a knack for understanding the essence of what needs to be explained to people who are learning how to use graphics software. I particularly like the way Dan employs real-world objects such as teacups and keys in his tutorials instead of just relying on primitive shapes. The images you will create as you use this book are things to be proud of.

We at Luxology have put similar care into the development of modo itself. We set a bar for ourselves that goes beyond making modo work; we work hard to make it truly usable. If you can invest the time, I am confident that modo can become a powerful and enjoyable way for you to create 3D models and images of any variety.

In addition to this book, there are resources on the Internet that will help you to get the most out of modo. For the latest on modo software and to join the community of people who use modo, please visit www.modo3d.com.

Sincerely,

Brad Peebler

President and Co-Founder

Luxology LLC

Acknowledgments

I think it's best to point out that none of you would be reading this book if it weren't for my beautiful, talented, generous, and completely understanding wife, Maria. When I was putting in 16- and 17-hour days working at the studio and trying to meet book deadlines (most of which I missed), she was right there supporting me. Next in line is my little girl, who was very patient while I worked on the laptop, and put up with me continually saying, "Just a minute." Hey Amelia, Lobesha!

Then, there is Mr. Dion Burgoyne at Luxology. Since the beginning, Dion has supported my efforts in getting up to speed with the latest version of the software, and he took time to answer questions throughout the book process. And, I can't thank Dion enough for the outstanding cover image he graciously supplied. Awesome work and a testament to the power of modo. Special thanks goes out to Brad Peebler. I've know Brad for many years, and he and I have been down this book road before. Thanks for all of the support and help, Brad!

When it came to technical editing this book, I knew who to trap—uh, I mean ask—right from the start. Greg Leuenberger from Sabertooth Productions (www.sabpro.com). Greg's efforts as a technical editor have been nothing less than stellar, and I can't thank him enough. Maybe I'll send him a Chicago pizza. There's no good pizza in Sunnyvale, is there, Greg? Additional thanks go out to Andrew Brown, who was instrumental in answering some questions I had in the beginning stages of the book. Thanks Andy! I can't forget to thank Philip Lawson for his excellent models, which he graciously donated to the book for all of you to use. We'll use his slick martini glass scene to learn some interesting rendering techniques.

I certainly can't wrap up this section without a big thanks to Kevin Harreld at Thomson Course Technology PTR for getting this book off the ground and putting up with my delays. Thank you to Cathleen Snyder, who made editing this book painless and entertaining all at the same time. How does she do it? Thank you Cathleen and the entire team at Thomson for the opportunity to write this book.

Lastly, thanks to the Luxology community. Everyone has been exceedingly supportive on the forums and in personal e-mails as this book process took nearly a year. Thank you for the well wishes. I hope you enjoy the book.

About the Author

Dan Ablan graduated from Morgan Park Academy (Chicago) in 1985. Originally planning a career in photojournalism, Dan's focus changed during his next four years at Valparaiso University. He ended up minoring in photojournalism and majoring in broadcast journalism. After an internship at WBBM-TV/CBS in Chicago, Dan began his career in television at WLFI-TV/CBS in Lafayette, Indiana, as a news photographer and editor. From there, he headed back to Valparaiso to become program manager for Prime Cable. Two years later, he accepted a job as a corporate video producer for a franchising corporation. Along the way, Dan discovered 3D animation, and within a year had formed his own part-time animation business out of his one-bedroom apartment. Dan Ablan is now president of AGA Digital Studios, Inc., a 3D animation and visual effects company in the Chicago area. AGA Digital has produced 3D visuals for broadcast, corporate, and architectural clients since 1994, as well as post-production services in conjunction with Post Meridian, LLC. Dan has created 3D animations for United Airlines, NASA, Northrop Grumman, Abbott Labs, and many more. In between animation jobs, Dan writes books on the subject. He is the author of many best-selling international books on 3D animation from New Riders Publishing (Peachpit): *LightWave Power Guide* (v5.0), *Inside LightWave 3D* (v5.5), *Inside LightWave 6, LightWave 6.5 Effects Magic, Inside LightWave 7*, and *Inside LightWave 8*. He coauthored *LightWave 8 Killer Tips*. He also is the author of *Digital Cinematography & Directing*, and he served as technical editor for *Digital Lighting & Rendering*. Dan was also a contributor to *After Effects 5.5 Magic* from New Riders Publishing. His latest books are *Inside LightWave v9* and *Digital Photography for 3D Imaging and Animation*.

Dan is the founder of 3D Garage.com (www.3dgarage.com), a Web site dedicated to 3D learning. He has written columns and articles for *LightWave Pro* magazine, *Video Toaster User* magazine, *3D Design* magazine, *3D World* magazine, and *NewTek Pro* magazine. Dan has been teaching seminars since 1995 across the country and at AGA Digital Studios, Inc. Some of the companies Dan has trained include Fox Television, ABC-TV New York City, CBS-TV Indianapolis, WTTW-TV PBS Chicago, Lockheed Martin, and many others.

In addition to his daily duties at AGA Digital Studios, Inc., Dan also served as editor-in-chief of *HDRI 3D* magazine (a magazine dedicated to animation and digital imaging) for two years.

Contents

Chapter 3
Working with the Tools   55

Chapter 4
modo 201/202 Jump Start   83

PART II
CREATING AND BUILDING 123

Chapter 5
Basic Building Blocks   125

Introduction

3D imagery is everywhere. In fact, there's more 3D work in television, movies, and even on the Internet than you realize. A good majority of "non-effects" films actually include many visual effects. Filmmakers use 3D imagery to add digital sets, open windows on buildings, add leaves to trees, or simply add birds to a scene. With the advances in technology and improvements in software performance, digital content creators have been able to visualize their dreams while controlling budgets.

In 2004, a new product hit the ground running, allowing 3D modelers and animators to reach even higher goals. Formed by the original programmers and team that built LightWave 3D, Luxology, LLC created what is considered to be the best 3D modeling package on the market. modo 103 not only made 3D modeling easy, but more fun than people ever imagined. A user coined the phrase "Model at the Speed of Thought." This is a phrase Luxology has adopted because it truly describes the power of the program. With the release of modo 201 and 202, the user has even greater power, all of which we'll cover in this book and on the included DVD-ROM. Evolution is inevitable, and it hasn't been more clear than with this current release from Luxology.

Getting the Most from This modo Guide

The Official Luxology modo Guide is designed to help you understand the power of the world's most powerful 3D modeler. This second-generation program now offers 3D painting and texturing, as well as advanced rendering capabilities. *The modo Guide* will hold your hand from starting the application to saving your final render. Unlike many books that simply talk about concepts and functionality, *The modo Guide* will have you actually working in the program. The book is designed in four sections: Part I, "Getting Started with modo 201/202"; Part II, "Creating and Building"; Part III, "Working Projects"; and Part IV, "More on Lighting and Rendering." To maximize this printed resource, it's recommended that you start at the beginning of the book and work your way through to the end. You'll begin by being introduced to the program, and before long you'll create a small project. Chapter 1 will introduce modo 202 and break down the program and its power. Chapter 2 takes you on a tour of the advanced user interface. From there, we'll break down the core concepts and work our way through the program. So even if you're experienced with modo, it's not a bad idea to take some time and go through the book from the beginning because you might pick up a tip or a trick you weren't aware of.

About the Creation of This Book

The Official Luxology modo Guide was written on a MacBook Pro, 2.0 Intel Core Duo with 2 Gigs of RAM and an ATI x1600 video card. Some portions were written on a Macintosh PowerBook G4 laptop with a 1.67-GHz processor, 2 Gigs of RAM, and a 128-MB ATI video card. Tutorials were tested for this book on a PowerBook G4 laptop, a Macintosh G5 desktop PowerPC, a Sony Vaio Pentium 4 PC running Windows XP Media Center operating system, and a Dell Optiplex 260 Pentium 4 PC running Windows XP Professional. Luxology has created an application that runs identically on both PC and Macintosh computers. The only difference you'll experience is based on the processor, RAM, and video graphics card you have installed on your system. There are a few keyboard variances, which will be noted.

Read the modo Manuals

The Official Luxology modo Guide is designed as a companion to the modo manual supplied with your purchased software. Read through the information provided by Luxology, and you'll get the greatest bang for your buck when it comes to mastering modo.

Experiment and Practice

Every once in a while, you might find yourself with some free time. Either at work in the afternoon, waiting for a render or a client call, or perhaps at home, late at night. Use those times to experiment with modo. Simply take a look around you and model what you see. How about starting with the computer monitor on your desk? There's no better reference than a physical object directly in front of you! Pay attention to the bevels, the depth of the buttons, and how the light reacts to these areas. Practice modeling the details and discover how easily modo handles the task. If you get stuck, keep going and work through the kinks. Before you know it, you'll be zipping through the interface, modeling almost anything you can imagine, while not worrying about finding the right tool. Before long, you'll be modeling at the speed of thought.

Now, I tried to make this book as informative as possible, but as you know, no single resource can be the only information you use. Although modo is a young product and this book is one of the first on the market, there certainly will be more coming, as happens with any software release. Another excellent way to get a grasp of this powerful software is by participating in Internet discussions and viewing training videos. The Luxology.com site has an excellent forum where you can not only ask questions, but also view others' work and expand your knowledge of what modo can do. Additionally, you can visit 3DGarage.com for up-to-date video training courseware for modo.

But don't just look to modo-specific software books and videos. There are more resources for learning animation, lighting, texturing, and rendering than you might realize. Principles in camera techniques, lighting techniques, and more can be applied in modo. I've compiled a list of additional resources, which you'll find in the appendixes at the back of this book.

Conventions Used in This Book

Throughout this book, you'll come across Note listings within the chapters. These provide you with additional information and helpful tips about the program. Any control area that opens will be referred to as a *panel*. Many panels have additional areas of control, which are called *tabs*, while buttons that have a small down arrow will be referred to as *drop-down menus*.

There's one more thing to remember: Always work with the Caps Lock key off! Throughout this book, you will come across many keyboard shortcuts, and there are significant differences between a lowercase shortcut and an uppercase shortcut. The essential and immediate shortcuts used regularly are assigned to lowercase keys, while less-used commands are assigned to uppercase keys. What's important to remember is that some of the uppercase commands are more complex functions, and if you're not prepared to execute such a command, you might get odd and unexpected results.

Lastly, when it comes to conventions and usage, can I give you one piece of advice? Stop clicking! Yes, that's right—stop clicking! When someone is learning software, any software, and he or she is not quite seeing the expected results, or there's no response from a tool, the user tends to click. Users often click anywhere, and in modo this could be a problem. For example, you've selected a group of polygons and you would like to rotate them all. However, after you thought you selected the Rotate tool, when you click and drag something else happens entirely. You click some more, and in your haste, you deselect the polygons. Now, you can undo and get back to your selection without much trouble. But the point is, work deliberately. Select a vertex, edge, polygon, light, or camera. Select a tool, click, and go. You'll find that not only will you learn the software faster, you'll do so with fewer problems.

System Considerations

Ah yes, the system question. People are always asking what the best system is to get. Should you spend $10,000 on a custom-built 3D workstation? What about dual 64-bit machines or quad processors? In the end, it comes down to your wallet and what works for you. But what is crucial and is often a mistake made by many—don't overdo the processor and forget the memory. You're better off getting a Pentium 4 2.7 GHz or a Mac G5 1.67 with two or three gigs of RAM, rather than the latest 4.0-GHz processor with only 512 MB or 1 Gig of RAM. Think of it this way: RAM (memory) is like money—you can never have too much. What's more, and very important for modo's best functionality, is the video card you use. Do you need to go out and spend $3,000 on the latest and greatest video card? No, not at all. If you've got it, by all means go for it. For the rest of us, a top-notch ATI or NVIDIA card with at least 128 MB of video memory will serve quite well. Be sure to check the compatibility and recommended video cards and drivers with Luxology at www.luxology.com.

Why This Book?

Unlike a book on Adobe Photoshop, a topic which has more published books than any one bookstore can shelve, this modo book is the first of its kind. A relatively new application, modo has already saturated the 3D market from hobbyists to professionals alike. Certainly, what you can create in modo is entirely up to you, and with version 202's new texturing and rendering capabilities, the possibilities are endless. You don't need to know 3D modeling to use this book, but if you do, you're a step ahead of everyone else. This book was created to introduce you to modo 202 and help guide you through the tools, interface, and controls available. To maximize the pages in the book, we'll use projects to help you learn and understand. Luxology has done a tremendous job of creating the modo 202 manual and additional learning materials, but this book was created to give you a succinct workflow from A to Z. For many, studying from a simple project to a complex one is more efficient. This book was written so you can learn the tools and what to do with them.

Who Am I?

Today, computer books are written by almost anyone. Some are good; some are not. I always tell people my books can be found in the bookstore right near the real books! In most cases, it doesn't matter who's writing the book—what matters is the content.

Before I entered the glamorous and fascinating world of 3D animation, I worked in a not-as-much-fun world of video production. After graduating college with a bachelor's degree in broadcast journalism, I promptly went to work for a very small CBS affiliate. If your idea of fun is standing in the center of Indiana with a 70-pound camera on your shoulder in the 20-degree Midwest cold, then I've got the referral!

For me, I wanted more, and I moved up to a program manager position for a large cable television outfit. There, I discovered 3D animation via NewTek's LightWave 3D and an Amiga computer. It was 1989, so you have to remember that today 3D is everywhere. Then, 3D was only prevalent in hugely expensive systems in the top video production studios, and mostly in an experimental state. Either way, one look at a small red apple rendering one pixel at a time (I think it took an hour or so), and I was hooked. From there, I produced corporate videos for a couple of years, and along the way submerged myself into 3D. In 1994, I went to work for an Amiga dealership, selling and training Video Toaster and LightWave systems. Also in 1994, I was fired from the Amiga dealership because Commodore stopped making Amigas. However, I had started doing 3D work on the side, and with the help of unemployment checks from the state of Illinois, I was able to forge ahead with my own business, AGA Digital Studios.

While creating 3D animations for corporate accounts such as Bosch and Kraft Foods, I also began submitting articles to the only LightWave publication at the time, *LightWave Pro*. From there, I wrote tutorials every month, and I also contributed to their sister publication, *Video Toaster User*. I was "Dr. Toaster," and I would answer questions for readers. (I did not choose the name of the column, by the way.) Avid Media Group, publishers of *Video Toaster User* and *LightWave Pro*, were bought out by Miller Freeman Publishing, so I started writing for a new magazine called *3D Design*. Around 1995, I met with a representative from Macmillan Publishing, and we discussed the idea of a LightWave book. They knew who I was through my articles in the trade magazines, and in 1996, the first book on LightWave was published, *LightWave Power Guide*, from New Riders Publishing.

Now, 12 years later, AGA Digital Studios, Inc. is located in the Chicago area, and we create animations for corporate and industrial clients such as United Airlines, NASA, Lockheed Martin, the FAA, Blue Cross and Blue Shield, Allstate, McDonald's Corp., and many others. In addition to daily animation work, in 2003 I founded a new division to AGA Digital, dedicated to 3D learning courses. 3D Garage.com is a training source with material that is presented as project-based courses. Visit www.3DGarage.com for more information.

The book you are reading represents my ninth book on 3D modeling and animation. For more information on my other books and photography, visit my Web site at www.danablan.com.

Words to Work By

It's truly amazing what you can do with a simple desktop computer (or laptop) and a few key software packages. Today's technology has grown beyond anyone's imagination, and it's only getting better—modo 202 is proof of that.

Whether you're a hobbyist or a professional in the field of 3D modeling and animation, you're in it because you enjoy what you do. You have a passion for creating. And although you might have a job or a client along the way who makes you want to quit the whole thing, deep down you know you can't. You know that your best work is yet to come, and *The Official Luxology modo Guide* is here to help.

Note

modo has so many great features, there simply wasn't enough room in this book to show you everything! So, head on over to www.courseptr.com/downloads and download the two bonus chapters that are part of this book.

Part I

Getting Started with modo 201/202

1

Interface Configurability

Most 3D programs have some ability to customize the interface. There are others that only allow you to add a button or change a color. However, Luxology's modo is an entirely different breed.

Built around a unique architecture, modo allows you to create a completely custom interface. Although colors and fonts remain primarily the same, the strength comes from the ability to rearrange panels and tool palettes in any way possible. You have the flexibility of quickly duplicating panels or starting with a completely blank interface and building your own from the ground up. What's more, modo understands your need for adjustments, and rearranging panels instantly changes them from listings to icons, depending on the size.

This chapter will introduce you to the modo 201/202 interface and run you through a few different ways you can configure and use the program. You'll learn how to create and save your own custom interface.

Note

The screenshots in this book were all taken in the modo 202 interface, which is slightly updated from the 201 version you might be using on your machine.
If you are currently running modo 201, the 202 upgrade is free (and 202 is faster!). Nevertheless, if you choose *not* to upgrade to 202, you will still find much value in the information covered in this book. Your interface will simply look a bit different than the images in this book.

Understanding the Basics

By this point, you most likely have worked with modo a bit. Either you've followed along with our Getting Started video tutorial from the book's DVD, or you've simply clicked through the interface and tried a few tutorials from the resources provided by Luxology when you purchased the software. However, this chapter will start by assuming you've not used the program at all, and it will ramp up from there.

When you start modo 201/202, you're presented with a default interface, as shown in Figure 1.1.

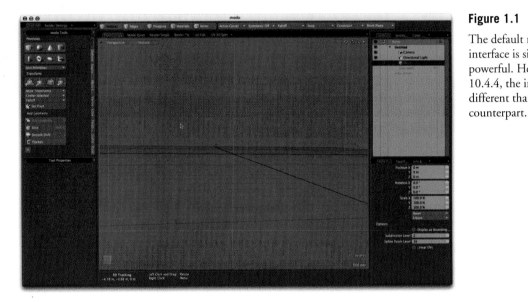

Figure 1.1

The default modo 201/202 interface is simple, yet powerful. Here on Mac OS X 10.4.4, the interface looks no different than its Windows PC counterpart.

To begin understanding the interface, you first need to understand viewports.

Viewports

Viewports are literally your windows to the world when it comes to modo. You can have as many as you like, and you are not limited to where you place them. A viewport can contain a model view, such as the large main work area you see in Figure 1.1. Or, a viewport can contain lists for objects, textures, or images. Everything in modo's interface is built within a viewport.

3D Model View

3D workspaces, tool bars, Item Lists—what does it all mean? Well, if you consider that first you have a viewport, you can understand that you have the ability to add whatever view you want to that viewport. For example, consider the main workspace in the default view shown in Figure 1.2. This is a viewport with a 3D Model view applied. When a 3D Model view is applied to a viewport, you have what looks like Figure 1.2. There are viewport position, rotation, and zoom controls automatically added to the top-right corner and a 3D position icon automatically added to the bottom-left corner.

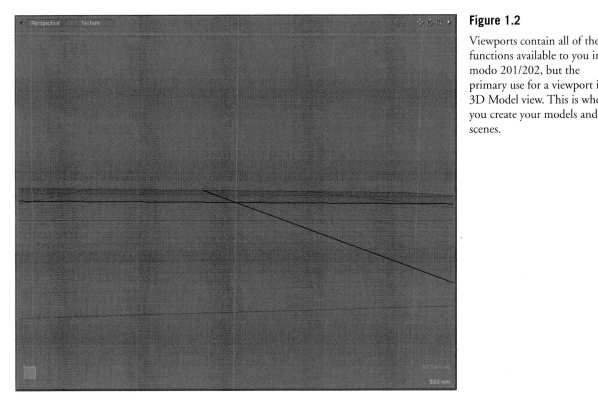

Figure 1.2

Viewports contain all of the functions available to you in modo 201/202, but the primary use for a viewport is a 3D Model view. This is where you create your models and scenes.

The 3D position icon that appears in a 3D Model view is your visual compass to axis control in modo. It is sort of a GPS (*Global Positioning System*) for your program! Here, you can determine the primary axis. That is, it will help you model in one large viewport. For example, in most 3D applications, if you want to build a box that is flat on the ground, you'd work in a Top, or Y Axis, view. In modo you can do that, but a faster way to work is to rotate your view so that the 3D position icon at the bottom-left of the viewport is highlighted to the Y axis. When you draw out a flat box, it will be lying flat on the X and Z axes. The axis keeps you oriented in 3D space. However, the semi-transparent white plane represents the orientation of the workplane. The workplane constrains your transformation and object creation tools. This might sound confusing, but as soon as you start working with the tools in Chapter 3, "Working with the Tools," it will make perfect sense and you'll wonder how you got along without it!

The viewport style buttons appear at the top-left of the 3D Model view. There are two buttons; if you click either, you'll be presented with viewport style choices. The first button on the left currently reads *Perspective*, informing you that you're working in a Perspective view. This is the Viewport Type list. With a Perspective view, you can rotate around the entire 3D scene and also have control of your tools on all axes. The second button sets your viewport style. You can view your work as wireframes, solid objects, textured, or even cell-shaded for a cartoon-like look.

There are quite a few viewport styles to choose from, and each will be appropriate at some point in your modo career. You'll use many of the viewport styles in the tutorials in this book. Figure 1.3 shows the choices available for both viewport style buttons at the top-left of the 3D Model view.

The grids you see in the 3D Model view are your references for modeling, rotating, moving, and more. There are both horizontal and vertical grids; you'll see how these are used in Chapter 2, "Editors, Action Centers, and Work Planes."

Figure 1.3

A 3D Model view also has viewport style controls. The list on the left lets you choose your viewport type; the list on the right determines your viewport display style, such as wireframe or shaded.

Tool Viewports

A viewport is nothing more than a blank panel—sort of a canvas to which you can assign work elements. At the top-left of the modo default interface, you'll see a panel of tools labeled *modo Tools*, as shown in Figure 1.4.

Perhaps for some reason you don't want this viewport to be a modo Tools viewport. No problem! Suppose you want to change the modo Tools viewport to a Filter Editor. Look at the right-facing triangle at the top-right corner of the desired viewport, as shown in Figure 1.5. Click the triangle; as you can see in Figure 1.6, there is a slew of things you can change this panel into. If you select Filter Editor, you'll see the viewport change, as shown in Figure 1.7.

Figure 1.4

One of the main work areas within modo is the modo Tools viewport.

Figure 1.5

To change a viewport, click the right-facing triangle in the upper-right corner of the desired viewport.

Figure 1.6

When you click the triangle, you see a huge list of options for your viewport.

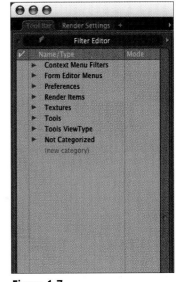

Figure 1.7

Choosing one of these options, such as Filter Editor, changes your viewport from a modo Tools viewport to a Filter Editor viewport.

As you can see, it's pretty easy to change viewports to anything you like. Perhaps instead of the Filter Editor, you can choose the Preferences or Event Log. It's totally up to you. You can even make this small modo Tools viewport into an additional 3D Model view, like you see in the main window of the interface.

Go back to the triangle drop-down list and change the viewport back to a modo Tools viewport. You can also do this by simply going to the Layout menu and choosing Layouts, 201/202 Default Layout.

Copy a Viewport

Perhaps you want a copy of a viewport—maybe you'd like to have two sets of the Item List, found on the right side of the interface. You can add a viewport and change it to what you like, or you can simply copy the existing viewport. Try this out:

1. In the main view of the interface, you'll see the large 3D Model view, as shown earlier in Figure 1.2. This is the scene area where you'll build your models. Hold the Ctrl key on your keyboard and click the tiny dot, the thumb, in the top-left of the viewport, as shown in Figure 1.8. This will duplicate the viewport. If you click and swipe left or right, the viewport splits horizontally. If you click and swipe up or down, the viewport splits vertically (see Figure 1.9).

2. Once this copy is made, you can click the right-facing triangle in the upper-right corner, as already mentioned, and change the viewport to anything you like—perhaps a list of images you'll use for texturing objects. Now, one more thing to know about the tiny dot in the top-left of the viewport. (Well, two things, really.) First, right-click on this dot and you'll see a list of options, as shown in Figure 1.10.

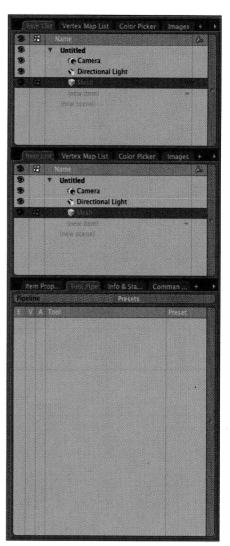

Figure 1.9

Holding the Ctrl key and clicking the dot in the upper-left corner of the viewport makes an instant copy.

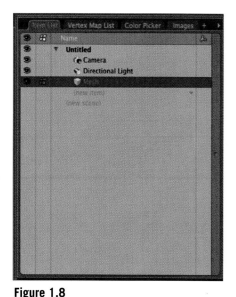

Figure 1.8

The dot at the top-left of the viewport, known as the thumb, is pretty powerful, allowing you to instantly split or duplicate viewports.

Look closely at the list. You'll see that you can duplicate, copy, detach, or even delete a viewport. What's more, you can save the viewport, which is pretty cool. Take some time and click these different options to see the results. Remember, you can always go back to the original viewport by choosing the 201/202 default layout from the Layout menu at the top of the interface.

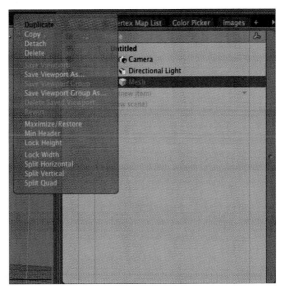

Figure 1.10

Right-click on the dot in the upper-left corner of the viewport, and you'll find a list of options.

Tip

If you happen to change to a viewport style that eliminates the little dot in the upper-left corner, don't think that you'll be unable to access the options. You can still right-click to get the options; however, you'll have to right-click directly on the upper-left corner of the viewport. The trick is to move your mouse to the upper edge of the viewport—when you see an orange rim highlight the viewport, you're good to go! Right-click at that point to access the options. If your viewport has Min Header checked, the headers, including the thumb button, will be minimized. Uncheck this setting in the Viewport Controls for the particular viewport to regain header information. Viewport Controls are accessed by clicking the small triangle at the top-right of each viewport.

Tabbed Viewports

Take a close look at the top-right of the modo interface. Assuming your modo interface is set to a 201/202 default layout, you should see an orange highlighted listing named Item List. Next to it is Vertex Map List, and next to that is Color Picker. These headings are called *tabbed viewports*. Figure 1.11 shows two tabs.

Figure 1.11

Tabbed viewports are noticeable in the 201/202 default layout, such as those at the top-left of the interface, for Tool Bar and Render Settings.

You can have as many tabbed viewports as you want. For example, Figure 1.11 shows two default tabbed viewports that allow you to change your viewport from a tool bar to render settings with the click of the mouse. The benefit of tabbed viewports is that you don't need multiple viewports open to access tools. For example, you're not always going to be using render settings, so why have the viewport taking up valuable screen real estate? Figure 1.12 shows the default tabbed viewports; currently selected is the Item List.

Figure 1.12

The default tabbed viewports show tabbed areas including Item List, Vertex Map List, and Color Picker.

As you might have guessed, clicking any one of these tabbed viewports changes the viewport.

Custom Layouts

Now that you are somewhat familiar with the viewport panels in modo 201/202, you should also be aware of how to arrange them. This first section will guide you through rearranging the interface, and then you'll follow along with a project to build your own interface from the ground up and save it.

1. Make sure you're working with a default modo 201/202 interface. Go to the Layout menu and choose Layouts, 201/202 Default Layout.

2. Click the Tool Bar tab at the top-left of the modo interface, if it's not already selected.

3. Hold the Ctrl key and click any of the primitives, such as the torus (or donut, if you're from Chicago). What you'll see is a perfect ring added to the main viewport. This Ctrl-click command adds a 1 Meter primitive to the viewport. It is a really easy way to add instant boxes, balls, discs, and so on for further modeling—or, in this case, interface testing.

4. With the torus in the viewport, press the **a** key. The object will fit to view, as shown in Figure 1.13.

5. Now that there is some geometry in the 3D viewport, click the right-facing triangle at the top-right corner of the 3D viewport, as shown in Figure 1.14.

6. When you click the triangle, you'll see a long list of viewport options. Here, you can change a viewport to a Tool Properties panel or an Input Editor—whatever you like. This tiny triangle lives in the upper-right corner of all viewports, so you can change any of them just as easily. For now, in the list that appears, choose the Render Tri setting, as shown in Figure 1.15.

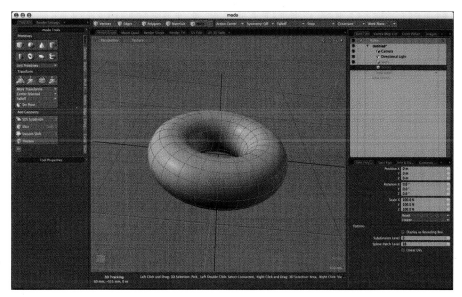

Figure 1.13

Holding the Ctrl key and then clicking on a primitive shape instantly creates an object in the 3D viewport. Pressing the **a** key fits that object to view.

When you click the Render Tri viewport option, your current 3D Model viewport changes to three views: a Preview viewport at the top-left showing a render, a Camera view at the top-right, and a Perspective view in the larger centered window. Figure 1.16 shows the change.

Figure 1.14

Click the right-facing arrow in the upper-right corner of the 3D viewport to change the viewport layout.

Figure 1.15

Clicking the right-facing triangle (Viewport Controls button) in the upper-right corner of a viewport offers a range of viewport choices, such as the Render Tri option.

Tip

If your render (Preview) doesn't appear right away, click and drag the Zoom, Rotate, or Move tool in the upper-right corner of the Camera view.

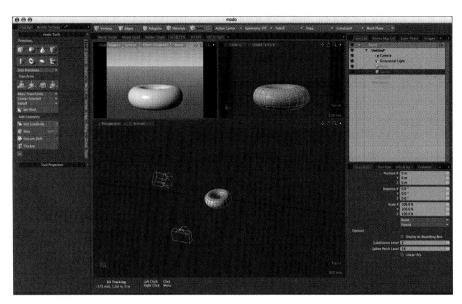

Figure 1.16

The Render Tri viewport setting changes your current viewport—in this case, the 3D Model view—to a Preview (render), Camera, and Perspective view all in one.

Tip

If you don't see the camera and light icons in the Perspective view, click the viewport style button in the top-left of the particular viewport, then go to Visibility Options, and you'll see a Show Cameras option and a Show Lights option. Figure 1.17 shows the menu. However, a quicker way to adjust viewport options is to simply press **o** (not zero) on your keyboard. This calls up a floating viewport options panel. Move your mouse off of the panel to remove it.

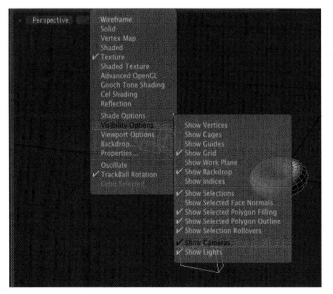

Figure 1.17

If you want to see your light and camera icons in the Perspective view, make sure you set the Visibility Options to Show Cameras and Show Lights.

7. Take the layout a step further. Click the Color Picker tab at the top-right of the modo interface. You'll see modo's cool Color Picker appear in that particular viewport.

8. Carefully move the mouse up to the top-left of the viewport, toward the little dot mentioned earlier in the chapter. You'll also see an orange frame appear around the viewport, as shown in Figure 1.18.

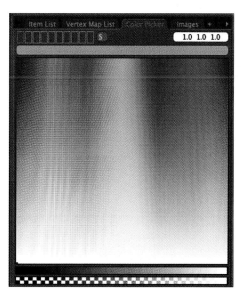

Figure 1.18

Move the mouse to the top-left of the Color Picker viewport until an orange frame appears around the edge.

9. Click and hold your left mouse button on that little dot in the upper-left corner of the viewport. Then, as you're holding the mouse, drag the viewport over between the Camera and iView (render) viewports at the top of the screen. You'll see an orange line appear between the viewport panels when you're locked in, as shown in Figure 1.19. When you see it, let go of the mouse, and your viewport will be relocated. Figure 1.20 shows the moved viewport.

If you look carefully at the top of the Color Picker viewport, you'll notice that the tabbed viewports remain. Your Item List and Vertex Map List are also moved, along with the Color Picker. But suppose you want to still have your Item List at the top-right where it originally was, but you want to leave the Color Picker in this new position.

10. Click on the Item List tab of the Color Picker viewport.

11. Click and hold the mouse on the Item List tab and drag it over to the spot where it was originally located (or anywhere else you want). You'll see that familiar orange line appear, signifying where your new viewport position will be. Release the mouse when you find that new position, and *voila*! Your Item List is now its own viewport outside of the tabbed viewport. Figure 1.21 shows the moved viewport.

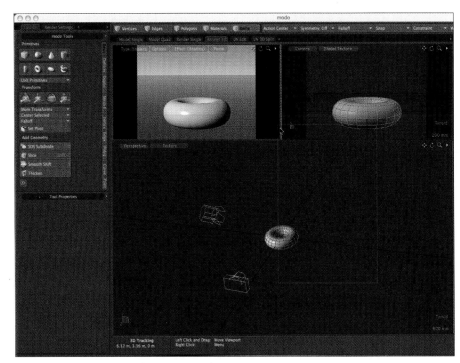

Figure 1.19

Move the viewport over until you see an orange line appear between the Camera and iView viewports. Letting go of the mouse when you see this line means that's where your moved viewport will reside.

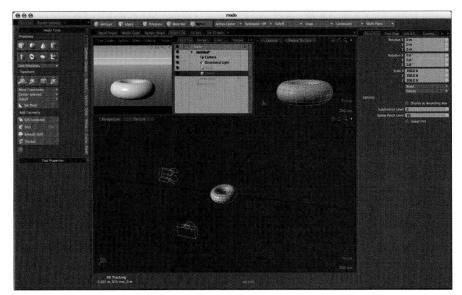

Figure 1.20

The Color Picker viewport is now moved and positioned between the Camera and iView viewports.

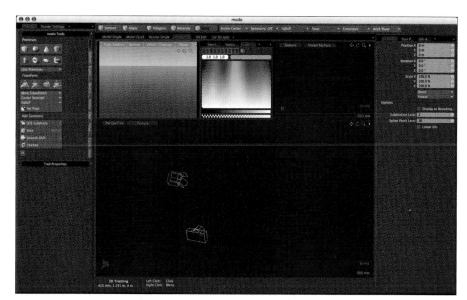

Figure 1.21

Clicking and dragging from the tabbed viewport listing pulls that particular viewport out of the tabbed viewport list, allowing you to reposition it.

Tip

So what if you want to make a non-tabbed viewport list a tabbed viewport? Click that little right-facing triangle at the top-right of the panel and choose Applications, Tabbed Viewport.

12. Oh no! You wanted that Item List as part of the tabbed viewport after all? Not to worry. Back over at the Color Picker viewport, you'll see a tiny plus mark to the right of the tabbed listings, as shown in Figure 1.22.

13. Click the plus sign to see the list of options, and then choose Item List from the Data Lists category, as shown in Figure 1.23.

Figure 1.22

When you move the mouse over the plus sign of a tabbed viewport, you'll see a New Tab listing appear. Click the plus sign to add a new tab in the viewport.

Figure 1.23

To add another tab to a tabbed viewport, just click the plus sign at the top-right of the column and choose what you want.

14. Now that your new layout is in place, how about saving it? Go up to the Layout menu and choose Save As, as shown in Figure 1.24.

15. In the panel that appears, enter a name such as My Cool Layout and click OK, as shown in Figure 1.25.

16. Any time you want to recall this layout, go to the Layout menu, select Layouts, and choose My Cool Layout, as shown in Figure 1.26.

Figure 1.24

To save your new layout, click the Layout menu and choose Save As.

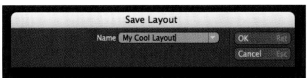

Figure 1.25

Enter a name for your layout and click OK.

Figure 1.26

Any time you want to recall the layout you've created, just choose it from the Layout menu.

As you can see, configuring viewports is not that difficult. It's actually kind of fun rearranging panels and tools to fit your own workflow. But what if this entire setup is just not for you? Maybe you're sort of a "roll your own" type of person. No problem! Read on to configure your own custom interface. Well, it won't be your custom interface—it'll actually be mine—but the next section will show you how to create a modo interface from the ground up.

Tip

Try choosing other layouts that the Luxology team has provided for you. You can always go back to the default 201/202 layout by selecting it from the Layout list. However, if you make a change to the default layout, modo remembers. Here's the trick: Go to the File drop-down menu at the top of the interface and select Reset. The layout will go back to the default settings that it had before you modified it.

Roll Your Own Interface

Suppose you're the type of person who always orders off the menu, a person who takes the road less traveled, or who simply wants things his or her way. Luxology has designed modo so you can configure it how you like. Perhaps you have a smaller workspace and only use a few modeling tools. No problem. Or, maybe you're lucky enough to be working on a new 30-inch LCD display. Either way, modo can accommodate you.

1. Start modo and don't worry about what layout you're currently using. From the Layout menu at the top of the interface, select Clear, as shown in Figure 1.27.

   Selecting Clear from the Layout menu obviously clears your interface, so now you have a blank slate to work with. Figure 1.28 shows the empty workspace.

Figure 1.27

Select Clear from the Layout menu.

Figure 1.28

Choosing Clear from the Layout menu does what it says—it clears your interface!

2. When you build your own interface, you need to take into consideration what tools you need most. And remember, you can make as many interface options as you want, such as a power-modeling interface with only your key modeling tools or a power-render interface with just a few render buttons and an item preview window. It's up to you. For now, you can begin by adding a new window from the Layout menu, as shown in Figure 1.29. You'll be presented with a blank viewport, as shown in Figure 1.30.

Figure 1.29

To begin making your own interface, select New Window from the Layout menu.

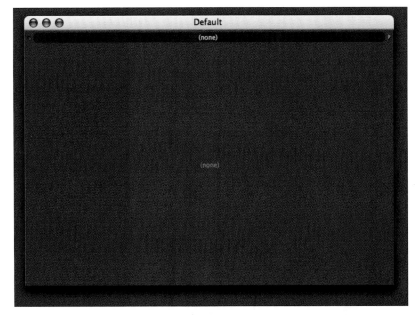

Figure 1.30

Adding a new window from the Layout menu presents you with a blank viewport.

Tip

In the Layout menu, you'll also see an option called New Palettes. The only difference between a palette and a window is that palettes can be instantly hidden by pressing the (`) key. This is the key directly to the left of the number 1 key at the top of your keyboard. It shares the key with the tilde character.

3. One of the first things you usually do in modo is build a basic primitive shape or curve. So, click the right-facing triangle at the top-right of the empty viewport and choose Toolbars, modo Tools, as shown in Figure 1.31. Figure 1.32 shows how the panel looks once the modo tools are added.

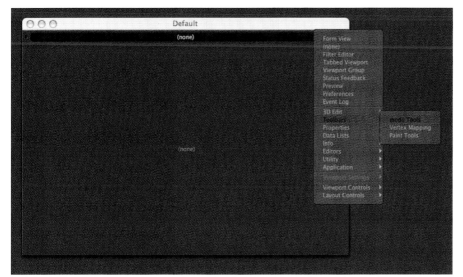

Figure 1.31

To begin creating your own interface, add a modo Tools viewport.

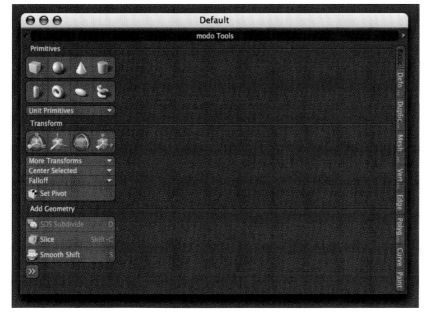

Figure 1.32

A modo Tools viewport has been created, but now has to be configured into the interface.

4. Now that you have a viewport to work with, you can start positioning it within your interface. Move the mouse to the tiny dot in the upper-left corner of the new modo Tools viewport. You'll see an orange frame appear around the viewport. Click and drag the viewport up to the very left of the modo main interface, until you see an orange line appear, as shown in Figure 1.33.

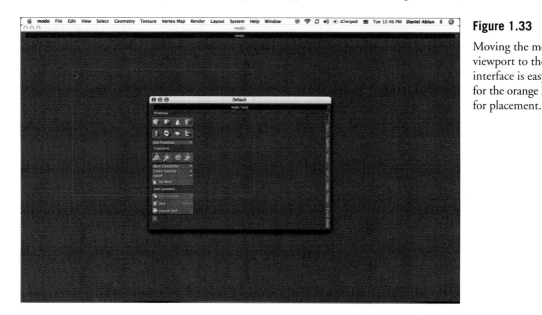

Figure 1.33

Moving the modo Tools viewport to the left of the interface is easy—just look for the orange line to appear for placement.

5. When you see the orange line appear, let go of the mouse button. The modo Tools viewport will be placed in the interface, as shown in Figure 1.34.

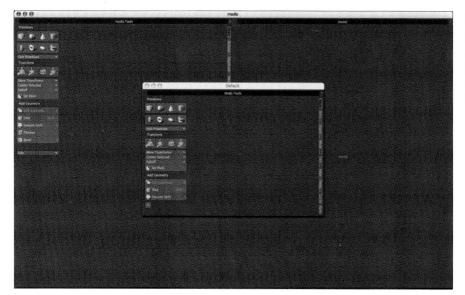

Figure 1.34

Moving the modo Tools viewport to the left of the interface and letting go of the mouse positions the viewport in the interface.

6. Click in the main interface, and then move the mouse to the right edge of the modo Tools viewport. Your mouse will change to a double-headed arrow icon. Click and drag to decrease the width of the modo Tools viewport.

7. Because the modo interface currently has no other viewports, you only will have the option to move the viewport to the top, left, bottom, or right side of the interface. You'll see that your original viewport still exists. Click the right-facing triangle in the upper-right of the floating viewport to open the Viewport Options and choose Properties, Tool Properties, as shown in Figure 1.35. The Tool Properties panel will be blank at this point because no tools are selected. When you select a tool such as the Move tool (**w** on the keyboard), the Tool Properties become active.

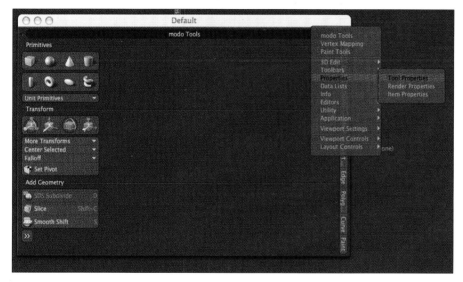

Figure 1.35

Your original viewport remains floating outside of the main interface, so change this to a Tool Properties viewport.

8. As you did in Steps 4 and 5, click and drag the new viewport to a position in the interface. Remember not to let go of the left mouse button until you see that familiar orange line appear. This will help you align the viewport. Figure 1.36 shows the Tool Properties viewport positioned to the right of the modo Tools viewport.

9. Now that you have a few viewports in place, close the floating viewport.

10. In Figure 1.36, you can see that the modo Tools and Tool Properties viewports are placed on the left side of the interface. On the right side is a blank viewport. Click the right-facing triangle at the top-right of this blank viewport and choose 3D Edit, 3D Model View, as shown in Figure 1.37.

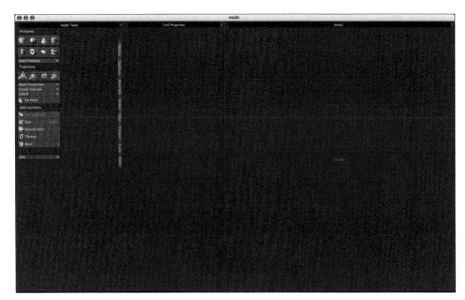

Figure 1.36

The Tool Properties viewport is positioned in the interface next to, rather than under, the modo Tools viewport.

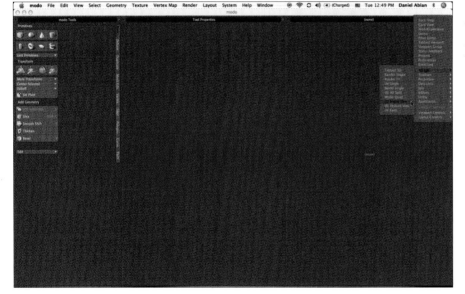

Figure 1.37

You can choose to add a 3D Model view to the large viewport within the interface.

11. Choosing 3D Model view converts this large blank viewport into a 3D Model view, and, if you notice, you can change the viewport style here to Camera, Top, Side, and so on. It currently defaults to Perspective. The viewport Move, Rotate, and Zoom controls are automatically loaded with this particular viewport at the top-right. Figure 1.38 shows the addition.

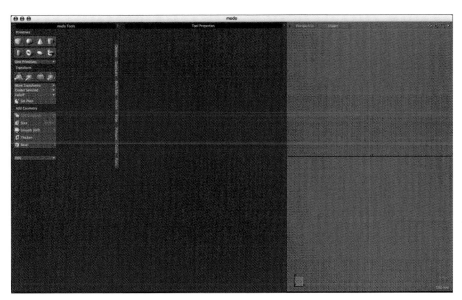

Figure 1.38

Changing the large blank viewport in the interface to a 3D Model view creates a nice large workspace for modeling.

12. You could use an Item List to see what object, lights, and cameras you have in your scene. Add a new window from the Layout menu. Make this new window an Item List by clicking the right-facing triangle at the top-right corner of the panel and choosing Data Lists, Item List, as shown in Figure 1.39.

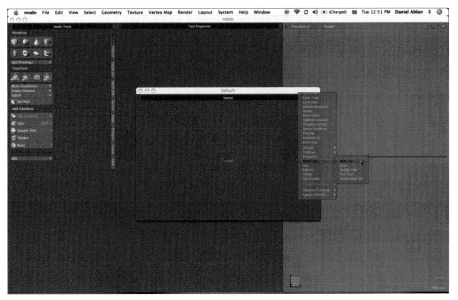

Figure 1.39

Create a new viewport and make it an Item List to see what objects, lights, and cameras are in your setup.

13. Position the new Item List interface above the 3D Model view, as in Figure 1.40.

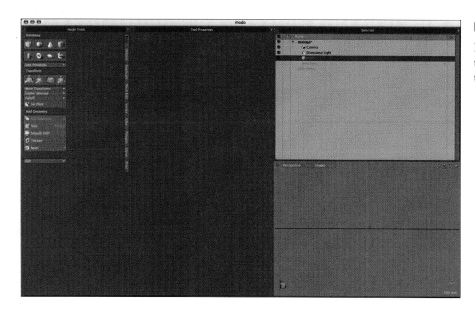

Figure 1.40

Position the new viewport into the layout by dragging it above the 3D Model view.

14. Scale the size of the Item List viewport by clicking and dragging the separation bar between it and the 3D Model view.

15. How about one more viewport? Add a new window from the Layout menu. Make it an Item Preview from the right-facing triangle menu at the top-right of the viewport. Then, position the new viewport to the right of the Item List. When you click and drag the viewport, you'll see the familiar orange bar appear, but if you carefully move the mouse, you'll see the bar jump between the right side of the Item List and the right side of the entire interface. Figure 1.41 shows the newly positioned viewport.

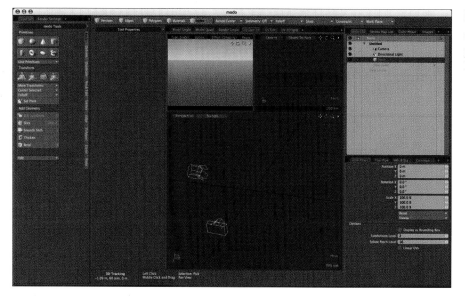

Figure 1.41

Create one more viewport and position it to the right of the Item List.

16. Choose Save As from the Layout menu and give your new custom layout a name.

As you can see, creating and rearranging viewport panels in modo is pretty easy. The interface setup you've created here is not really that exciting, but you can do much better on your own! Remember that you can add a Color Picker, a clips list to view what images are loaded, and so on. And, if you want to save space in a particular viewport, create a tabbed viewport. Additionally, remember that you can right-click on the little dot at the top-left of a viewport to detach it, delete it, copy it, and more.

Tip

If you want to share your configurations with other modo users, go to the File menu and choose Config (configuration) Export. To import a saved configuration file, either from a previous work session or from someone else, choose File, then Config Import.

As mentioned earlier, you can create a new palette rather than a new window. The only difference is that the palette can be instantly hidden with the ` key (on the tilde key). So if you create an entirely new interface, you can have a toolbar in a viewport that floats, rather than one that is locked to the interface. To do this, create a new palette from the Layout menu, and then add the desired tool set to it. Then don't put it into the interface. When you want to hide the panel, press the ` key. It's kind of a cool way to work—you can pull up one or many viewports with the click of a button. Again, it all depends on what you like, what screen real estate you have, and so on.

You've only scratched the surface of modo 201/202's configurability, so read on to Chapter 2 to learn about the customization you can perform with Form Editors, Key Editors, pie menus, and much more.

2

Editors, Action Centers, and Work Planes

Chapter 1 highlighted the ease of configurability with modo 201/202. But simply adding, changing, and rearranging viewports is just the tip of the iceberg when it comes to customizing your workflow. Rearranging the interface is great, no doubt, but to really get under the hood and make some modifications to the program to fit your specific likes and dislikes, you need to learn about the Input Editor and Form Editor. Additionally, there are certain preferences you can modify to fit your needs. This chapter will cover these options.

From there, you'll learn about the Action Center and Work Planes. The next step in your modo career is to understand how modo 201/202 allows you to have complete control over your vertices, edges, and polygons.

Preferences

Preferences in most programs are simple things such as file save locations, menu bar inclusions, and so on. In modo, there's a lot more to the preferences than you might think. This section will give you an overview of the Preferences panel and suggest when and why you should visit these controls. You can refer to your modo 201/202 manual supplied to you from Luxology. The manual has very specific tool information and is a great reference.

Take a look at Figure 2.1, which shows the Preferences panel. You access this panel by selecting Preferences from the System menu at the top of the interface.

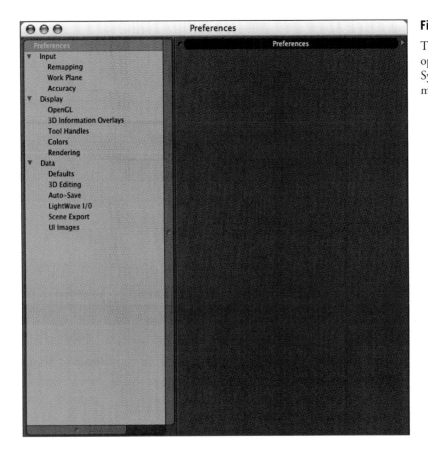

Figure 2.1

The Preferences panel upon opening, selected from the System menu at the top of the modo 201/202 interface.

Input Preferences

On the left side of the panel, you'll see three categories for Input, Display, and Data. These three main categories give you the power to change underlying preferences, which can truly change the way you work. Normally, you'll keep most of these at their defaults, but occasionally you might need a tweak or two, so this section will give you the rundown on each category.

Remapping

Click the Remapping listing under the Input category. You'll see variables pop up on the right side of the Preferences panel, as shown in Figure 2.2.

Here, you can change preferences, such as the maximum undo level, or select the type of input device you're using, such as a mouse or tablet. Another key preference here is the Input Presets selection. Click this drop-down menu and you'll be able to change modo's keyboard input commands to that of your favorite program, such as LightWave, Cinema4D, Maya, and others, as shown in Figure 2.3.

Figure 2.2

Select the Remapping listing, and the associated variables appear on the right of the panel.

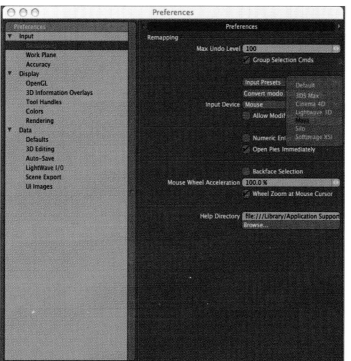

Figure 2.3

With so many options available to change in modo's presets, there's one initial preference you might be interested in—the Input Presets setting.

However, we're not going to be using these input presets in the book—we're working strictly with modo's own default input presets. Why? It's often better to learn a program natively so that you understand the tools and workflow fully. Then, once you're comfortable with the program, you can configure it any way you like.

Work Plane

Another key area within the Input category in the Preferences panel is the Work Plane options. Here, you can set a preferred plane bias, as well as the ability to lock the plane. You're probably asking yourself, what's a Work Plane? Ah, good question, young grasshopper! Work Planes are a powerful workflow enhancement that will be discussed in detail later in this chapter. But, to give you an introduction, the Work Plane in modo affects all mesh editing you do. It gives you control over alignment of various operations, such as Align to Selection or Align to Geometry. You might have seen many modo demos either in person or as preview videos on the Internet. In those videos, you probably saw that the demo person was working in a single viewport. While most 3D modeling programs work in a quad view, and modo offers that to you, the Work Plane enables you to work in a large single viewport. The Work Plane constrains your translation and object creation tools, making it very easy to work in a single viewport.

Accuracy

Depending on how you like to work, modo gives you the ability to work in measurements of metric, English, or SI (system internationale). Figure 2.4 shows the available options.

When you choose a specific unit system, such as metric, modo allows you to choose a default unit to work with. In the case of Figure 2.4, the unit value is set to Meters. This means that overall measurements throughout the program are based on this, such as the size of a cube or the movement of a mesh on the Y axis, and so on.

The Accuracy controls also give you options for Light Unit System. These two values are Radiometric and Photometric. Photometric measurements of light are based on luminance values, whereas radiometric is based on radiance values. With photometric values, every wavelength is measured according to how visible it is, such as a bright white box or a light bulb. Radiometric measurements are based on what is called *unweighted power*. The human eye responds better to green light than red. This means that a green source in your scene will have a higher luminous value than the same red source. The calculations modo performs when it comes to photometric or radiometric light unit systems can also be understood as the difference between watts (radiometric) and lumens (photometric).

Figure 2.4

How you work is just as important as what you work on. The accuracy with which you perform your actions can be adjusted in the Accuracy category of the Preferences panel.

The Accuracy settings allow you to change how coordinates are rounded off when set throughout the program—none to normal, fine, and fixed. Depending on what you're modeling, you might want to work with specific values.

Finally, modo has many values that you can adjust, obviously. You can tell the program to use a 0% to 100% scale, or 0 to 1.0 if you'd like.

Display Preferences

Probably some of the most used preference settings you'll change are the Display Preferences, as shown in Figure 2.5.

Many of the variables here can change often depending on what you're working on. Also, depending on the strength of your computer, you might want to adjust some of these values.

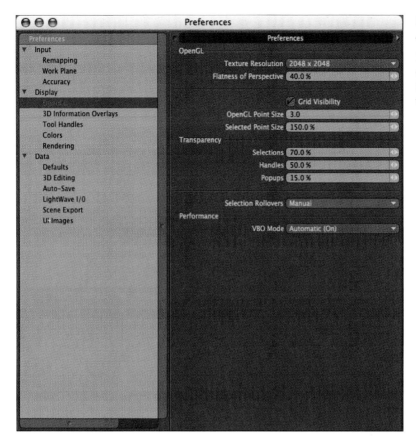

Figure 2.5

The Display category of the Preferences panel offers more of the most common controls for your everyday modo workflow.

OpenGL

OpenGL is an open graphics language method for computer displays. This widely distributed multiplatform function is an industry standard for computer games, 2D and 3D graphics, and even basic operating system functions. modo's OpenGL settings allow you to set a default texture resolution from 64×64 pixels up through 4096×4096. The more powerful your video card, the higher you can set this value. When you use textures and images in your 3D scene applied to models either as texture maps, normal maps, bump maps, and so on, the quality of the display is set here. This setting does not affect the render quality, but only the display.

You can control the flatness of perspective within the OpenGL settings in the Preferences panel. Essentially, what this setting does is change the amount of perspective in modo's Perspective viewport. Figure 2.6 shows a default cube in the Perspective view with a Flatness of Perspective value set to 0%. Figure 2.7 shows the same view with a Flatness of Perspective value set to 100%.

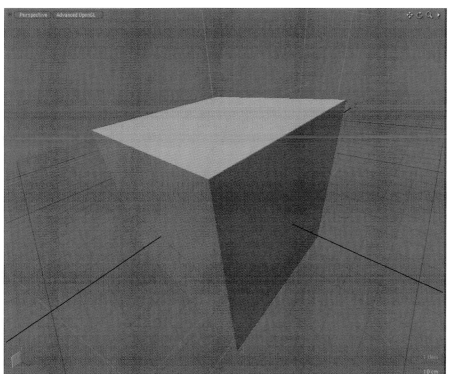

Figure 2.6

A Flatness of Perspective value set to 0% creates a wide-angle view in a Perspective viewport.

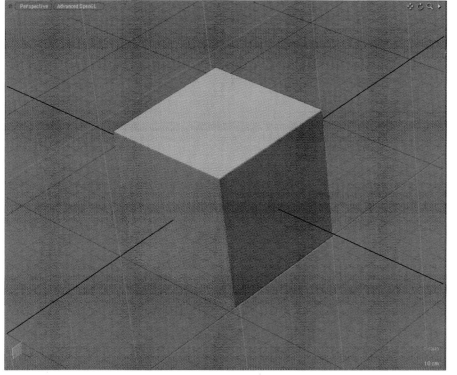

Figure 2.7

A Flatness of Perspective value set to 100% drastically changes the Perspective viewport.

Other OpenGL settings allow you to turn the grid on and off with Grid Visibility. You can change the OpenGL point size, as well as the selected point size. Again, these values don't affect your final render or model, simply their display.

When it comes to OpenGL transparency in modo, you can change preference values for selections, handles, and pop-ups. The default values work quite well, but perhaps you'll want to change your control handles' visibility, such as those for move and rotation. If so, change the transparency for them here.

You might have noticed when working in modo that moving your mouse over parts of an object automatically highlights the vertices, edges, and polygons, giving you easy direction for selecting the right element. The way this selection rollover happens can also be changed in the Preferences panel.

Your system might not be the latest and greatest, or maybe it is! But even so, at times you might find your performance lacking. modo offers control of the VBOs, or vertex buffer objects, with the VBO Mode settings. You should know that VBOs will help performance, not hinder it, in terms of both OpenGL and quicker viewport switching. If you set it to Automatic, modo won't dynamically change the VBO's on/off—it will simply default to on. Typically with a newer NVIDIA or ATI card, you're fine with VBO set to on (or Automatic), but there's a certain line of NVIDIA cards that needs it off. Also, some older ATI cards and things such as Intel integrated chipsets and Wildcat cards might not perform as well with VBO set to on. If VBO is set to off, you will lose some performance; however, video cards that VBOs don't work with are not strong performers to begin with. Also, if you change the VBO type, you have to restart modo for the effect to take place.

3D Information Overlays

A simple selection of preferences here allows you to turn on or off the overlays for the current selection, current tool, grid size, and morph map. What this means is that if you look at the bottom-right of the viewport when working on a model, you'll see values such as the number of polygons, vertices, or edges selected, as well as the tool you're using and so on. This the 3D Information Overlay, and if these values annoy you while you're working, turn them off.

Tool Handles

Tool handles are a very important part of the modo workflow, as you'll see throughout this book. They give you access to specific axis control for tool operations. Because of this, there are a number of preferences you can set to work them. You have the ability to change the size of the points on tool handles, including large points (pixels) and small points (pixels). Additionally, you can change the values for Handle Line Width and the Handle Line Hit Width. The "hit" value you see within these preferences is the pixel area that defines the handle. A large hit size makes it a little easier to select a tool handle when you move the mouse over it. The Handle Scale values change the visible size of the tool handles in the 3D viewports. If you selected the Rotate tool, for example, and changed the Handle Scale value, the rotational rings defining the Rotate values would be drawn larger or smaller, depending on what percentage you've entered in the Scale field.

Finally, Draw Style for tool handles can be set to Invisible, Basic, or Advanced. If you set it to Advanced, you'll see the amount of your movement, rotation, scale, and so on in the 3D viewport. This will help you make more specific adjustments if needed. Additionally, in Advanced mode, the handles can be dragged by the user to control adjustments. A good example of this is with the Loop Slice tool. If you use the Loop Slice tool to subdivide a loop of polygons, you can move individual slices with the Advanced mode. This mode also provides numeric feedback.

Colors

Figure 2.8 shows the preferences for colors. Here, you can change the colors to various schemes or create a new one. Additionally, you can change the colors of pretty much everything in modo, from the background, to selections, all the way down to the color of display text. Goof around with these and have some fun making up different color schemes for your modo interface. Although changing

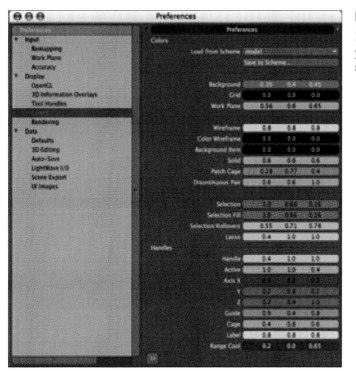

Figure 2.8

Preferences for colors allow you to work with different schemes or create your own.

colors might be fun, it can also be helpful if your eyesight is not the best or you're colorblind. This is just one more area where modo excels in its flexibility. However, note that changing these colors does nothing in and of itself. You have to apply the new color scheme to the viewports on a per-viewport basis, using the View, Viewport Color Scheme command.

Rendering

Rendering preferences give you the flexibility to tell modo how many render threads to work with. However, you can keep this setting at Automatic, and modo will determine whether you have one, two, or four processors in your computer and use them accordingly for rendering. You can set the cache size for geometry, giving you flexibility for larger modeling projects. The more memory you have in your system the better, and the higher you can set this value. You can also set a Default Exposure gamma, which essentially tells modo to have a base brightness for renders before other variables, such as light and environments. Also for rendering, you can set the Bake UV border size to something other than the default value of 3. This default value works quite well in most situations, but at times, depending on the UV map, you might need to increase or decrease this value. Baking a UV map means that you're rendering an image map based on a model's shape (which you've determined) and recording data into that map, such as color, light, and shadows.

Note

The Default Exposer gamma applies the gamma after rendering, during the Save Image process, as an image-processing command—not prior to rendering. The Display gamma just applies a gamma correction to the render window. The Exposure gamma helps add brightness to modo's physically accurate renders without having to unrealistically over-crank the global illumination settings. If you want to leave the setting at 1 because you might adjust gamma further down the render pipeline, you can adjust the Display gamma to the amount that is usually added during the compositing process (perhaps in Photoshop) and obtain a realistic preview of what the image will look like when it's gamma corrected.

Data Preferences

Data preferences are specific controls for 3D editing, saving, exporting, and user interface images.

Defaults

In most cases, it's a good idea to keep default names set to default so you know what they are. The Default preference settings allow you to change the default name to anything you want for default materials, default parts, or default texture maps. You can also tell modo to auto-create item masks. Depending on the type of texturing you're applying in the Shader Tree, you might enjoy having this option turned on to help save you a step. The Shader Tree will be discussed in Chapters 7 and 8.

On of modo's most powerful features is the ability to create instances. Instances can be applied to textures, objects, lights, and even cameras. An instance by definition is a suggestion or request. Unlike a copy of an object, for example, an instance does not duplicate the geometry; rather, it references the geometry. You would use instances for creating large copies of items to better manage your system resources. Using the MeshPaint tool to create grass or leaves could benefit from instances. In the Preferences panel, you can tell modo that when you're creating instances, it should create them as bounding boxes. This will help the redraw time, especially when you have hundreds or even thousands of instances.

Although modo is an excellent subdivision surface modeler, you also have the ability to build with spline curves. You can set default values for the Patch Display Level, Curve Display Level, Curve Display Angle, and New Spline Patch Display Level. Like many values throughout the Preferences, the default values here work quite well. Finally, modo allows you to set a default image format. This is especially useful when you're creating images for painting on 3D models.

3D Editing

With only two preferences to set within this heading, you have control over the flatness limit of your geometry and vertex deletion options. When deleting a vertex, you have the option to remove line polygons or keep all polygons. Depending on your model and what you're intending to create, you can change this preference. But in many cases, you'd use the default value of Remove Line Polygons. What this means is that when you delete a vertex (a point), you are telling modo to remove two-point polygons and stray vertices, rather than remove the entire polygon.

Auto-Save

For some, auto-save options are a lifesaver. For others, they are a tool of destruction. The Auto-Save feature in modo is not enabled by default. You can turn it on in the Preferences panel and set the time interval for saves, a backup directory, and the number of revisions. The reason an auto-save might be destructive is that if you make a change to your model that you don't like, and then the auto-save kicks in, you could very easily overwrite your existing model. When using any automated operation, make sure you're aware that it's on and what it's doing.

LightWave I/O

LightWave 3D has been around since 1990, and the developers of modo have a history with that program. Because of the way LightWave handles geometry, a special preference area has been created to handle LightWave models, such as Load SubPatch as Subdivided and Save Subdivided as Subpatched. When textured with images, LightWave models point to a specific directory. Therefore, modo has the option to set a content directory for LightWave models. This means that when a LightWave model with applied texture maps is loaded, modo will know where to look for the images.

You can also turn on Save Flat Transform, and either Convert Imported Textures or Lock Imported Textures.

Scene Export

When you build objects in modo and create a cool render scene, you might be inclined to put your name on it. The Scene Export preference allows you to set an author name, a copyright, and an absolute path.

UI Images

Perhaps your models are all cartoon characters and you never need image maps. No problem! But for everyone else who uses many images for textures, lighting, or reference, the preferences for UI images offer a good amount of control, allowing you to sort by age or numerically. You can also give modo a maximum images number, which will help you control your system resources. And like other geometry preferences, you can also set image preferences such as cache size and thumbnail size. Lastly, the UI Images preferences give you the ability to clear images from throughout modo, such as the backdrop or paintbrushes.

You might never need to open the preferences for modo 201/202. That's fine. The Luxology team has done a pretty darn good job of anticipating what will work best for most users and setting the preferences accordingly. If you do need to adjust them and at some point you get completely screwed up, you can revert back to defaults. To do so, simply delete your configuration files.

modo Configuration Files

Sometimes you need a fresh start. A clean slate. When it comes to modo, that might mean deleting your config files. They are located in different places on the Mac and PC. Configuration files are written when you close modo, so for any changes you make to your preferences, layouts, or other user interface options, the values are recorded in a configuration file. By deleting these files, you are erasing those settings and creating a brand-new file when you restart modo. It's a great way to get back to the original installed version of the program without reinstalling the entire thing.

Mac Configs

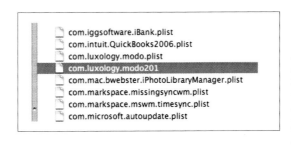

To reset modo to all of its default values on a Mac running the OS X operating system, you can delete the config files found in the Preferences folder of your user account. Go to your user:Library:Preferences:com.luxology.modo201, as shown in Figure 2.9. With modo shut down, just drag this file to your trash. Restart modo, and you're good as new.

Figure 2.9

Part of working with preferences is knowing where modo stores configuration files. At times, you might want to delete this file to reset modo to its full defaults. Here is the location of this file on an Apple Macintosh.

PC Configs

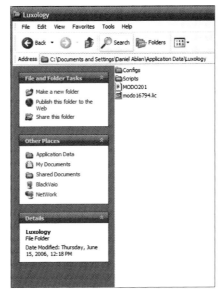

To reset modo to all of its default values on a PC running the Windows XP operating system, you delete the config files found within the Documents and Settings folder (see Figure 2.10).

Figure 2.10

Even though modo is cross-platform and works the same on both Mac and PC, the config files are located within the Documents and Settings folder on a Windows-based PC. This folder is normally hidden on the PC, so be sure to enable Show Hidden Folders in your system's folder options.

Form Editor

In the System menu at the top of the modo interface is a selection for the Form Editor. Selecting this calls up a panel with a lot of information, as shown in Figure 2.11.

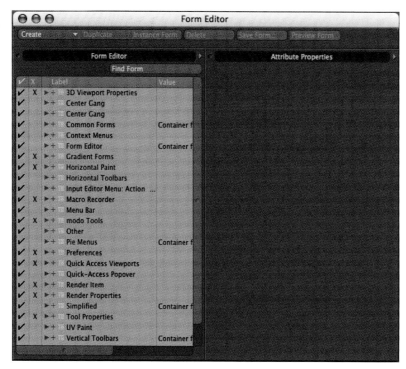

Figure 2.11

The Form Editor looks daunting, but is easy to use and quite powerful.

In many ways, the Form Editor is a deeper set of preferences for modo's many variables. But while the Preferences panel allows you to change and adjust certain values, the Form Editor actually allows you to create or duplicate specific operations. One of modo's unique capabilities is allowing the user to change key commands or add alternate commands to various functions. Take a quick tour of the Form Editor to familiarize yourself with the panel and how it works.

If you look at Figure 2.11, you'll see two main panels with the headings of Form Editor and Attribute Properties. The Form Editor section on the left side gives you access to all of the forms in modo, such as the modo Tools buttons you commonly use to create basic primitive shapes. The upcoming tutorial will show you how to quickly find a particular form to edit. When you find a form and select it, the Attribute Properties become active on the right side of the panel. For example, Figure 2.12 shows the modo Tools form selected, and what you'll see on the right under the Attribute Properties are common properties values, such as the label, description, a help URL, and more. You can set many of these values to aid in your workflow. You'll also see Form Properties to tell you whether the form is exported, which means that it's available to use in the modo interface. You can also choose whether the particular form is laid out vertically or horizontally, as well as whether the form should have an icon and, if so, what size. Take some time and change some of these values to see for yourself how they change your modo setup. Also, a form is a special type of viewport (a Form view) that is used to create many of modo's user interface panels. For example, the modo Tools panel is a Form view. You can add to, subtract from, duplicate, alter, or create your own unique Form views from within modo. Form views can be seen as a viewport pop-up, a pop-over, and a pie menu (special types of forms). The Alt/Option-space command pop-up is just another Form view.

Figure 2.12

The Form Editor is straightforward in that you find a form you want to edit on the left side of the panel, which then activates the attributes on the the right side of the panel.

The Attribute Properties for modo's forms are very similar; however, some have slight variations. Rather than listing all of the features in the Form Editor, these next few steps will guide you through the creation of an alternate command in modo 201/202 utilizing the Form Editor.

1. For this project, you'll add an alternate command for a modo tool. In the modo interface, select the Tool Bar tab on the left side of the screen to view the modo tools, as shown in Figure 2.13. Note that this is found within the Basic category, which is at the top of the vertical listing of tools.

2. Holding the Shift key, click on the Torus tool to make a quick toroid. Doing this creates a one-meter unit primitive shape. You'll see a donut shape appear in the viewport; when you do, press the **a** key to fit it to view, as shown in Figure 2.14. You can rotate the view by holding the Alt or Option key on your keyboard, then clicking and dragging in the viewport to see the object better.

Figure 2.13

Navigate to the modo Tools panel, found under the Tool Bar tab.

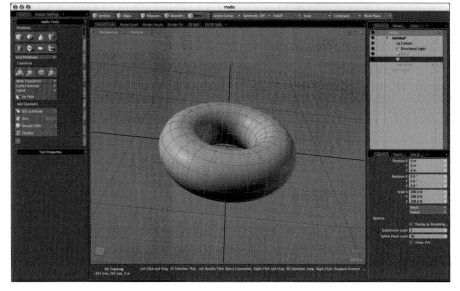

Figure 2.14

Holding the Shift key and clicking on a primitive shape creates a one-meter unit primitive.

3. Now that you have created an object, you can do something to it, such as move it. If you hold your mouse over the Move tool under the Transform listing, you'll see a pop-up telling you what the tool is, what its keyboard equivalent is, and what its alternate commands are, as shown in Figure 2.15.

4. Make sure the Form Editor is open by choosing Form Editor from the System menu at the top of the modo interface, or by pressing F3.

5. In the Form Editor, click Find Form from the top-center of the panel, and then click on the Move tool. The Form Editor will instantly open to the selected tool, making your search absolutely painless. Figure 2.16 shows the panel after choosing Find Form.

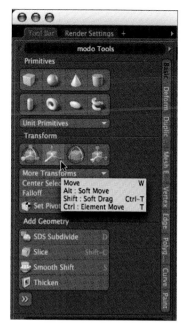

Figure 2.15

Holding the mouse over a tool for a few seconds calls up its commands.

Figure 2.16

Rather than searching through a plethora of forms in the Form Editor, use the Find Form function to quickly select the form you want to edit.

6. Looking at the Form Editor, you'll see that the modo Tools category is expanded to the Basic category, which displays the Transform category. There, you can see that the Move tool is selected. Click the small triangle to the left of the Move listing in the Form Editor to expand its commands. You'll see that there is an alternate command listing. Expand that, as shown in Figure 2.17.

Figure 2.17

Expanding the Move command in the Form Editor displays its alternate command.

7. From Figure 2.17, you can see that a Soft Move has a value of Alt, meaning the Alt key is the modifier to make the "alternate" happen. Similarly, you'll see Soft Drag assigned to Shift, and Element Move (a fantastic tool) assigned to Ctrl. Right-click on the Element Move command (Apple-click on single-button Macs).

8. When you right-click or Apple-click, you'll see a listing for Create Alternate Command, Edit, and Delete. For this tool, there are quite a few alternate commands already, but perhaps you'd like to change one. Easy—simply select Edit.

9. In the Create Alternate Command panel that appears, you can see that the modifier is Ctrl, the Command is tool.set "ElementMove" "on," and the Label is Element Move. Of course, you can relabel your tool here, but for now hold the Shift and Ctrl keys at the same time, and you'll see the modifier keys update, as shown in Figure 2.18.

10. Click OK, and you'll see your new alternate command modifiers listed in the Form Editor.

11. Close the Form Editor, and then hold the Shift and Ctrl keys. Look at the Move tool as you do, and you'll notice that the icon changes to represent the Element Move command. Choose it and then click and drag on your object in the viewport.

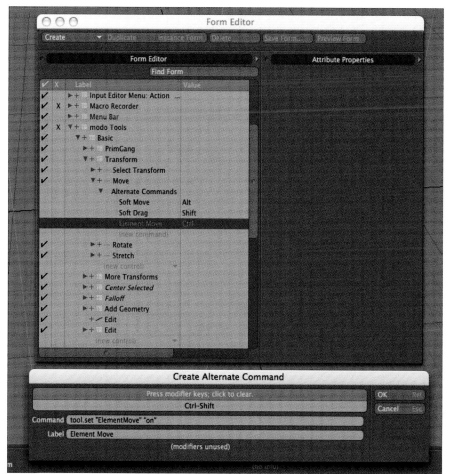

Figure 2.18

Holding the Shift and Ctrl keys at the same time, you tell modo to use those together as an alternate command for the Element Move tool.

Congratulations! You just modified your first tool! Obviously this is the tip of the iceberg when it comes to modifications, and we could probably write an entire book on using the Form Editor, modifying keys, and creating new ones. But this quick tutorial helped familiarize you with the Form Editor and what you can do with it. A few notes you should know:

■ To revert back to your existing settings after modifying, you can edit the command again. Or, you can delete your modo configuration files as described earlier.

■ Other Attribute Properties allow you to create your own icon. At the bottom of the Attribute Properties within the Form Editor, you can set a custom icon. Click the blank icon and then select Load Image from the pop-up that appears. Add your own image, and away you go!

- From the top of the Form Editor, you can create instances of forms (such as the modo Tools), and you can create new forms and new commands, and save them.

- Using the Form Editor, you can create your own custom interface tools. If you choose Layouts, Paint from the Layout menu at the top of modo, you'll see a variation of the Form Editor's capabilities. The horizontal icons across the top of the interface were assembled using the Form Editor and Attribute Properties. Be sure to click and drag the viewport windows down a bit to reveal the Paint Layout icons.

Input Editor

The Form Editor is cool, but so is the Input Editor. Also accessed from the System menu or by pressing F2, the Input Editor is your home for keyboard shortcuts and commands. Figure 2.19 shows the panel.

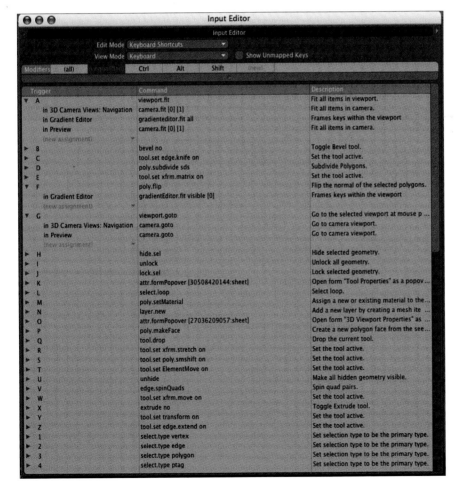

Figure 2.19

Selected from the System menu or by pressing F2, the Input Editor gives you access to all of your keyboard commands.

Across the top of the Input Editor panel, you can see the Modifiers listings. You'll see All, Unqualified, Ctrl, Alt/Option, and Shift. Select any one of these, such as Ctrl, and you'll reveal all of the commands in modo that use Ctrl as a modifier. A modifier key is simply a key command that you can use in combination with a keyboard equivalent, as an alternative. It will allow you to create even more keyboard shortcut combinations.

Figure 2.20 shows the Ctrl modifiers selected, and at the very top is Ctrl+A for the Trigger listing.

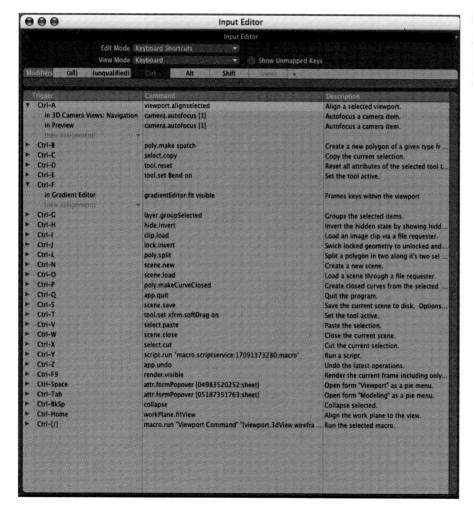

Figure 2.20

Selecting Ctrl from the Modifiers list shows all of modo's command that use the Ctrl key.

The next column shows the command. You'll see that Ctrl+A controls viewport.alignselected, and the description to the right shows that the tool aligns a selected viewport. Additionally, take a look beneath the Ctrl+A listing, and you'll see that the command acts differently in different viewports.

Similar to the Form Editor, if you right-click on a command, you are offered controls to vary its use. Most of these are things you may or may not want to change, but if you do, remember what you've changed so that you can get back to the default settings.

At the top of the Input Editor is the Edit Mode selection. By default you see Keyboard Shortcuts, but clicking the drop-down list shows that you can view key commands for Viewports and Tools. And as you might expect, you can modify, add, or delete any number of these commands.

You might never feel the need to use the Input Editor, and that's just fine. You should be aware of the Input Editor and the Form Editor, but there is not really a need to use them unless you specifically need to change a command or keystroke. The Luxology team has done a pretty good job of assigning keyboard equivalents and alternate commands to the toolset. For more specific info on these areas, view your modo manual and check out the forums at www.luxology.com. We want to make sure there's enough room in this book for model creation, texturing, and rendering!

Note

The Input Editor is not just for changing command or keystrokes, but for adding new commands as well. You can also add scripts and macro functions to selected keystrokes. You can even set up viewport-specific keystrokes or change or add popover forms to certain keystrokes. Quite powerful indeed!

Action Centers

There's nothing more frustrating in 3D modeling than not being able to control your mouse movements in the direction you want. This is especially true when you're trying to move or rotate a selected edge or polygon. But never fear, Action Centers are here! Okay, that was lame, but Action Centers are not, so follow along with this simple operation to see how they work.

1. From the File menu, select Reset to bring modo back to its original state.

2. From the Basic category, under the modo Tools, hold the Ctrl key and click the Sphere icon. This will drop a one-meter unit sphere into the viewport.

3. Press the **a** key to fit the ball to view.

4. Press the **t** key to activate the Element Move tool. Run your mouse (without selecting) over the ball, and you'll see the edges and polygons highlight as you breeze over them.

5. When you feel the urge, move over any edge and click and drag. Figure 2.21 shows the movement.

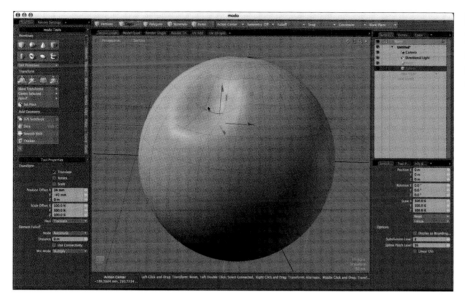

Figure 2.21

Element Move is a powerful tool that saves you time. You can click and drag on a vertex, edge, or polygon and move it.

6. Notice that when you move the edge around, it's hard to give it a specific direction. Okay then, click and drag on one of the handles, such as the green Y-axis handle. The edge moves up.

7. But perhaps you need to move that edge directly out from the ball. That is to say, you need it to move along the surface normal. From the top of the modo interface, select the Action Center drop-down, then choose Element, as shown in Figure 2.22.

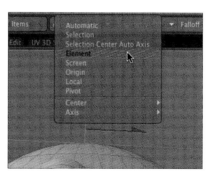

Figure 2.22

There are a number of Action Centers to choose from. For now, select Element.

8. Once you choose Element as the Action Center, go back to the viewport, click on an edge, and look at the handles—they're aligned to the selection. Click on the blue handle and drag, and you'll be able to pull the edge directly away from the object, as shown in Figure 2.23.

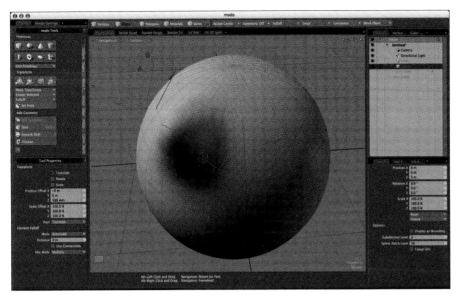

Figure 2.23

Once an Element Action Center is set, you can move the selected edge (or vertex or polygon) deliberately on a specific axis equal to the surface normal.

When using the Element Move tool, you're already in Element Action Center. You can look to the Tool Pipe at the bottom-right of the interface to confirm. But, you have no Action Axis defined unless there's already one in the Tool Pipe from a previous tool. Selecting Element Action Center does add the Element Action Axis component along with the Element Axis component, but the Element Action Center isn't what's giving the ability to move out from the Element's normal. It's the Element Axis—a big distinction because you can mix an Axis with an Action Center.

Here's one more quick example of the Axis and Action Center:

1. Create a unit sphere by holding the Shift key and clicking the ball in the tool bar.

2. Select a polygon, any polygon.

3. Press the **Esc** (Escape) key on your keyboard to clear out any Action Centers/Axis in the Tool Pipe.

4. Select Origin as the Action Center.

5. Select the Move tool from the Tool Bar tab, or press the **w** key.

6. Click in the viewport to activate the tool. You'll notice the handles are at the origin, and the axis conforms to the modo universe.

7. Now drag the selected polygon around slightly.

8. Press **q** on your keyboard to drop the tool.

9. Switch to Element Action Center from the Action Center drop-down at the top of the modo interface.

10. Select the Move tool again. Click in the viewport to activate the tool, and notice how it's aligned to the element—both its position (center of the polygon) and axis (Z axis aligned to polygon's normal).

Action Centers allow any action to be oriented to a desired specification you set. Generally, 3D modeling programs tend to use the pivot point or mouse position for the Action Center. modo uses these Action Centers, but also many others, enabling you to customize the axis and center for tool handles. Other Action Centers include Automatic (the default), Selection, Screen, Origin, and others. These Action Center presets also include a preset Action Axis as well. Now that you have seen how the Action Center can affect an action or transformation, here's a quick list of the Action Centers and their uses:

- Automatic Action Center uses the current selection, not geometry, as its guide. This goes for items and components. The key point is you can translate the Action Center to wherever you want it onscreen with a simple click of the mouse.

- Selection Action Center uses the selected geometry as its guide. The selected tool aligns itself to the selected geometry.

- Selection Action Center Auto Axis has the same axis as Automatic (aligned to the world). In fact, it's just like Automatic except you can't redefine where you want it with a click. It stays put in the center.

- Element Action Center aligns the axis to the element's normal, and the center to the center of the element.

- Screen Action Center is pretty cool in that it aligns the major axis of the viewport (X for right and left sides, Y for top and bottom, Z for front and back) with that axis of the tool. In Perspective view, it aligns the Z axis of the tool with the angle of the Perspective view. The center of the action behaves much like Auto Action Center in that you can click to reposition the center of the tool.

- Origin Action Center is useful for things such as scaling objects. It aligns the tool to the origin of the universe 0,0,0, with the axis aligned to the origin's axis as well.

- Local Action Center will transform an element or multiple elements around their local axis from the center of that element. You could use this setting for working with eyeballs in a character. This is why this tool is very useful.

- Pivot Action Center simply uses the selected item's pivot as its Action Center.

You can also set Auto, Selection, Element, Screen, Origin, and Pivot for the center and axis as well, directly from the Action Center menu. This additional level of control in modo 201/202 enables you to set the same Action Center type controls described above, but directly for the center and axis. The preset Action Centers supply an Action Axis as well, and you can mix and match them using the Center and Axis drop-down menu selections.

Each is useful in its own respect and is chosen based on the modeling task at hand. Remember that the Action Center applies to all of the modo tools, from Move, to Rotate, Scale, and so on. You'll choose and use these Action Centers throughout the book's projects.

Work Planes

Last but not least is the Work Plane. By now you've clicked around modo enough to be familiar with the interface, but one thing might be weighing on you: What the heck is that vertical grid? Until you understand how useful that second grid is to your modeling, it will only appear as a visible nuisance.

No matter what 3D program you're working in, you can only control up to two axes at a time, such as the X and Z. But with modo's Work Plane, the alternate grey grid plane you see in the Perspective viewport gives you a third axis to work in. The reason for this is that the Work Plane adjusts to your geometry or selected element. Rotating your viewport makes the Work Plane snap to the major axis, such as ZY, XZ, or XY. The Work Plane is used to assist and set the center and axis of tools you use to build and edit your 3D models. Step through the following instructions to get a feel for the Work Plane.

1. From the File menu, select Reset to bring modo back to its original state.

2. Then, from the Basic category within the Tool Bar tab, hold the Shift key and click the Teapot primitive, as shown in Figure 2.24. The Shift key is an alternate command to create a unit primitive as a new item, not just add some primitive geometry to an existing item.

3. With the teapot in the viewport, press the **a** key to fit it to view. Then, hold the Alt or Option key and click and drag the viewport left to right. Pay attention to the vertical light-grey grid and watch what it does. You'll see it "snap" based on the axis as it changes.

   What's happening here is the Work Plane is adjusting to the dominant axis. By rotating the view, you're changing that axis. How can you tell what the axis is? Take a look at the bottom-left corner of the viewport. Do you see the XYZ representation, as shown in Figure 2.25? Notice that it's highlighted in grey between two axes. This is the dominant axis and will change as you rotate.

If you were to build an object and you needed it to lay flat on the Y axis as you created it, you would rotate the Perspective viewport until this icon showed the dominant axis between the Z and X. You'll do this later in the book as you build objects.

Figure 2.24

Holding the Shift key gives you access to a few additional primitive shapes, such as the industry-standard Teapot.

Figure 2.25

Pay attention to the icon at the bottom-left of the modo viewport. The grey highlight between two axes is showing your dominant axis.

4. Select the Polygons button from the top of the modo interface.

5. Click and drag over some polygons to select them on the teapot.

6. If you choose a tool such as Move or Rotate at this point, you can control how the selected polygons will be adjusted through an Action Center setting. But what if you wanted even more control, perhaps to build additional objects from the selection? At the top-right of the modo interface is a Work Plane drop-down menu. Click it and choose Align Work Plane to Selection, as shown in Figure 2.26.

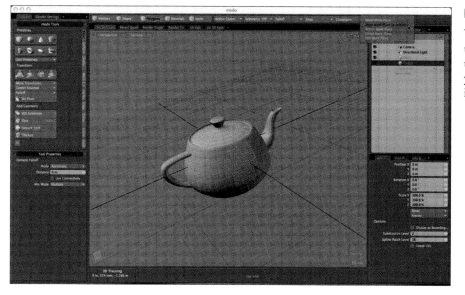

Figure 2.26

You can align the Work Plane to your selection, allowing you to have greater control over your tools and how they interact with your model.

7. The adjusted Work Plane will constrain the selected tool to the new position set by the axis of the Work Plane. From the Work Plane menu, you can also choose to reset the Work Plane, offset it, or rotate it based on your needs. Experiment with these settings.

As you can see, just a few key areas within modo are quite powerful. Here's one more example for you to try:

1. Drag out a primitive cone. Hold the Ctrl key to keep it proportional. Drag it out with the Work Plane aligned to the XZ and XY. You can set this by rotating the viewport until the white transparent square is drawn between the X (red) and Z (blue) references in the small XYZ icon in the bottom-left of the viewport. You can see the difference and how the Work Plane affects geometry creation.

2. Next, select the Scale tool and drag in the viewport. You'll notice that the cone is only scaling on the plane (the XZ). The Work Plane is constrained to where you drag. When you drag tools instead of using the handles, the Work Plane keeps the tool constrained to two axes.

3. Now select some polygons on the cone, and align the Work Plane to the selection by choosing this option from the Work Plane drop-down menu at the top-right of the interface.

4. Hold the Ctrl key, drag out a new cone primitive, and see how it's aligned to the selection.

5. Press the **End** key on your keyboard to reset the Work Plane, or simply choose Reset from the Workplane drop-down selection.

Be sure to check out the Workplane video on the book's DVD for a visual explanation of this powerful feature.

This chapter guided you through some of their uses, but not all. The best way to understand how each of these key areas works is to see them in action in a full-blown project. But before you get to that, read on to learn about selections, falloffs, and the amazing modo Tool Pipe.

3

Working with the Tools

To gain the most from modo, it's important to understand how the tools work. Although you can get by just clicking around in the program until you build something you like, you'll actually save much more time with a clear knowledge of what the key tools do in modo 201/202. Specifically, this chapter will discuss working with selections, falloffs, and the Tool Pipe.

Selections

modo's selections and tools work in a similar fashion to most 3D applications—you choose a selection mode, click and select particular geometry, and modify the selection in some way. And, as in most applications, if nothing is selected, what you do (such as move or rotate) applies to everything. But modo goes a step further by making selection and deselection easier than you thought possible. In the end, your workflow is greatly improved. There are five selection modes available to you in modo 201/202: Vertices, Edges, Polygons, Materials, and Items.

Take a look at Figure 3.1, which shows the various selection modes available at the top of the modo interface. You see the five selection modes available; however, what is discussed here primarily focuses on the three selection modes you'll use most often, Vertices, Edges, and Polygons. Note that the default 201/202 layout is used here.

Working with Selections

The best way to understand how modo's selections work is by trying them out for yourself. This brief tutorial will instruct you on creating an object and using it to work through various selections.

1. Start up modo and make sure you're working with a default 201/202 layout, which you can set from the Layout menu at the top of the interface.

2. Next, in the Tool Bar tab on the left side of the screen, hold the Shift key and select the Torus primitive. This is within the Primitives category of the modo Tools panel. Figure 3.2 shows the region.

Figure 3.2

To start working with selections, you need to have some geometry! Create a Torus primitive.

3. Next, press the **a** key to fit the new primitive shape to view.

> **Note**
>
> Holding the Shift key and selecting a primitive will offer a few more shapes, such as a teapot and a flat plane, and it will give you a unit primitive in your current mesh item. Conversely, you can press the Ctrl key and select a primitive shape, and you'll get a one-meter unit primitive, which will be placed in the Item List as a new item.

4. To begin working with selections, start with the most common selection type—polygon. Click the Polygons button at the top of the modo interface to tell the program you want to work with polygons. This means that when you click on your model, you'll be selecting the polygonal geometry, or the surface of the model.

> **Note**
>
> It's important to pay attention to the mode buttons at the top of the modo interface. This will tell you what selection mode you're working in. Additionally, you can repeatedly press the spacebar to toggle through the three main selection modes.

5. With the Polygons mode button selected, click and drag over a few polygons on the torus shape. When you select, you'll see the selected polygons highlighted in orange. Figure 3.3 shows the selection. This is often referred to as *painting a selection.*

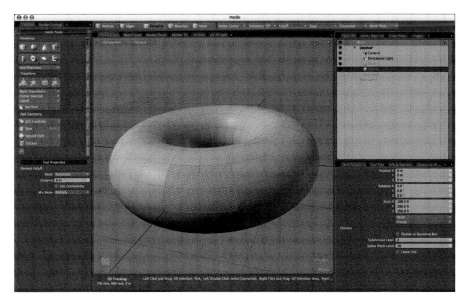

Figure 3.3

When you click to select a single or multiple polygons while in Polygons mode, the selected geometry is highlighted in bright orange.

6. With a few polygons selected, press Shift+A. The selected polygons will fit to view. Consider this keyboard shortcut when you are working on specific areas of models, whether you have polygons, edges, or vertices (points) selected. Now press just the **a** key to fit the model to view, rather than the selection.

Note

Be sure to note the heads-up display (HUD) visible in the bottom-right of the viewport interface. This will tell you how many vertices, edges, polygons, or materials are selected. If none are selected, the HUD reads "All Polygons" for Polygons mode, and the rest accordingly.

7. With these polygons selected, whatever tool you choose to use will apply to just these. With that said, press the **b** key on your keyboard to activate the Bevel tool. You can find this tool under the Mesh Edit vertical category listing on the left side of the interface. When you turn on the Bevel tool, the Tool Properties become visible at the bottom left of the interface, as shown in Figure 3.4. The Bevel tool will also appear within the Basic category under the Add Geometry heading.

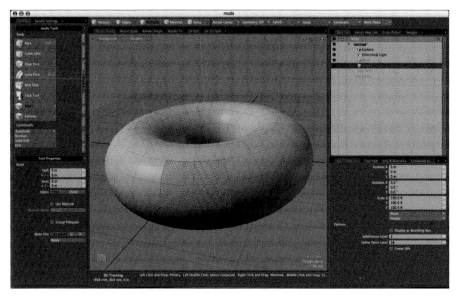

Figure 3.4

When you activate a tool, the Tool Properties become visible. Here, the Bevel tool is active.

8. With the Bevel tool active, click once in the viewport. You'll see a red and blue handle appear, as shown in Figure 3.5.

   If you click and drag the red handle to the right or left, you change the inset value of the bevel. Try it. If you click and drag the blue handle, you change the shift of the bevel.

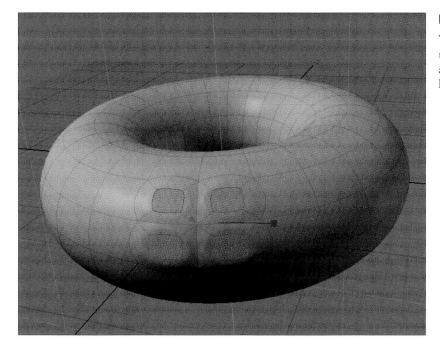

Figure 3.5

Turning the Bevel tool on and then clicking in the viewport activates the tool's control handles.

9. After you've played around with these tools, press Ctrl+z to undo. Then, click and drag in the viewport, making sure not to click on either handle. You can perform a change to the Inset and Shift values for the bevel at the same time.

10. One thing you might have noticed is that each of the selected polygons bevels independently. This is fine in some situations, but mostly you'll want to bevel these together as one. To do so, press Ctrl+z a few times to undo your bevels, returning to just the selected polygons. Then, in the Tool Properties panel on the left side of the interface, click the Group Polygons button.

11. Click and drag in the viewport, either freeform or directly on one of the handles. Figure 3.6 shows the bevel operation with Group Polygons on.

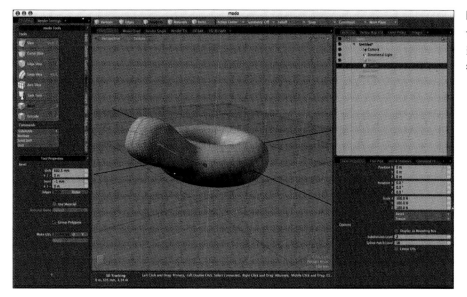

Figure 3.6

With Group Polygons selected in the Tool Properties panel, selected polygons bevel as one.

12. If you now turn off the Bevel tool by pressing the **b** key again or clicking on the Bevel tool, then turn it on again, you activate a new bevel. And because your polygons are still selected, you're now beveling from your existing bevel. But, a better way to quickly bevel again is to hold the Shift key and click once in the viewport. Make an adjustment, beveling more, then hold the Shift key and click, and bevel again. The process can continue to create complex and interesting shapes very easily. You can drop the Bevel tool by pressing the **q** key on your keyboard.

You'll use the bevel process a lot in your modeling tasks, and you'll see this first-hand later in the book. Let's try a few more selection tasks and then move on to a few more complex controls.

Selection Methods

Probably one of the best things about working in modo is how easy it is to select vertices, edges, polygons, or materials. Unlike a lot of other 3D applications, modo allows you to get down to business quickly because you're not spending a lot of time selecting the necessary elements to edit. Take a quick look at this section to see the various ways you can select geometry.

1. In modo, go to the File menu at the top of the interface. Select the Reset command from the bottom of the list, as shown in Figure 3.7. This clears the viewport and resets it back to its default views. Note that you'll get a request asking whether you want to save your work. Choose what's right for you.

2. Select the Basic vertical category on the left side of the modo interface to access the primitives. Holding the Shift key, click the Teapot primitive icon to create a one-meter unit. Note that you won't see a Teapot icon until you press the Shift key.

3. When the Teapot primitive is created, press the spacebar to toggle to the Edges selection mode, visible at the top of the interface. Then, press the **a** key to fit the model to view. Feel free to press the period key on the keyboard to zoom in or the comma key to zoom out.

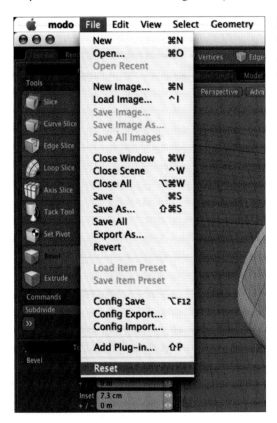

Figure 3.7

To clear out your work and start fresh, choose the Reset command from the File menu.

Note

Remember that you can hold the Alt/Option key and click directly in the viewport to rotate the view. Conversely, you can hold the Alt/Option and Shift keys at the same time, then click in the viewport to move it around or use Alt/Option and Ctrl to zoom.

4. When you move your mouse over an edge while in Edges selection mode (or any other mode, for that matter), you'll see the element highlight. This helps you choose the selection. Figure 3.8 shows a highlighted edge as the mouse moves over it. You should be in Edges selection mode to see the edge rollover with modo's default settings. You can change your Selection Rollover option under Display, OpenGL in the Preferences panel. If you change this setting to Closest, you'll be able to roll over vertices, edges, and polygons no matter what selection mode you're in.

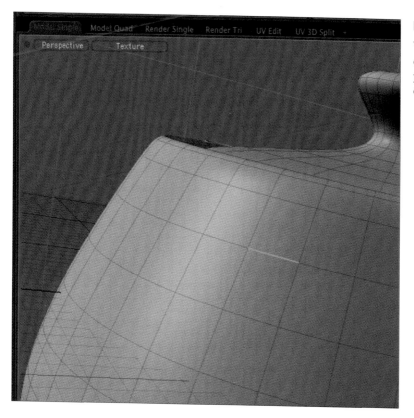

Figure 3.8

When you move your mouse over any element, modo helps you select that particular element by highlighting it.

Note

If you don't like the selection rollovers, you can disable this feature. From the System menu at the top of the interface, choose Preferences. From the Display category, choose OpenGL. There, you'll find options for selection rollovers—Manual, Closest, or None. Manual sets the rollovers to the particular selection mode you're working in. Closest highlights polygons, edges, or vertices, depending on which is closest to the mouse cursor. Or, you can simply choose None for no rollover selection at all. Figure 3.9 shows the options.

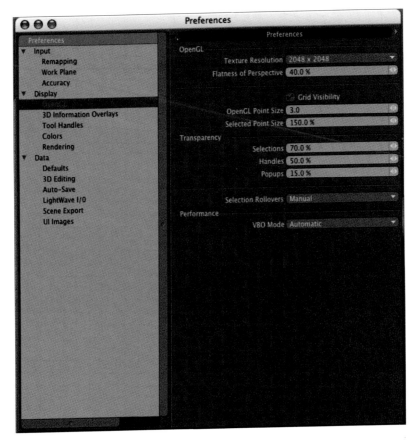

Figure 3.9

In modo's Preferences panel, you can choose not to use rollover selections.

5. When the mouse highlights an edge you want to select, simply click on it. The edge will be selected and will turn orange. You can hold the mouse down and select more than one edge, by dragging the mouse over the desired selection. Try clicking and dragging over a few edges to select them.

6. If you accidentally select extra edges, hold the Ctrl key and click on the edge you don't want. This will deselect it. To continue adding to a selection, hold the Shift key and choose the edges you want to select. Note that this method applies to all selection modes.

7. The great thing about modo is the quick way you can select elements. Find an edge in the middle of your Teapot primitive and double-click it. One click will select the particular edge, while a double-click will select the entire edge loop, as shown in Figure 3.10. Try it out!

8. When this edge is selected, you can slide it, move it, size it, bevel it, extend it, and so on. Press the **b** key to select the Bevel tool, as you did earlier. Then, click and drag in the viewport to bevel the selected edge. Figure 3.11 shows the result.

Figure 3.10

Double-clicking on an edge will select the entire edge loop.

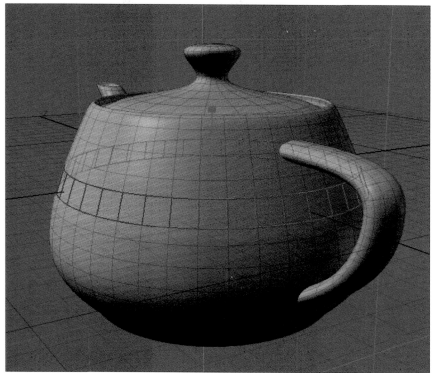

Figure 3.11

After a quick edge selection, you can bevel the selection to add more geometry.

9. A cool thing about modo is how you can change from one selection mode to another. After you've beveled the single edge, as Figure 3.11 shows, you are left with multiple edges selected—the original edge plus the new ones created with the operation. But what if now you want to multiply the polygons created by the edge bevel? Rather than deselecting the edges and then reselecting polygons, simply hold the Alt/Option key on your keyboard and look at the selection types across the top of the interface, as shown in Figure 3.12. They each now say Convert. So, if you have a group of selected edges, as in Figure 3.11, hold the Alt/Option key and click the Polygons selection mode. You will convert the selected edges to selected polygons. Figure 3.13 shows the result.

Note

Another cool feature of selections is that you can old down the Ctrl key, instead of the Alt/Option key, and choose Boundary mode. This will select the boundary of the current selection, such as an edge on an open end of a tube.

Figure 3.12

Holding the Alt/Option key down allows you to convert a selection.

Figure 3.13

Selected edges are quickly converted to selected polygons.

10. You can see that by starting with a simple edge selection, you've quickly added geometry and converted the selection to polygons in a matter of clicks. Now, you can choose a tool such as Bevel (press the **b** key) and click and drag to bevel out the selected polygons. Make sure Group Polygons is on in the Bevel Tool Properties panel.

11. Bevel the selected polygons two or three times, similar to the process you performed earlier in the chapter. After you've beveled once, hold the Shift key and click on the viewport to start a new bevel. Figure 3.14 shows a few bevels on the selected polygons.

Figure 3.14

Because the conversion from edges to polygons was easy, you can now bevel the polygons to modify the geometry.

As you can see, working with selections in modo is pretty painless. This chapter, although not too exciting, is important to understand because it is the foundation of all the work you will do in the program. You will continually be selecting and deselecting any time you work with a model. This is especially true when you start working with multiple objects or objects with multiple parts.

Note

As your modeling skills progress and you begin making more complex models, you can create selection sets. This is a way to tell modo that you want to save a selection of vertices, edges, or polygons. Why? Well, perhaps the desired selection is intricate and encompasses multiple surfaces. Perhaps it's a group of edges that need to be adjusted often based on a client's needs. Why go back and worry about selecting the exact element every time? Instead, select the desired vertices, edges, or polygons, and then, from the Select menu at the top of the modo interface, choose Assign Selection Set. Give the set a name and click OK. Then, any time you want to select that same group of elements, simply choose Use Selection Set from the Select menu.

Here are a few more ways you can select in modo 201/202:

- Select two elements in order (vertices, edges, or polygons) and then press the up arrow on your keyboard. This will allow you to continue selecting in the same direction.

- Use your down arrow on your keyboard to deselect in succession.

- Select one polygon or edge and press the left or right arrow on the keyboard to quickly select a selection loop.

- Hold the right mouse button (or Apple key and mouse button on the Mac) to lasso select. This method allows you to quickly draw out around an element you want to select. This works for vertices, edges, or polygons. If you take a look at the Select menu at the top of the modo interface, you can change the lasso style to a rectangle, circle, or ellipse shape.

- Double-click on a polygon to select all attached polygons.

- Double-click on an edge to select the edge loop.

- Double-click on a vertex to select all attached vertices.

- Hold down the mouse button while you pass the cursor over the model to select everything in the path. This is a paint style selection. Releasing the mouse, and then holding it down again while you pass over the model will deselect everything in its path. Remember that what is selected depends on the selection mode you're in, set at the top of the interface—Vertices, Edges, or Polygons. Remember also that if you release the mouse, then start a paint style selection again, you will start an entirely new selection.

- Select one element, and then let go of the mouse button and select another to deselect the first selection. To continue a selection after releasing the mouse button, hold the Shift key.

- Hold the Ctrl key and click on an unwanted selection to deselect it without deselecting everything.

- Click in the layout, off of the model itself, to deselect anything selected.

- For faster selections, right-clicking brings up a relevant pop-up menu of commands for that element type. To switch selection modes, use the middle mouse button (provided you have one). A two-button wheel mouse will also work; just click the wheel. This works nicely with rollovers set to Closest.

- You can grow and shrink selections (expand and contract) using the Shift+up arrow combination and Shift+down arrow combination.

- Left and right arrow keys will also allow you to crawl up or down loops. Holding Shift while doing this will select the polygon or edge loops as you crawl up or down them.

- Invert Selection is important because it's often easier to make a small selection, then press the left bracket key (to the right of the P key on your keyboard).

- Select an edge, and then press **L** on your keyboard to instantly select a ring of edges. This is for Edges mode only.

- Another way to quickly change selection modes is to right-click away from the model to get an instant pop-up menu. Figure 3.15 shows the pop-up menu.

- Also try pressing Alt/Option+q to call up a selection pie menu, as shown in Figure 3.16.

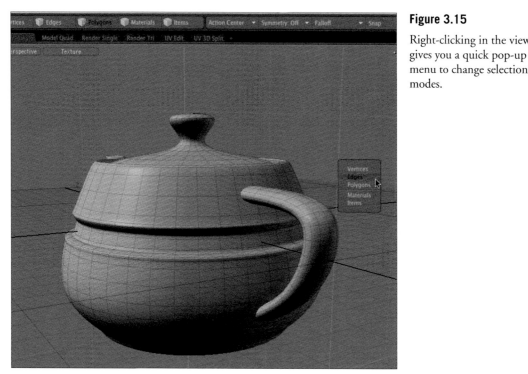

Figure 3.15

Right-clicking in the viewport gives you a quick pop-up menu to change selection modes.

Note

When you select an element with the viewport set to a shaded mode (default), you will only select what's visible to you. That is to say, you won't select elements on the other side of the model. If, however, you're working in a wireframe view, any selections you make will be on all visible geometry. Here's a tip, though: If you have a three-button mouse, use the middle mouse button to select through the model in a shaded mode. This works great for lasso-style selection. If, however, you're in wireframe mode, using the middle mouse button only selects those elements facing the camera. The middle mouse button and right mouse button selection modes are the most effective way of working with selections in modo.

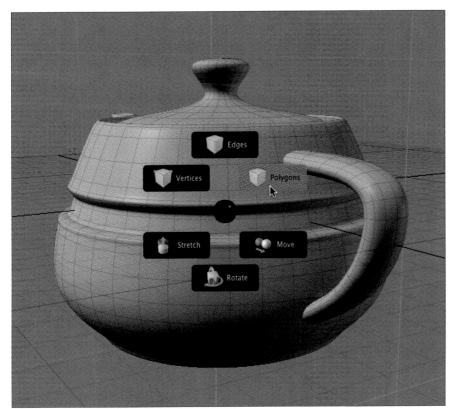

Figure 3.16

Pressing Alt/Option+q calls up a pie menu for changing selection modes.

Items Selection Mode

At the top of the interface, you'll see another selection mode labeled Items. Because modo 201/202 offers cameras and lights in addition to models (or meshes), you have the ability to select these various items.

Using the selection modes of Vertices, Edges, or Polygons allows you to select elements within a particular mode, as does the Materials selection mode. But the Items selection mode gives you the freedom to select different items in the modo viewport. So how would you use this selection mode? Easy—suppose you have a large scene with two cameras, six objects, and four lights. By choosing Items selection mode, you can just click on whatever item you want in the viewport, then choose a tool to adjust it, such as Move or Rotate.

Items selection mode makes it easy to work on multiple items without a lot of thinking. You don't have to worry about heading over to the Item List, choosing an item, editing the item, and so on. Just use Items selection mode!

Note

The quickest way to jump to Item mode is to press Shift+spacebar.

Quick Access Selection

There's one more thing to learn about selections, and then it's on to falloffs. The last thing you need to learn about selections is the Quick Access selection bar. This is a really cool way to work with selections, especially if you're not good at remembering keyboard equivalents. It's an easy way to see all the available options in one place.

1. Working with the same model you were using earlier or any primitive shape, mouse over a group of polygons to select them, as shown in Figure 3.17.

Figure 3.17

Select a group of polygons, remembering to first switch to Polygons selection mode at the top of the interface.

2. Then, press Alt/Option+spacebar. You'll be greeted with the Quick Access selection bar, as shown in Figure 3.18.

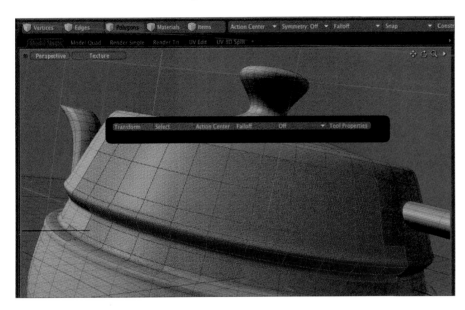

Figure 3.18

Pressing the Alt/Option key and the spacebar calls up the Quick Access selection bar.

3. By clicking the Select button in the Quick Access selection bar, you can choose what to do with the selected elements. You can invert the selection, select connected, and so on, as shown in Figure 3.19.

Figure 3.19

From the Quick Access bar, you can choose what to do with your selected elements, all in one handy location.

Experiment with these various selection modes using just simple primitive shapes as we've done here in these few pages. There are multiple ways to change selection modes, as you can see, and which method to use is completely up to you. Get comfortable with this process and try the different methods.

Falloffs

You might have heard about modo's advanced feature set, and you've even probably heard something about falloffs. More than just a term, falloffs are important to the way you control how a tool works in modo 201/202. Falloffs allow you to ramp a tool's effect based on the falloff type you choose. By doing this, you can create great effects with less effort. To grasp this cool concept, follow along with this quick tutorial.

1. From the File menu at the top of the modo interface, choose Reset to restore modo to its default views and clear out the primitive shapes you've worked with.

2. Because you've not yet created any models, use the Teapot primitive for this exercise, as you did previously. The goal of these few steps is to gain an understanding of the falloffs available in modo 201/202. Holding the Shift key, click the Teapot primitive from the Tool Bar tab on the left side of the interface. Press the **a** key to fit the model to view.

3. From the top of the modo interface, choose Automatic from the Action Center drop-down list.

4. Then, from the Falloff drop-down list, choose Radial, as shown in Figure 3.20.

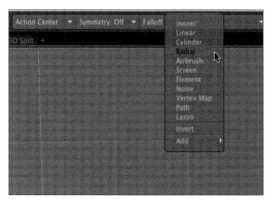

Figure 3.20

Set the falloff type to Radial in the Falloff drop-down list at the top of the modo interface.

5. Holding the right mouse button (or the Apple key on a single-button Mac), draw out a small region for the radial falloff in the viewport, around the pour spout of the teapot. Make sure you rotate the view to drag out the radial in each of the X, Y, and Z directions, as shown in Figure 3.21.

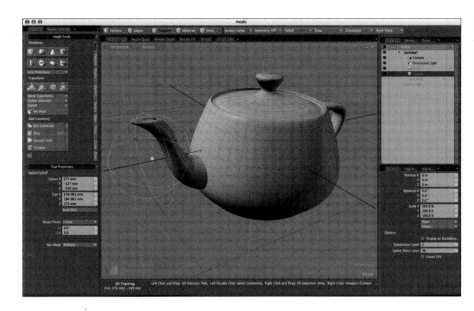

Figure 3.21

With the Falloff type set to Radial, draw out a region with the right mouse button.

> **Note**
>
> When the preliminary region is drawn out, as in Step 5, you can rotate the Perspective view and simply click and drag on the red, blue, or green squares to size the region. If you click and drag on the red, blue, and green arrows, you can move the region.

6. With the region drawn out, press the **w** key to quickly select the Move tool, which is located in the Basic vertical category.

7. Now, click and drag in the viewport. The Move tool will affect the region within the radial falloff. Figure 3.22 shows the effect.

   As you can see in Figure 3.22, the falloff is affecting how the Move tool applies to the mesh. At the center of the falloff, you have 100% of the Move tool applied. With the outer edge of the region of the radial falloff, you have 0% of the Move tool applied, hence the term *falloff.*

> **Note**
>
> When using falloffs, be sure to also try using your middle mouse button to vary the effects.

Figure 3.22

With the Falloff type set to Radial and the Move tool applied, the action affects the area within the region you determined in Step 5.

8. Now try something cool. Click and drag the light-blue square, which is located in the center of the radial falloff. Drag it around, and you'll see the falloff can shape your model simply by moving it. Remember that this radial falloff is combined with the Move tool to gain this effect. Figure 3.23 shows the falloff moved to the top of the spout, essentially flattening it out.

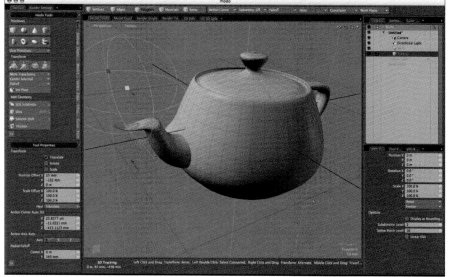

Figure 3.23

The Radial Falloff tool applied with the Move tool can shape and deform your model simply by moving it around.

9. Here's one other example to see falloffs in action. Press the **q** key on your keyboard to turn off the Move tool. Then, from the Falloff menu at the top of the interface, select Linear.

10. Click with the left mouse button at the top corner of the teapot spout and, keeping the mouse button pressed, drag to the bottom of the spout, as shown in Figure 3.24. You'll see a light and elongated triangle of sorts, representing the linear falloff.

Figure 3.24

A linear falloff is set by clicking in one spot, then dragging out.

11. Press the **e** key on your keyboard to turn on the Rotate tool.

12. Click toward the bottom of the spout, at the joint where it extends out from the teapot. You'll see the rotation handles appear, as shown in Figure 3.25.

13. Now click and drag the red rotational handle to the right to rotate the object. Notice what happens? You're deforming the object. Only a portion of it is rotating. This is because the linear falloff is telling modo to apply 100% of the tool at the bottom and 0% at the top—the narrow end of the Falloff tool. Figure 3.26 shows the deformation.

14. Now click and drag on either of the light-blue squares from either end of the Linear Falloff tool and drag it around. You'll see how the model deforms, similar to the radial falloff movement you did earlier.

You can see that by using the Falloff tools in modo, you have even greater flexibility for creating organic shapes. Imagine trying to actually model a bent, ugly teapot from scratch. In modo, you don't have to go through all that trouble.

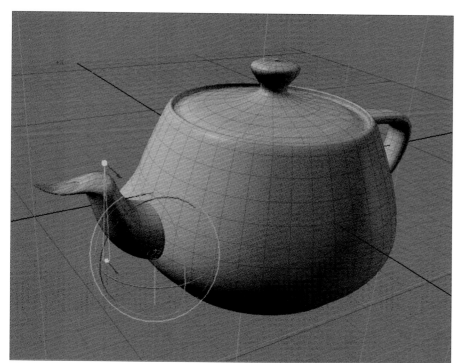

Figure 3.25

Selecting the Rotate tool and clicking in the viewport in a specific area determines where the rotation control handles will appear.

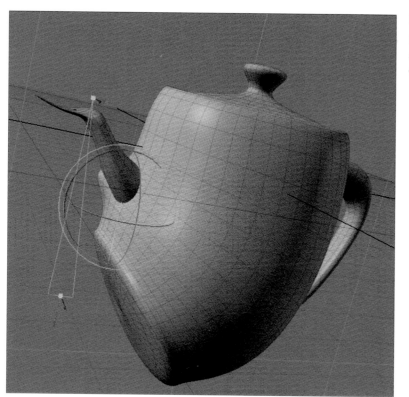

Figure 3.26

Rotating the object with a linear falloff results in a deformation of the object.

It's as easy as just applying a few tools with falloffs applied. But there are more than just the two falloffs described here. Take a look at the Falloff drop-down list at the top of the interface and try the same steps you've just performed with the different falloff types. See what you can come up with. This next project will show you a pretty powerful combination of tools to create some cool shapes.

1. Using the Teapot primitive from the previous exercise, press the spacebar to turn off any tool that might be on. You can also press Ctrl+z to undo your deformations to return to a less deformed shape. Or, feel free to reset your program from the File menu and create a new primitive shape.

2. From the Falloff drop-down list, select None.

3. Press the spacebar until your selection mode is set to Edges. Look for this at the top of the interface.

4. Now press the **t** key to activate one of modo's most powerful tools, the Element Move tool. This tool allows you to simply click and drag on any element to move it. It's excellent for shaping objects. This tool is located under the Deform tab of the modo Tools form, as shown in Figure 3.27.

Figure 3.27

Select the Element Move tool from the Deform category.

5. Find an edge on the model and click and drag it. The Element Move tool allows you to click and drag on any element (saving you the trouble of selection), choose a tool, perform the action, drop the tool, drop the selection, and then repeat. This saves huge amounts of time when modeling.

Notice in Figure 3.28 that the edge is moved. It looks like a little bump in the object. What if you wanted to really dent the object? How would you do that? There are some other modeling tools you could apply, but one easy way is to add a falloff to the Element Move tool.

Figure 3.28

Using the Element Move tool makes it easy to pull and shape elements such as edges.

6. Press Ctrl+z to undo your previous Element Move operation. From the Falloff drop-down list, select Element.

7. Press the **t** key again to turn on the Element Move tool. Then, with the right mouse button, draw out a falloff region as you did earlier. Figure 3.29 shows the example.

8. Click and drag on an edge of the model. Now instead of just the edge moving, you'll see that the edge takes a lot more of its neighboring geometry with it. Figure 3.30 shows the deformation.

You can see that by using a simple falloff, you can achieve great results. Once you've set up a tool like this, you can rotate around the view (hold the Alt/Option key, then click and drag) and start dragging edges, polygons, or vertices to shape the model. Figure 3.31 shows a dented teapot using just the Element Move tool with an Element falloff type.

At any point, you can change the falloff region. To do this, use the right mouse button (hold the Apple key on those single-button Macs) and then set your falloff region. Then, with the left mouse button, click and drag on an element. Rinse and repeat until you have the model you want.

Figure 3.29

As you did with other falloff tools, you create a falloff region by using the right mouse button.

Figure 3.30

Using a falloff, the element move has more influence on the selected edges' neighboring geometry.

Note

Remember that using the Element Move tool doesn't mean you're stuck moving just edges. You can click and move any element of your model, vertex, edge, or polygon. That's the beauty of the tool.

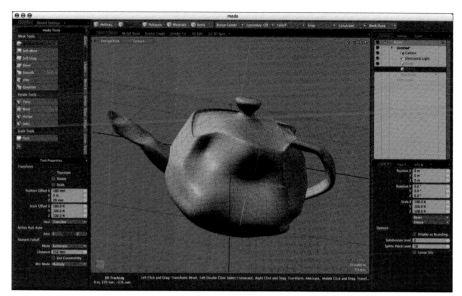

Figure 3.31

Using just the Element Move tool with an Element falloff, you can take out your frustrations on a defenseless teapot.

Falloffs are quite powerful, and when combined with the right tools, who knows what you can create! Although we could go on and on with different crazy examples, there's one other important area you should learn about before moving on.

Tool Pipe

Finally, we come to the Tool Pipe. You might have heard this term passed around on a forum or two, or perhaps in some marketing material. Contrary to what you might think, the Tool Pipe has nothing to do with pipes or modeling them, but rather is a melting pot of components and tools. With the Tool Pipe, you're able to take falloffs, for example, further by combining them with other modeling and creation tools. Tools in many programs have limited falloffs, but modo is different. The Tool Pipe is where all actions come together, by joining modifiers and tools. Figure 3.32 shows the Tool Pipe at the bottom-right corner of a default modo 201/202 interface. Here, you can see the Element Move tool combined with an Element falloff type.

If the Tool Pipe sounds scary, it's not. Guess what? You've been using it this entire time without even knowing it! Every time you use a tool, you're using the Tool Pipe. The Tool Pipe is a palette that can combine tools with Action Centers, Action Axes, falloffs, snapping, and constraints to give the tools more power. Or, you can literally create entirely new tools.

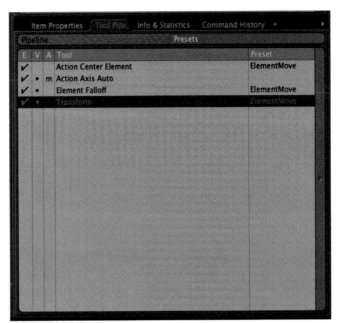

Figure 3.32

The Tool Pipe is where all modo actions and modifiers come together, creating more powerful commands and presets.

Taking a closer look at Figure 3.32, you can see that the tools being used to deform the teapot are all listed. There is a Move command, along with an Element falloff, set with an Automatic Action Center. The end result is a tool that does more than meets the eye.

The Tool Pipe is not something you really ever have to worry about working in, but it can be if you choose. It's the Tool Pipe that makes modo's functions so powerful. For example, if you choose an Airbrush falloff and then the Bevel tool, modo's Tool Pipe combines these to give you a more powerful modeling operation.

1. Using an object such as the teapot or another model or primitive, select the Airbrush falloff from the top of the modo interface.

2. If you're using the Teapot primitive, press the **d** key one time to subdivide the entire model. This creates more geometry to work with.

3. Click over to the Polygon category from the vertical list on the left side of the interface, and choose Bevel (or just press the **b** key).

4. With the right mouse button (hold the Apple key on single-button Macs), click and drag out a range of influence for the tool. Figure 3.33 shows the action.

5. Making sure that the Shift value has a setting of about 1 cm or so in the Tool Properties panel on the bottom-left of the interface, click and drag on your model.

Figure 3.33

Just like the other falloff tools, you select the falloff you want, choose a tool, then right-click in the viewport to set a range of influence. The Tool Pipe remembers your combination of tools.

6. The Tool Pipe has combined the Polygon Bevel tool with the Airbrush falloff. The result is that you can not only change the way your modify tools work, as shown earlier in the chapter, you can change the way geometry is created. Figure 3.34 shows the airbrushed bevel operation.

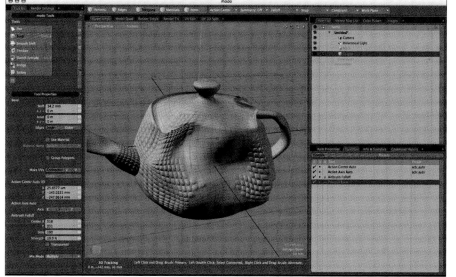

Figure 3.34

The Tool Pipe not only combines modify functions, but geometry creation as well. Here, an Airbrush falloff type is combined with the polygon Bevel tool. The result is the ability to "paint" on the bevels.

This poor teapot has had enough abuse for one chapter, don't you think? But hopefully the examples have shown you what the core modo tools can do. The combinations of Action Centers and falloffs all come together in the Tool Pipe, and in the end, you have the ultimate control. Although at first it might seem a bit daunting, you'll soon come to learn that there is a method for this madness. As the chapters progress, you'll see all of these core tools in action. You'll use them for yourself and create objects and scenes that are definitely more attractive than a busted old teapot. So if you're ready, grab a snack and head on into Chapter 4, "modo 201/202 Jump Start."

4

modo 201/202 Jump Start

Trying to learn computer software is often a lot of fun, but as you might know, it can also be frustrating. The element of 3D compounds the challenge in your quest to master a new software application, such as modo 201/202. This adds even more facets to the amount of information you'll need to absorb to create anything more than a blob of 3D geometry—or so you think! Although Luxology's modo is an easy-to-use application, it does take a little getting used to. But in the next few pages, you'll soon see results and you'll realize that this killer application from Luxology is not as hard to learn as you once thought.

Here's the deal: I just returned from the bookstore, where I was skimming through the new line of books on various topics. I looked at the Maya books, the Flash books, and the general 3D graphics books. While the information is good, there's so much talk! Argh! You don't want that, do you? Granted, you don't want a "point-and-click" book; rather, you want a book that will help you understand the tools. I first came upon this situation when writing *Inside LightWave 8* (New Riders Press, 2003). At the time, I was looking to use Flash more, and all of the books I found talked about the same thing. They all started out the same way, either covering the tools of the interface or having you build silly little character shapes. Somehow it was left to me to sift through 500 pages and then figure out how to make some simple interactive menus.

Because of the frustration I get from most software books, I want my books to help you learn differently. For example, if you were to sit down with me right now in my studio, I'd show you modo. We'd start with a "Hey, check this out!" and a

"Here's how this works" type of approach. Would you ever sit down in a training session with someone and have that person talk about theory and the history of 3D, and blah, blah, blah? You want to learn the software! Or, what if you went to a trade show to see modo in action. Imagine Luxology's Brad Peebler sitting there and discussing coordinates, the history of 3D, or principles of lighting. You'd walk. You'd be there to see the software and what it can do. So why should a book on the subject be any different?

To quickly accelerate you from a novice to a somewhat dangerous 3D modeler, I created this "Jump Start" chapter. I designed it to take you through the entire process of creating, surfacing, and rendering a model in modo 201/202 without much effort. Note that this chapter will not discuss in detail workflow, tools, and interface. Rather, it will provide a show-and-tell method of learning that quickly walks you through the necessary steps to gain a keen understanding of the modo 201/202 process. And with that, you'll be able to work in the program and get results right away. The idea is not to have you read 30 or 40 pages, only to find that you created a ball, moved and rotated it, and copied it to three layers. I know you're smarter than that!

When you start up modo 201/202, you're presented with a cool, modern-looking interface, as shown in Figure 4.1.

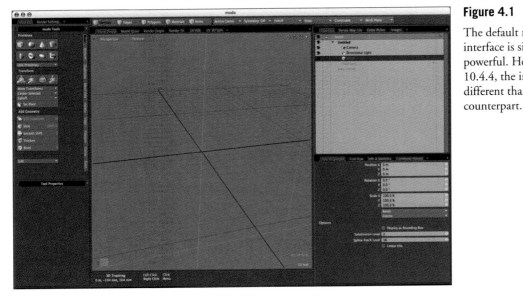

Figure 4.1

The default modo 201/202 interface is simple, yet powerful. Here on Mac OS X 10.4.4, the interface looks no different than its Windows PC counterpart.

Model Preparation

If your modo interface does not look like Figure 1.1, be sure you're using the default interface setting. You can find this setting by going to the very top of your screen and clicking the Layout drop-down menu, navigating to Layouts, and then selecting the modo 201/202 default layout. Figure 4.2 shows the selection.

The project you'll be working on in this chapter will give you a working knowledge of modo 201/202. You'll create a cool pair of sunglasses, from the modeling steps through texturing and rendering. Along the way, you'll get a feel for how to approach most projects in the program.

Figure 4.2

To set your modo 201/202 interface to its natural state (that is, its default settings), choose the default setting from the Layout drop-down menu.

Tip

Although selecting the 201 default layout option appears to reset your viewports to their natural state, there's a little trick you can do if the interface is not quite right. Select the 201 default layout option again! Suppose you move a few panels around, and then quit modo. When you restart, the panels will be where you left them. If you change your view again but select the 201 default layout option, your view will return to the adjusted state, not the default. So, selecting the 201 default layout option two times returns your view to modo's original state.

When you see outstanding models from artists around the world, certainly many of them are created from the artists' own creative minds. But a good majority of models begin with a sketch or photograph. This project will use background images to help you model the first object.

1. At the top-left of the modo viewport, change your view from Perspective to Front by clicking the Viewport icon. A drop-down list will appear.

2. To the right of the Viewport icon is the Viewport Style icon. Click this and, in the list that appears, select Backdrop, as shown in Figure 4.3.

3. In the backdrop panel that opens, click the Load Image icon. Choose the Glasses_Front.jpg image in the Chapter 4 folder of the Projects folder from this book's DVD.

4. You'll see an image of a pair of simple eyeglasses appear in your viewport, as shown in Figure 4.4. The image will serve as a reference. This technique can be used for almost anything, from characters, to cars, to everyday objects.

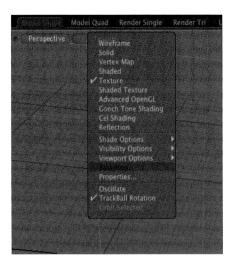

Figure 4.3

At the top of the modo viewport, change to a Front viewport style and select the Backdrop option to add an image to modo's background.

Tip

One of modo's cool features is its pie menus. Although you can easily change viewport styles from the top-left corner of each viewport, there's another way to do so as well. First, press Ctrl+spacebar. A pie menu will appear. Move the mouse to the viewport you want, click, and go. Another option with this technique is to click Alt/Option and the **q** key to choose different selection modes. You can also press Alt/Option and the spacebar to gain quick access to Transform tools, Action Centers, falloffs, and more.

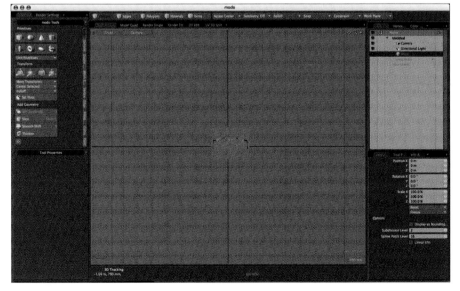

Figure 4.4

Adding an image to the backdrop allows you to model over the image as a reference.

Note

If you don't have a DVD-ROM player and you can't access the project files on the book's disc, visit http://www.danablan.com and download the project files.

5. The image is a bit small in the interface and, while you can adjust it, you also have the option to zoom into it. In the top-right corner of the viewport, you'll see three small white icons—a crosshair to move the viewport, a magnifying glass to zoom in and out, and a tiny arrow to quickly change the viewport to other options. Click, hold, and drag to zoom in on the eyeglass image.

Note

When navigating the viewports, the Move, Rotate, and Zoom controls are easy to use in the upper-right corner. However, another way to work is to use Alt/Option and click in the viewport to rotate (Perspective view). Hold Alt/Option and Shift, and then click in the viewport to pan. Finally, hold Ctrl and Alt/Option, and then click in the viewport to zoom.

6. Using backdrop images is an excellent way to build almost any shape you want. Much of your modeling will rely on your talent and intuition to sculpt details into your objects, but the backdrop image is almost always a great way to start a project. Sometimes, though, the backdrop image you use is too dark or light, making your geometry hard to see. To adjust the backdrop image, select Adjust Backdrop Image from the View menu at the top of the modo interface, as shown in Figure 4.5.

7. Take a look at the bottom-left side of the modo interface. You'll see a new set of tools appear under the Tool Properties heading, called Background Image 3D. If the Tool Properties panel appears to extend below your screen (you'll see two small right arrows), move your mouse to the top of the Tool Properties window, then click and drag to slide the panel up. Figure 4.6 shows the Background Image 3D controls within the Tool Properties panel.

Tip

Whenever you select a tool, be it a box, tube, or some function, the properties for that tool will appear in this same area, under Tool Properties.

Figure 4.5

To adjust a backdrop image, first open the Adjust Backdrop Image controls from the View menu.

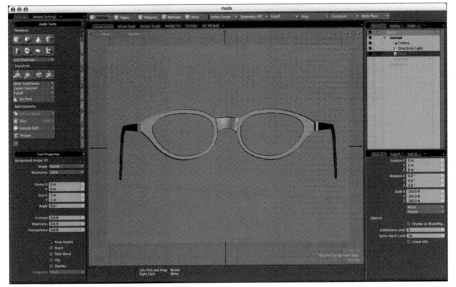

Figure 4.6

Opening the Adjust Backdrop Image controls shows the options in the Tool Properties panel. To view all or less of the panel, move your mouse to the top of the panel, and click and drag.

8. To adjust the backdrop image once the Adjust Backdrop Image controls are opened, click directly on the backdrop image in the viewport.

9. You'll see light-blue handles outline the image, with visible corners. You can click and drag on the corners to size the image larger or smaller, or you can click and drag the image to position it. Conversely, you can use the Center, Size, and Angle controls in the Tool Properties panel to adjust the image. For now the position of the image is fine, but it's too bright. Depending on the image, you can adjust the Contrast, Brightness, or Transparency. For this particular image, bring the Transparency setting to 50%. You can manually enter the value or click, hold, and drag the tiny arrows to the immediate right of the value. Figure 4.7 shows the adjustment.

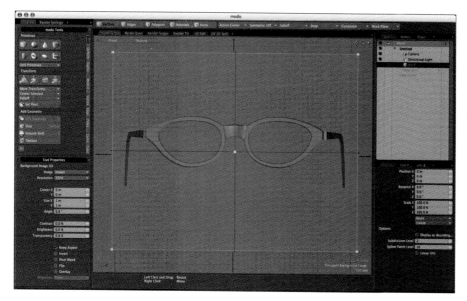

Figure 4.7

Depending on the image, you can adjust the brightness or contrast of the backdrop image. Here, the transparency has been adjusted for better visibility of the model you'll create.

10. Press the **q** key on your keyboard to turn off the Adjust Backdrop Image tool.

Creating the Basic Lens

Now that your backdrop image is in place, it's time to start creating the model.

1. Make sure the Tool Bar tab is selected at the top-left of the modo interface. Then, click the Basic list button, which lies vertically on the left side of the viewport. If you can't see all of the letters in these buttons, drag the Tool Properties panel down. Figure 4.8 shows the area, with the Basic button selected and highlighted in orange. This Basic button refers to basic geometry and basic functions, such as primitive creation, rotation, transformation, and so on.

2. Click the Box icon in the Primitives list to activate the Box tool. You'll see the Tool Properties panel at the bottom-left fill up with controls. For now, click and drag over the right lens of the backdrop image in the main viewport.

3. If you let go of the mouse, you'll see red and green handles appear around the geometry, as in Figure 4.9.

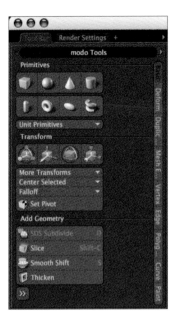

Figure 4.8

Many of your models will begin with the basics; therefore, start this project by clicking the Basic button to reveal the primitive object-creation tools.

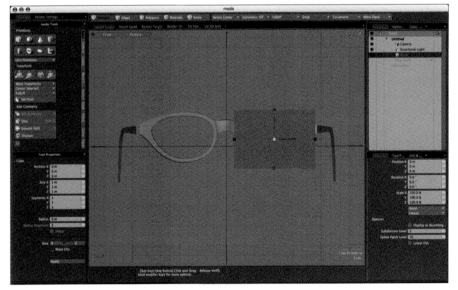

Figure 4.9

Red and green handles appear around the geometry.

4. Before you do anything, add some segments to this flat box. This will help you shape it. You can add segments in two ways at this point—either numerically in the Tool Properties panel at the bottom-left of the interface or, better yet, by clicking and dragging with your right mouse button. If you're on a Mac without a right mouse button, you can hold the Apple (Command) key. If you click and hold the right mouse button and move the mouse to the right, you'll add segments on the X axis. Moving left removes them. Create four segments; you should see three vertical lines.

5. Next, hold the right mouse button and move the mouse up to create three segments on the Y axis. You should see two lines horizontally.

6. One last setting in the Tool Properties panel: Add a Size value of about 1.8 cm to the Z axis. You can type this value into the field in the Tool Properties panel or just use .018, since the default unit of measurement in modo is meters. Once you've made your segments and added size to the Z axis, press the **q** key to turn off the Box tool. Figure 4.10 shows the box with four segments on the X and three segments on the Y. You won't see the size added to the Z axis just yet, but you will later.

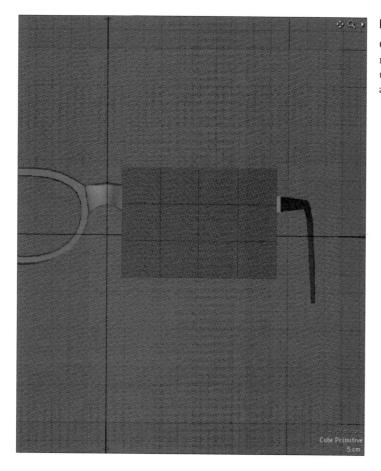

Figure 4.10

Creating primitive objects with multiple segments is easy by using the right mouse button and dragging.

You should note that you can create segments in all of your primitives by using the right mouse button. And it should also be noted that if you turn off your tool—in this case, the Box tool—you can't reactivate it and make the segments with the right mouse button. Instead, you would either need to rebuild the object or use modo's other tools to subdivide your object.

7. Because the backdrop image has some grey in it and your geometry's base surface is grey, go ahead and change the view style. This will help you not only see what you're working on; you'll also have a clearer view of the backdrop image. At the top of the viewport, change the viewport style to Wireframe by clicking the selection list, which should read Texture at the moment. Figure 4.11 shows the choice.

8. At this point you can start adjusting the shape to fit the eyeglass lens. Press the **t** key to activate the Element Move tool. For the record, this tool is located within the Deform list, as shown in Figure 4.12.

Figure 4.11

To view your model better and see the backdrop image, change your viewport style to Wireframe from the selection at the top-left of the viewport.

The Element Move tool will become one of your best friends in modo. This tool allows you to literally click and drag on a vertex (point), edge, or polygon. This one-click operation will aid your modeling efforts faster than you thought possible. Selecting it and dragging over your model will automatically highlight the element, such as an edge or polygon. Now, it's a little tricky to get used to, so be patient. You might accidentally move an edge when you wanted to move a point. Don't worry, though—Command+z (Mac) and Ctrl+z (PC) will undo!

Figure 4.12

The Element Move tool is located within the Deform list.

9. Begin at the top-left of the Wireframe box and, using the Element Move tool, click and drag the top-left corner vertex (point) down to match the outer rim of the eyeglass. Figure 4.13 shows the operation.

10. Remember, by using the Element Move tool, you do not need to select, move, and then deselect items. Simply click and drag the element and move on. So, repeating what you did in the previous step, move the other points on the outer edge of the box to match the shape of the eyeglass image. Figure 4.14 shows the rest of the points in place.

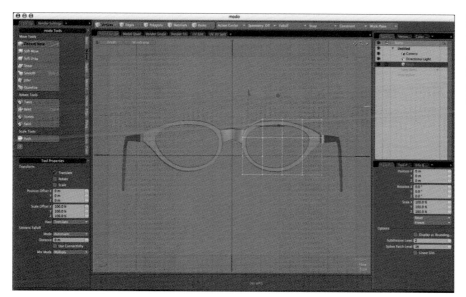

Figure 4.13

Using the Element Move tool, clicking and dragging on the top-left point allows you to quickly move it into position based on the backdrop image.

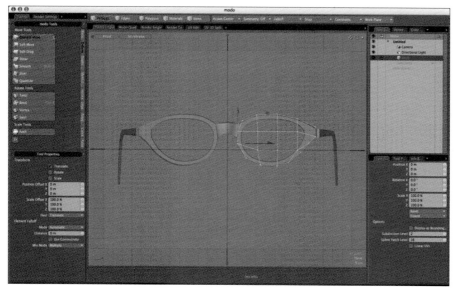

Figure 4.14

Continuing with the Element Move tool, the outer edge points of the box are moved to match the shape of the backdrop image.

Note

You might find that when using the Element Move tool, the control handles can get in the way. These are the two or three arrows that appear when you click an element. If they get in the way, just click off of (or away from) the object to move these handles. Then, go back and click and drag the desired point, edge, or polygon. You can also use the Tool Pipe to uncheck visibility by clicking the dot under the V heading. (V stands for visibility.) However, be sure to turn visibility back on again when needed.

11. Press Ctrl+spacebar and change the viewport to a Perspective view.

12. Hold the Alt/Option key, then click and drag in the viewport to rotate it. Figure 4.15 shows the view rotated.

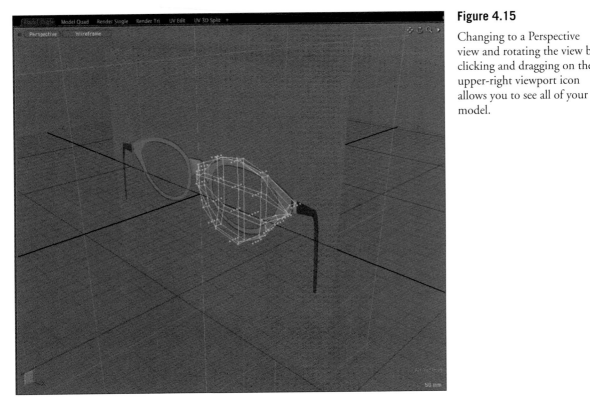

Figure 4.15

Changing to a Perspective view and rotating the view by clicking and dragging on the upper-right viewport icon allows you to see all of your model.

You can see that what you've created so far isn't that exciting. But, when you created the box, you added size on the Z axis. The object has depth, as you can now see.

13. Back at the top-left of the viewport, change the view style to Shaded. This will make the geometry appear solid.

14. Press the Tab key on your keyboard. This activates Subdivision mode, and you'll see your model smooth out. At this point, feel free to adjust the shape using the Element Move tool. When the basic shape is to your liking, save it and move forward with the tutorial. Remember to move back and forth between the Perspective view and Front view. You can use the **2** key on your numeric keypad to quickly jump to Front view.

Creating the Lens Details

You can see that using a backdrop image allows you to quickly create a general shape. From there, you can continue to use the backdrop image or go for it freestyle! This next section will show you how to create more detail in the eyeglass lens. From there, you'll build the rest of the eyeglasses, then surface and render.

1. Zoom into the eyeglass lens by clicking and dragging the magnifying glass icon in the upper-right of the modo viewport.

2. Next, at the top of the modo interface, click the Polygons button to tell modo you want to work with polygons. When you do so, the button will be highlighted in orange.

3. From there, click on the top edge of the eyeglass lens, selecting just one polygon. You can tell that you have one polygon selected by looking at the bottom-right of the viewport. You should see how many polygons, points, or edges are selected depending on what item mode you're using.

4. Holding the Shift key, select the polygon directly next to the polygon you've already selected. It can be in either direction, but make sure it's on the edge, not on the front or back. Figure 4.16 shows the two polygons selected.

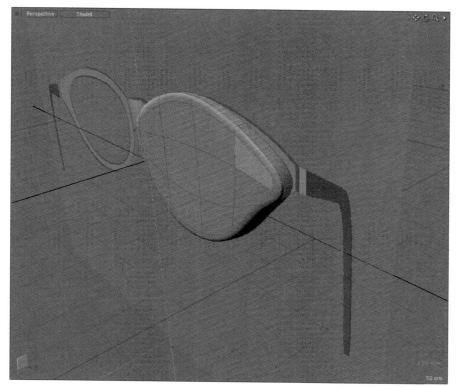

Figure 4.16

Select two polygons in order on the edge of the eyeglass.

Tip

One way to quickly select points, edges, or polygons is to click and drag the mouse. If you click a selection, then let go of the mouse button, holding the Shift key allows you to continue your selection. Conversely, holding the Ctrl key lets you click and deselect.

---

5. Now that you've told modo which way you will select polygons, the program selects the rest for you. Press the up arrow on your keyboard. The next polygon in succession will be selected. You can keep pressing the up arrow, or simply hold it down and the selection will continue around the entire edge. Figure 4.17 shows the full selection.

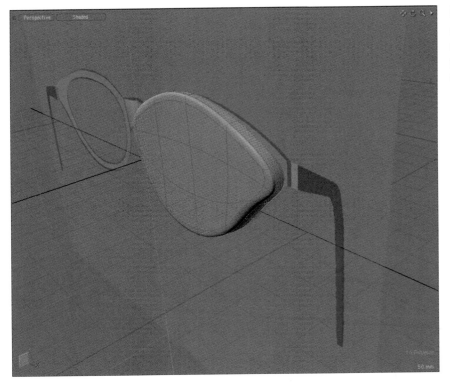

Figure 4.17

Once two polygons (or points or edges) are selected in order, you can use the up arrow to continue the selection.

This select loop feature is exceedingly handy and, as you might figure, using the down arrow deselects. Try using the right and left arrows as well, and see what happens. You'll use these throughout the book, so take some time to get a feel for them. Remember that Ctrl+z (PC) and Command+z (Mac) will undo your selections or de-selections, so if you mess up, just undo back to where you were. And of course, save often!

6. With all the outer-edge polygons selected, press the **b** key to select the Bevel tool, which resides within the Mesh Edit tools. After you activate the tool by pressing the **b** key, look in the Tool Properties panel at the bottom-left of the interface. Click the Group Polys option. This tells modo to bevel all polygons together. If you left this option unchecked, you'd bevel each selection separately.

7. Once you check Group Polys, click and drag in the viewport. You'll see the edges of the model sharpen up, but not too much. Figure 4.18 shows the bevel.

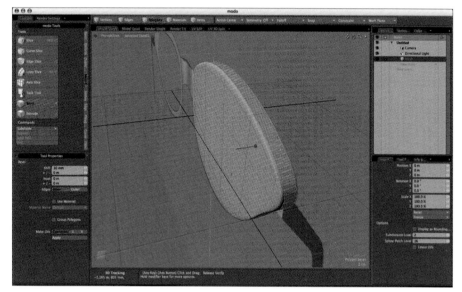

Figure 4.18

Beveling the selected polygons around the outer edge of the eyeglass helps shape it.

8. Press the **q** key to turn off the Bevel tool, and then click anywhere in the viewport away from the model to deselect the polygons.

9. To create the separation between the lens and the frame, you can work with the edges. First select Edges at the top of the modo interface (to the left of where you selected Polygons) to tell modo you want to work with edges.

10. Go to the front of the lens and, as you did for your polygon selection, select two edges in order on the outer area of the front of the lens, but make sure to cross over the corner, as shown in Figure 4.19. Then use the up arrow to select the loop. Your selection should look like Figure 4.20.

11. If you rotate your view around toward the front, you can see that the selected edge is not perfectly even with the outer edge of the object itself. Now, thinking ahead, you'd want that edge to be even because one side of the edge will be the frame and the other will be the lens. So, using the Element Move tool (press **t**), adjust the edge and vertices (points) to simply shape the selection. Figure 4.21 shows how your selected edge should end up.

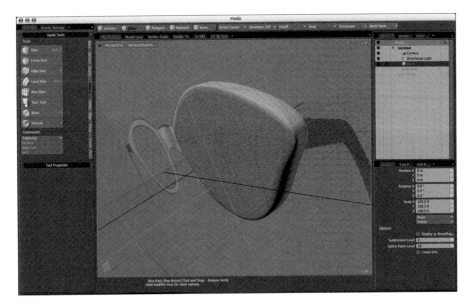

Figure 4.19

Select two edges crossing the corner of the front of the lens.

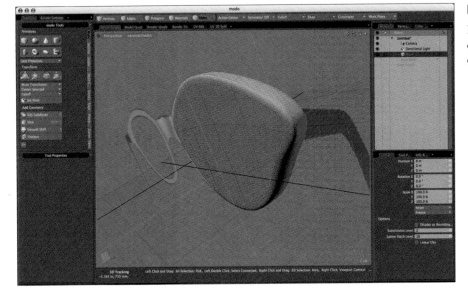

Figure 4.20

Pressing the up arrow continuously selects the edge loop.

12. Don't be too concerned with obtaining a perfect shape here. The idea is for you to understand the process of working with and editing points, edges, and polygons. Press the spacebar to turn off any tool you're using, then click a blank area in the viewport to deselect the edges.

13. At the top of the modo interface, select the Polygons button to tell modo you want to work with polygons. Then, run the mouse around the front portion of the eyeglass (the area on the inside of that edge you just selected).

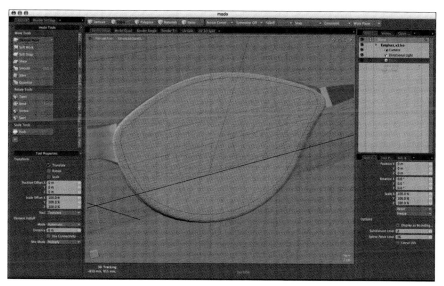

Figure 4.21

Adjusting the selected edge using the Element Move tool allows you to help shape the geometry.

14. This next step is a little more advanced, but it is really easy to do. It will help you save your steps for use later. Once the polygons are selected, go to the top of the modo interface and, from the System drop-down menu, select Record Macro (see Figure 4.22). You'll come back to this shortly. Figure 4.22 shows the selected polygons.

If you accidentally select more than you should, remember to hold the Ctrl key and click the polygon you do not want selected. This will deselect it while keeping the rest of your selections intact.

15. Making sure you're still in Polygons mode (click the selection at the top of the modo interface), press the **b** key to activate the Bevel tool.

16. At the bottom-left of the modo interface, look to the Tool Properties panel, and you'll see the bevel controls. Make sure Group Polys is selected. This will bevel all selected polygons as one.

Figure 4.22

Select the polygons on the front of the eyeglass that will make up the lens, and then choose Record Macro.

Tip

Here's a cool way to work in modo. With the polygons selected, hold the Ctrl key and watch the item buttons at the top of modo (Vertices, Edges, Polygons). You'll see the Edges button change to Boundary. While still holding the Ctrl key, click that Boundary button. The current polygon selection will change to an edge selection around the boundary of what you had previously selected.

17. In the main viewport, click once. You'll see a blue and a red handle. But look more closely: The blue handle has a little arrow at the end, and the red handle has a square. If you have trouble seeing the handles, rotate the view around by clicking and dragging the viewport rotation control in the upper-right of the interface.

Tip

A quick way to rotate around while in Perspective view is to hold down the Alt key, then click and drag directly in the view.

18. Click and drag the red handle, making sure you're clicking directly on the square of the red handle. When you move the mouse over the handle, the handle will be highlighted. Clicking and dragging changes the Inset value. Drag the red handle to inset the selected polygons inward, about 2 cm. You can watch the value in the Tool Properties panel.

19. Now you want to bevel again, but you need to create a little more geometry. Holding the Shift key, click once in the viewport. This creates a new bevel from the selection. It essentially starts a new bevel.

20. Bevel the inset one more time by clicking and dragging the red handle to 2 mm. Figure 4.23 shows the operation.

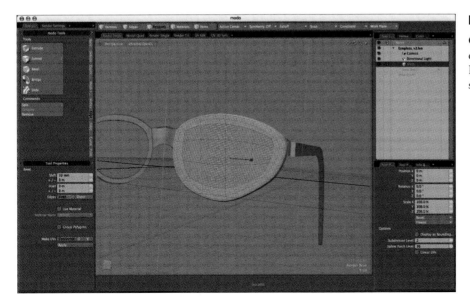

Figure 4.23

Clicking and dragging directly on the red handle with the Bevel tool active insets the selected polygons.

21. This time, instead of using the red handle, click and drag directly on the blue handle. This will allow you to shift the selected polygons. Shift them in toward the eyeglass –2 mm. Figure 4.24 shows the operation.

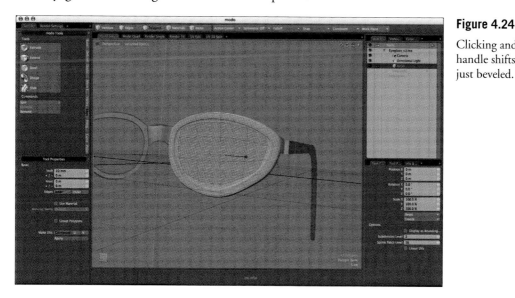

Figure 4.24

Clicking and dragging the blue handle shifts the polygons you just beveled.

22. Again, holding the Shift key, click once on the selected polygons. This creates a new bevel.

23. Inset the new bevel by clicking and dragging the red handle to about 3 mm. And, shift them by clicking and dragging the blue handle to 3 mm as well. You're pulling the selection out after you've beveled it so that it looks something like Figure 4.25.

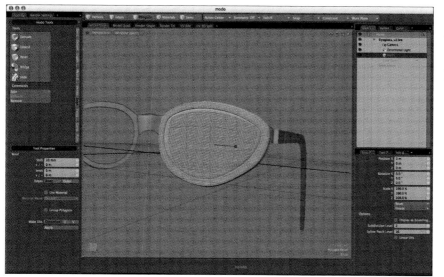

Figure 4.25

Another bevel operation to both inset and shift the polygons helps form the lens from the frame.

24. One last time, hold the Shift key and click once on the selection to create a new bevel. Then, click and drag the red handle to inset the selection to 2.6 cm. Click and drag the blue handle to shift the selection to 5 mm. Note that the inset here is centimeters, and the shift is millimeters. Figure 4.26 shows the result.

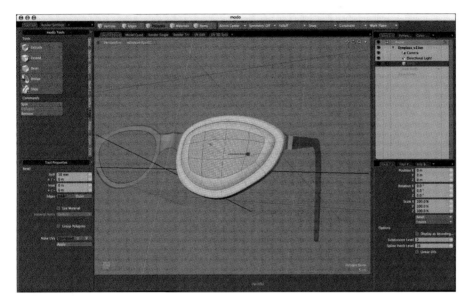

Figure 4.26

One last bevel operation has the lens defined from the frame.

25. You're almost there! Hold the Shift key, but this time press the right arrow on your keyboard twice. This will expand the selected polygons so that your entire lens will be selected.

26. There are other tools in modo that can help refine your geometry, which you'll learn about throughout this book. However, try one now. On the left side of the interface, change to the Deform tools by clicking the vertical button at the left of the viewport. Then, under the Move Tools category, click the Smooth tool. (You can also select the Smooth tool by pressing Shift+S.)

27. Once the Smooth tool is turned on, click and drag on the polygons in the viewport. Watch them smooth out. Hold the mouse button down and move the mouse back and forth to see the geometry even out. Your goal here is to simply smooth out the bevel operations.

28. After you have smoothed out the selection, press the spacebar to turn off the Smooth tool. Then, click a blank area in the viewport to deselect the polygons.

29. Now go back up to the System drop-down list and uncheck the Record Macro option.

30. Save your work.

31. Now go back to the System drop-down list at the top of the interface and choose Save to File. When you selected Record Macro at the beginning of these bevel operations, modo stored your actions in a file that is currently held in memory. Save this file to a place on your hard drive so you can use it in the future.

32. Rotate the Perspective view around to the back of the eyeglass and select the area that would make up the lens, as you did previously at the beginning of your bevel steps. Figure 4.27 shows the selection.

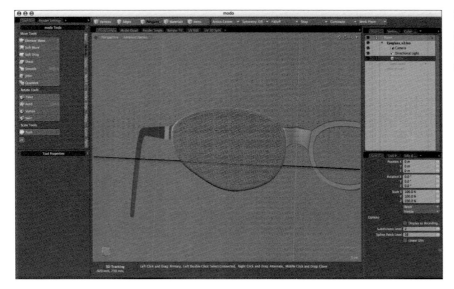

Figure 4.27

Select the polygons on the back of the eyeglass that will make up the lens.

33. If your macro is still in memory, you can select Replay from the System drop-down menu. If not, you can simply call the macro from file (since you saved it) by selecting Run Script from the System drop-down menu or by pressing F6.

34. Once you run the script, you'll see the selected polygons quickly turn into a lens, similar to the lens you manually beveled on the front of the eyeglass. Pretty cool!

You can see how useful Record Macro can be. Think about things like windows, doors, or bottles. You can create a slew of macro scripts so that whenever you need a similar function, you can save yourself a lot of time.

Creating the Frame

This last modeling section will use some of the same techniques as the previous sections. You'll select polygons, bevel, and so on. There can be a lot more details with this model, but for now this will give you a good idea of how to begin creating models in modo. But before you build the frame of the eyeglasses, shape the lens.

1. Making sure that the work you've created is saved, click the Backdrop button from the viewport display type at the top-left of the viewport. This is the same place where you added the backdrop image earlier in the lesson. When you click Backdrop, a panel opens. Instead of loading an image this time, select the icon that says None. This will remove the image from the backdrop.

2. Next, make any changes you see fit to your model's shape using the Element Move tool.

3. Save your work.

4. Click the Deform list of tools from the vertical listings on the left side of the interface. There, you'll find the Bend tool under the Rotate Tools category. Select it and click to the center of your eyeglass object in the viewport where your model resides.

   What you'll see when you click is a blue ring and a long handle sticking out. It's a bit confusing at first, but you'll soon realize its power. Figure 4.28 shows the tool.

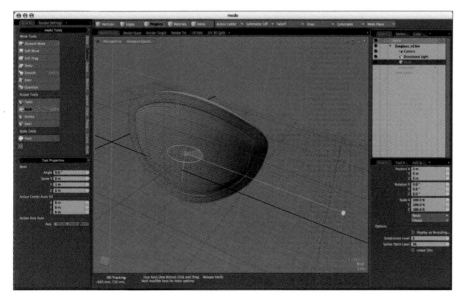

Figure 4.28

Activating the Bend tool by clicking in the viewport displays its simple yet powerful controls.

First, the handle is your control to bend. If you look over at your Tool Properties on the left of the interface, you'll see a setting for Action Axis Auto. If you change the axis from Z to X or Y, you'll see the blue control ring change direction in the viewport.

5. Change the axis to Y. The ring should lay flat in the viewport. Remember, you can hold the Alt key and rotate the view around to see the workspace better. You should be working in the Perspective view.

6. Now click, hold, and drag the blue ring. You'll see the model bend, as shown in Figure 4.29.

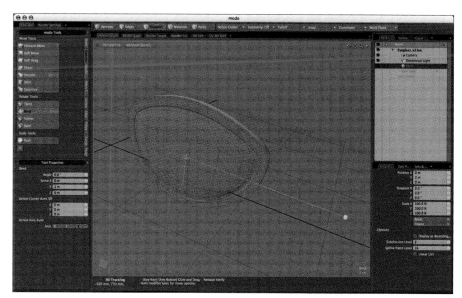

Figure 4.29

Dragging the blue handle for the Bend tool allows you to easily bend the object.

7. The long handle sticking out of the ring with the light-colored square at the end is the falloff. Click and drag that little light-colored square around and watch what it does to your model. Essentially, it changes how much the Bend tool affects your model.

8. One last thing to try: If you click, hold, and drag in the very center of the blue ring, you'll change where the bend operation begins. modo is interactive, so you'll be able to see the effects of moving the tool around right away.

9. Figure 4.30 shows the approximate bend you should go for with your lens. A good place to position the blue control ring is toward the left side of the object. Remember, you've been modeling the right side of the eyeglasses, so this is the side that would bend around the face.

10. Press **q** to turn off the Bend tool, and save your work.

11. To make the rest of the frame for the glasses, rotate the view around to the back. Select the polygons within the upper corner of the object, as shown in Figure 4.31. Make sure that one polygon resides on the side of the object.

12. Under the Mesh Edit list of tools, select Extrude. Click once, and then drag the blue handle in the viewport to extrude the selection, as shown in Figure 4.32. Drag the selection about 10 cm or so. Feel free to drag the other handles to position the extrusion as you like.

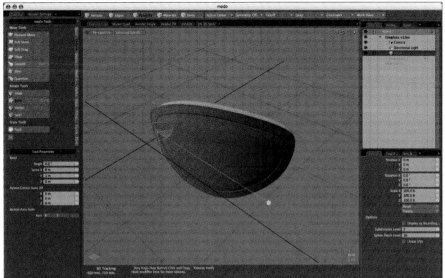

Figure 4.30

Using the Bend tool, you can easily shape the right lens of the glasses.

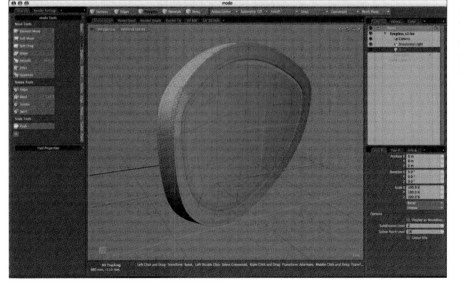

Figure 4.31

The next phase means selecting just a few polygons in the upper-back corner of the lens.

13. Hold the Shift key and click again on the polygon selection. Then, drag the blue handle again to extend the eyeglass frame a little farther, about –7 cm on the Z axis. Figure 4.33 shows the seven extrusions.

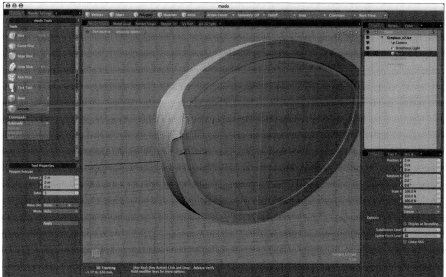

Figure 4.32

Select the polygons on the back of the eyeglass that will make up the lens.

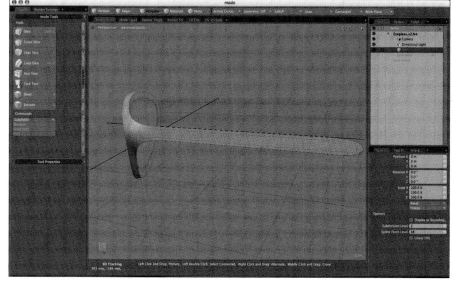

Figure 4.33

Once you create the initial extrusion of selected polygons using the Extrude tool, repeat the step seven times.

Note

While you have repeated the bevel steps seven times, you can also extrude one time, then change the Sides attribute in the Tool Properties to give it additional segments.

14. Now that you have the frame of the glasses extended, all that's left is to make the loop for the ear. Back under the Deform tool list, select Bend. Click toward the back of the frame you just extruded, as shown in Figure 4.34.

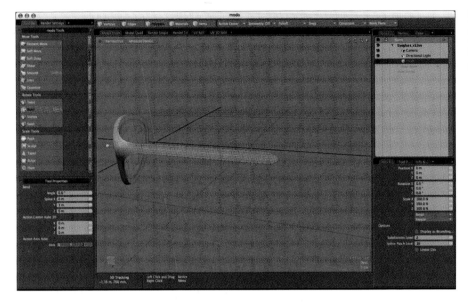

Figure 4.34

The Bend tool will help make the final curved portion of the eyeglass frame.

15. Make sure the axis for the Bend tool is set to X by checking the setting in the Tool Properties panel on the left of the interface.

16. Make sure the falloff control is to the back of the object. Click and drag the highlighted light-blue square so that it resides slightly behind the frame. Then, click and drag on the blue handle to bend the end of the frame. Remember, you can rotate around your view, move the Bend tool, and move the falloff control handle to interactively shape the model. Figure 4.35 shows the result.

17. Press the spacebar to turn off the Bend tool, and save your work. Of course, you can add a lot more detail to the model, perhaps by beveling the edges more or cutting in small details on the frame. For now, though, you should have a good idea of how the modeling process works, as well as how to work with the tools and interface. However, there are a few more steps to complete before you texture and render this model, so keep going!

18. Rotate your view around to see the front of the model. From the Duplicate tool list, select the Mirror tool.

19. Click on the very left of the model to mirror it over. This tool (like most modo tools) is very interactive, and you can experiment by holding the mouse button down on the Mirror tool's highlighted square and dragging it around. Figure 4.36 shows the mirrored object.

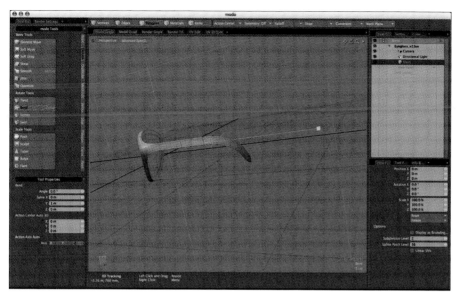

Figure 4.35

Using the Bend tool again, bend the end of the glasses.

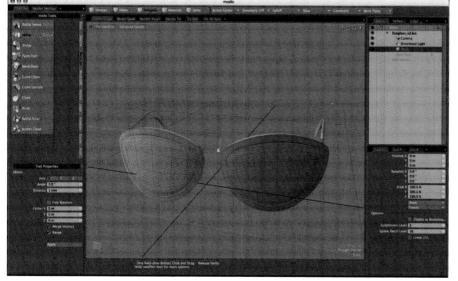

Figure 4.36

The Mirror tool comes in handy to make a perfect copy of the model.

20. You're going to use one more tool to make your model complete. Press **q** to turn off the Mirror tool. You should still be in Polygons mode (from the top of the interface). Then, select the polygons that make up the upper inside edge of each lens. Figure 4.37 shows the selections.

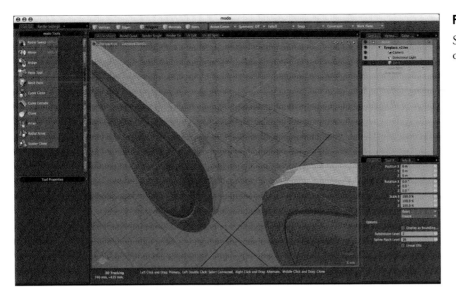

Figure 4.37

Select a few polygons
on each lens.

21. Under the Duplicate tool list where the Mirror tool was, you'll also see a tool
called Bridge. Select this. Then, click in the viewport. The two opposing polygons will connect. If you continue to hold the mouse button and drag, you can
add segments to the bridge, giving it more detail. Add about five segments. You
can view how many segments you're adding by watching the value in the Tool
Properties on the bottom-left side of the interface. Figure 4.38 shows the result.

The Bridge tool can also connect smoothly, or linearly. The default mode is
Curve, which is perfect for the bridge of the glasses. You can change the mode
in the Tool Properties.

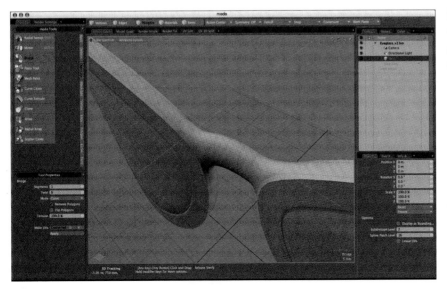

Figure 4.38

The Bridge tool with the mode
set to Curve is a perfect way to
create the bridge of the glasses.

22. Press **q** to turn off the Bridge tool, and then save your work. Press the **a** key to fit the model to the viewport, and admire your work.

There is more you can do here, such as selecting the edge of the new bridged area. You can easily double-click on the upper edge of the bridge, press **b** for bevel, and click and drag to sharpen the geometry. The same techniques can be applied to all four corners of the bridge. And, at any time you can undo your actions by choosing Undo from the Edit drop-down list or pressing Ctrl+Z (PC) or Command+Z (Mac).

Congratulations! You just completed a model in modo 201/202!

Basic Surfacing

As you can see, modeling in modo is pretty straightforward. What's more, once you're completely comfortable with the tools, you can model without thinking about what you're doing. That is to say, you won't worry about which tool to use or how to control the shape; you'll just do it. But there will be much more modeling throughout the book. For now, how about adding some simple textures to this model?

1. Making sure the model you've created is saved, while you're still in Polygons mode, select all of the polygons that make up the lenses, as shown in Figure 4.39.

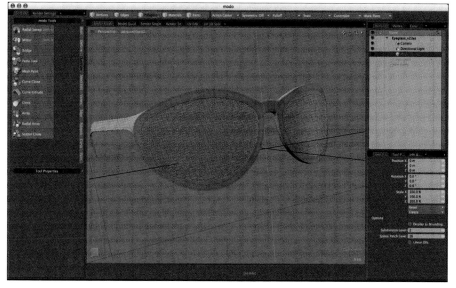

Figure 4.39

Select the polygons that make up the lenses.

2. Press **m** to call up the Polygon Set Material dialog box. Enter the name for the selected polygons as Eyeglass Lens and give them a light-blue color or something similar, as shown in Figure 4.40.

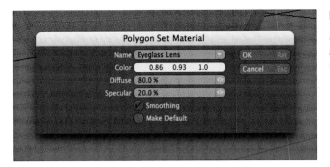

Figure 4.40

Set the material for the selected polygons by pressing the **m** key.

Note

Note that you are creating a material group. This is a group of polygons that you can see in the Info panel. By creating this group, modo will automatically create a mask for you in the Shader Tree that references this group of polygons. modo has also created a material for you and put it inside that mask. There is a distinction to be aware of here because you are not creating a material—you are creating a material group. It is a mask that references this group and a material inside the mask simultaneously.

3. When you're finished, click the OK button or press Enter (PC) or Return (Mac).

4. Now invert the selection by pressing the left bracket key ([) on your keyboard. This is the key to the right of the P key. You can also find this command under the Select drop-down menu. What this will do is deselect what's currently selected (the lenses) and select what's not currently selected (the frame).

5. After the Invert command, you should see only the frames for the glasses selected. Press **m** to again call up the Polygon Set Material dialog box.

6. As you might have guessed, give these selected polygons a material name of Frames and set the color to a color you like.

7. Press Enter (PC) or Return (Mac) or click OK to close the Polygon Set Material dialog box, and then click a blank area in the viewport to deselect the polygons.

8. Save your model!

9. At the top-left of the interface, there are two tabbed viewports. One reads Tool Bar, which is the one you've been working in. To the right of it is Render Settings. Select this option.

10. New tools will appear, and at the top you will see a column labeled Shader Tree. Move your mouse over the edge of the column between the viewport and the tools, and a little double arrow will appear. When it does, click and drag to widen the tool area.

11. Then, in the Shader Tree, click the little arrow in front of the Render listing. You'll see expanded settings, as shown in Figure 4.41.

12. You'll get into the Shader Tree much more throughout the book, but this chapter will give you a quick overview to surfacing and rendering an object. Expand the EyeGlass_Lens material listing by clicking the triangle to the left of the listing.

13. After you expand the listing, you'll see a listing labeled Material (2). Select this, and you'll see this surface's values below in the Render Properties panel, as shown in Figure 4.42.

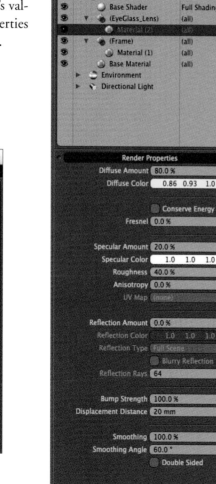

Figure 4.42

Selecting the material for the eyeglass frames calls up the appropriate settings in the lower panel.

Figure 4.41

The Shader Tree is a cool, complex, powerful place within modo 201/202.

14. You're not going to change the surface too much at this point, but you will later in the book. Change the Reflection Amount to about 20%. Adjust the color if you'd like, and leave everything else alone.

15. Vertically on the right side of the Render Properties panel, you'll see Material Ref, which is the tool list you're working in now. You'll also see Material Trans. Select this.

16. In the properties that appear, change the Transparent amount to about 85%.

17. Change Refraction to about 1.3.

18. Save your work.

19. Back in the Shader Tree, select the Material:Frame listing. Click the triangle in front of the listing to expand. Select Material (2); here, you can adjust the color and other basic settings. Change the Specular Amount to 60%. Also, click on Double Sided at the bottom of the panel.

    For now, these settings are just fine for the lens and frame, but if you're comfortable, adjust as you like. Remember to save often and that you can always undo to get back to a setting you inadvertently changed. The Shader Tree is an amazing new addition to modo 201/202. You'll use the Shader Tree extensively later in the book.

Basic Rendering

You've made it to the last point of the tutorial! Here, you'll get a quick lesson in rendering in modo 201/202. There are significant tools when it comes to rendering, all of which you'll work with throughout the book. This section will have you set up a camera, a light, and an environment.

1. Working with your previous lesson results, look to the right side of the modo interface, under the Item List. You'll see a camera listed. Click it and watch. Nothing happens!

2. It's okay that nothing happened because all you did was select the camera. Your current view is a Perspective view. Change this to a Camera view by clicking the drop-down list at the top-left of the viewport. Depending on your setup, you might see something like Figure 4.43 when switching to Camera view.

Note

You should get into the habit of rendering with the selected camera. However, you can render your current view. To do so, click Render Visible from the Render menu at the top of the interface. You can also just press Ctrl+F9.

Figure 4.43

Switching to Camera view means you'll have to set the camera in position for the render.

3. The reason you can't see a good view of your object is because the camera is not set up. However, the camera is selected from the Item List, so all you need to do is move it in place. Hold the Alt and Ctrl keys on your keyboard, and then click and drag with the left mouse button. You're now moving the camera in and out on the Z axis. Move it in toward the model. Holding Alt/Option and using the left mouse button translates the camera around the center of the view. Basically, the camera is orbiting the object.

4. Holding the Alt and Shift keys while clicking with the left mouse button will move your camera around the X and Y axes. Holding the Alt key and clicking the left mouse button rotates the view. Work with these settings to move the camera into a comfortable view of the glasses, something like Figure 4.44. Also, holding the Alt/Option key and using the right mouse button will rotate the camera. If the bank movement becomes awkward, move the cursor toward the edge of the viewport and hold the Alt/Option key, and then use the left mouse button and drag up or down to fix.

5. Back in the Item List, click New Item. It's slightly ghosted, but it's just below the Camera listing. This will create a new object in a new layer. Your glasses will seem to disappear, but don't worry; they're just in another layer.

6. On the left side of the modo interface, change the Render Settings tab back to Tool Bar. And in the Basic list of tools, select the Box tool. This is pretty much the first step you did at the beginning of this chapter.

7. With the Box tool selected, change your view to a Top view. Draw a large flat box, as shown in Figure 4.45.

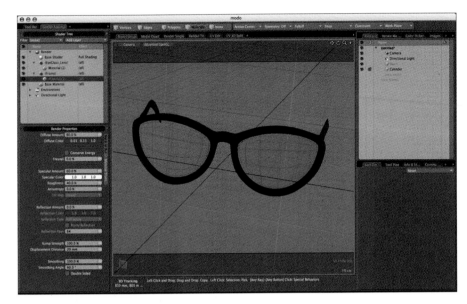

Figure 4.44

Working in a Camera view, you can position the camera into view to set up the scene for a render.

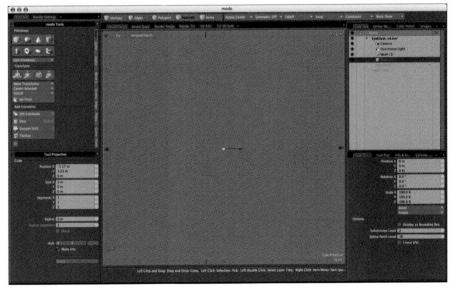

Figure 4.45

From a Top view, draw a flat box.

8. Change back to the Camera view, and then, in the Item List, click the eyeball icon to the left of Mesh (1), as shown in Figure 4.46.

9. You can see that the eyeglasses are now a background layer. Take a look at Figure 4.46. Mesh (2) is selected—you can determine that because a large grey bar covers the listing. Selecting the eyeball icon for other meshes on other layers makes them visible in the backdrop. Currently, the backdrop is set to Wireframe, and although you can change this, leave it as is for right now.

10. Make sure you're in Polygons mode (from the top of the modo interface), and double-click on the flat box you created. Conversely, you can press Shift, and then click the spacebar to jump to Items selection mode. This will allow you to avoid using the Item List to select.

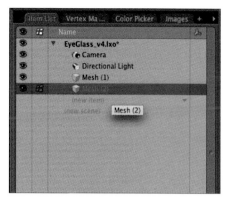

Figure 4.46

Click the eyeball icon in the Mesh List to make it visible in the background.

11. Press the **w** key to activate the Move tool, and then click and drag on the green handle to move the box down under the glasses, as shown in Figure 4.47.

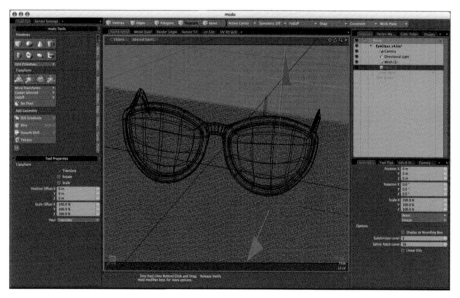

Figure 4.47

Using the Move tool, move the flat box down on the Y axis by clicking and dragging on the green handle.

12. You can also click and drag the blue handle to move the flat box on the Z axis. And if your box doesn't fill your scene, press the **r** key to activate the Stretch tool. Click and drag on the appropriate handle to stretch the object on any axis. Clicking and dragging the center box of the Stretch tool scales it equally on all sides.

13. While the polygons are still selected for the flat box, press **m** to call up the Polygon Set Material dialog box. Name this selection Floor and give it a simple grey color.

14. Save your work.

15. Press F9 on your keyboard. If you're on a Mac laptop, you might need to press Fn+F9. Figure 4.48 shows your first render.

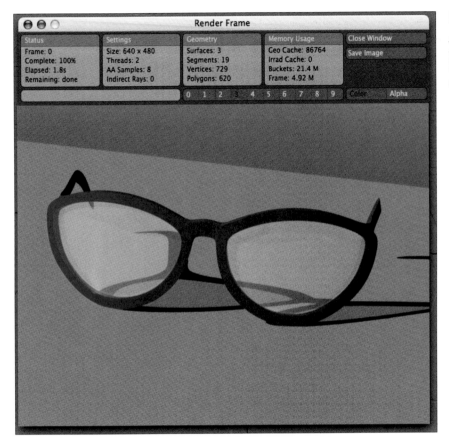

Figure 4.48

A default render of the model you made. Nothing to write home about, but a few settings can give it a much better look.

16. At the top-left of the modo interface, select the Render Settings tab. Click the Render listing in the Shader Tree.

17. Below the Shader Tree, under Render Properties, click the Global Illumination button on the vertical list on the right side of the panel. In the panel, click the Enable button, as shown in Figure 4.49.

18. At the top of the Render Properties panel, bring the Ambient Intensity up to 0.07 to brighten the scene a little bit more.

19. In the Shader Tree, select the Directional Light listing. Expand the listing and select Light Material.

20. In the Render Properties panel below the Shader Tree, bring the Opacity to 0%. This essentially turns off the light.

21. Save your work.

22. Press F9 to render the scene again (or Fn+F9 on a Mac laptop). Figure 4.50 shows the render. It's a bit blue, but you can fix that.

23. The reason your render has strong blue overtones is because the default environment has a blue sky. Turning on global illumination diffuses that blue color throughout your scene. Go back up to the Shader Tree and select the Environment listing. Expand the listing and select Environment Material.

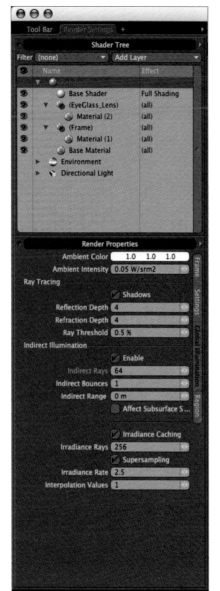

Figure 4.49

Enable Global Illumination for your scene for a much more realistic look.

24. Below the Shader Tree in the Render Properties panel, change Environment Type from 4 Color Gradient (you can see how much blue is there) to Constant. Change the Zenith color to a soft white or grey.

25. Press F9 to render again. Figure 4.51 shows the change.

Figure 4.50

Global Illumination rendering on the glasses looks more realistic than a basic light, but there is an overall blue cast to the scene.

Figure 4.51

Changing the environment color affects the overall global illumination of the scene.

Tip

If you look closely at the Shader Tree, the small thumbnail images are actual Preview renders. modo has a feature called iView that provides a quick render of your scene without actually rendering. When changing colors and environments, take a look at the thumbnails in the Shader Tree for a quick reference. Also, you can change the size of these thumbnails by right-clicking directly on the Shader Tree heading of the panel.

26. Overall, the render is pretty boring. But you can see how drastic the change is from the first render, and all you did was make one change to the environment. Using a 2 Color Gradient as the Environment Type instead, you can add some warmth to the render. Figure 4.52 shows the final render with an orange-colored Nadir setting and an off-white Zenith. And, a 15% Reflection value has been added to the Floor surface.

Figure 4.52

Using 2 Color Gradient for the Environment Type in the Render Settings panel, you can add warmth to the render.

Overall, you can get a lot more out of a simple render such as this. You can add more color and additional lights. You can also add more detail to the glasses, which would create more interest. But the goal of this chapter was to walk you through the entire modo workflow. You modeled, moved around the interface, changed views, created surfaces, worked with a camera, and rendered a globally illuminated scene. Not bad!

From this point, experiment on your own. I encourage you to put the book down and work in modo for a few hours. Try just texturing and lighting simple geometry. When you're comfortable with that, try modeling some other objects around your desk, such as a computer mouse, a monitor, or a lamp. Then, when you're ready, move through the rest of this book to learn about all modo 201/202 has to offer.

Part II

Creating and Building

5

Basic Building Blocks

By now you should have a good sense of how modo 201/202 approaches the creation process. But what is better than actually creating something to see the process for yourself? The first four chapters, Part I of the book, introduced you to the program, the interface, the tools, how to select and deselect, and how the key tool controls work. This next section will take you through four more chapters, introducing you to modeling with modo and perhaps a little bit more. With each chapter, you'll learn how to create models from the ground up. Then, you'll learn all about the Shader Tree and how to texture your models.

Building Blocks, Literally

You probably thought that because this chapter was titled "Basic Building Blocks," you'd learn about fundamentals of the program, tools to create models, and so on. No way! You're through with those boring chapters. In this chapter, you're actually going to build blocks!

1. Take a look at Figure 5.1, which shows what you will create in this first tutorial. You'll learn about the basic modeling tools and how to navigate your way around the Item List.

2. Begin with a default 201/202 layout by selecting this option from the Layout menu at the top of the modo interface.

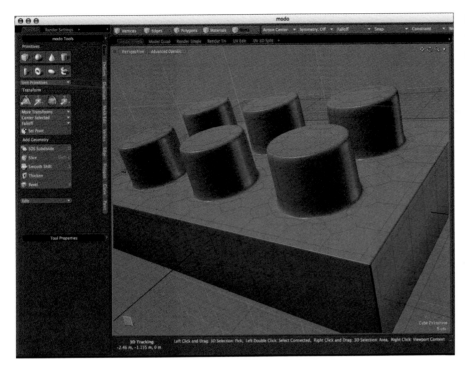

Figure 5.1

Basic building blocks you will create in this first tutorial.

3. You'll start building many objects with simple primitive shapes. On the left side of the interface under the Tool Bar tab, select the Cube primitive. When you do, the Tool Properties panel at the bottom-left of the screen will populate, as shown in Figure 5.2.

4. Rather than drawing out a box in the Layout viewport, you can create one more specific to your modeling task. Adjust the Cube primitive settings to the following:

Position	X	0
	Y	0
	Z	0
Size	X	1.8m
	Y	35cm
	Z	1.1m
Segments	X	10
	Y	2
	Z	7
Radius	0	
Axis	Z	

Note

Selecting the modo 201/202 default layout two times in a row will reset it back to its original state.

Figure 5.2

Select the Cube primitive within the Tool Bar tab.

5. After you've entered the settings, click the Apply button at the bottom of the Tool Properties panel. If you can't see it, simply click and drag the panel upward from the top edge of the panel. Figure 5.3 shows the Cube primitive with the applied settings.

6. Press the **q** key to deactivate the Cube primitive.

7. Over on the right side of the interface, look in the Item List. You'll see that the new cube you've created is listed just as Mesh. Because you only have one object created in one layer, this is more than fine. However, it's a good idea to get in the habit of naming your models as you build them, regardless of how complex or simple they are. Select the name Mesh in the Item List, right-click, and select Rename, as shown in Figure 5.4. Rename the mesh Toy Block or something similar.

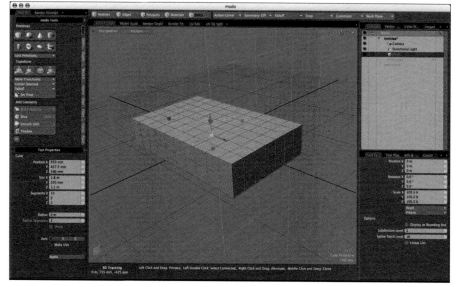

Figure 5.3

A specific Cube primitive shape is created numerically. The segments play a key role in the creation of the toy block.

Figure 5.4

Note

When you right-click on an item in the Item List, not only can you rename the item, but you can duplicate, delete, and more. Pay close attention to the options when you right-click.

Any time you create a new mesh, right-click on its name in the Item List and rename it to keep organized.

8. Now is a good time to save, so if you're on a Mac, press Apple+s. Choose a name and a place to save your current scene. If you're on a PC, press Ctrl+s.

   This project will give you a good idea of how powerful the modo tools are, even on the simplest level. You've created a basic cube with a specific number of segments for a reason. With the subdivided top surface of the mesh, you can select specific polygons and edges to create more detail. This same principle applies to almost anything you'll create.

9. If you press the Tab key, you'll see the cube round out. The Tab turns on subdivision surfaces, as shown in Figure 5.5.

10. You'll want your final model to be subdivisional, but as you can see here, it's too smooth. This is a good thing because you want to always be adding more detail rather than trying to take it away. Press the Tab key again to return to your original square cube.

11. Rather than adding unnecessary geometry to your entire model by creating more polygons, you can work with just the edges to create the sharp lines your model needs. Select the Edges mode button at the top of the interface to tell modo you want to work with edges.

12. If you double-click on the closest edge, you'll select the entire length of that edge. Figure 5.6 shows the example.

13. By pressing the up arrow multiple times (on your keyboard), you'll begin selecting the contiguous edge. Keep pressing until your selection loops around, encompassing the object. Then, repeat the process until you have all outer edges selected. Figure 5.7 shows the full selection. Note that you should see a listing of 76 edges in the bottom-right of the viewport when all the outer edges are selected. And, don't forget that you can hold the Alt/Option key, then click and drag the view to rotate around to select the edges on the other side of the cube.

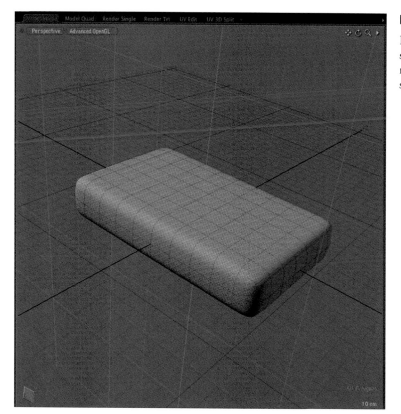

Figure 5.5

Pressing the Tab key to turn on subdivisional surfaces for your model shows that it's too smooth at this point.

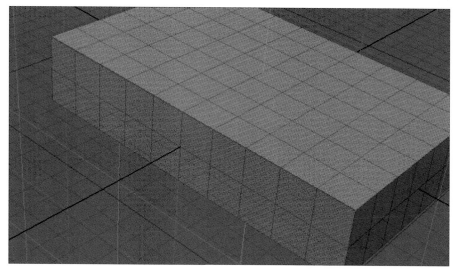

Figure 5.6

Double-clicking on an edge selects the entire length of the edge.

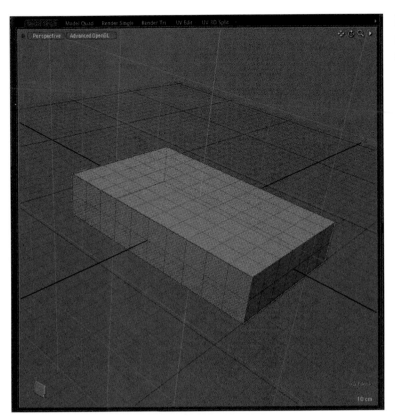

Figure 5.7

Select all outer edges of the cube.

Note

You can also hold the Shift key and double-click on each edge length you want to select.

14. Now that the outer edges are selected, press the **b** key to activate the Bevel tool. Click and drag on the model to bevel the selected edges. Take a look at the Tool Properties for the Bevel tool on the left side of the interface. Bevel mode should be set to Inset, with a value of 4.1mm. You can manually enter this value if you want, and also add a Round Level of 2. Figure 5.8 shows the result.

15. Press the **q** key to drop the Bevel tool. Then, click a blank area of the layout to deselect the edges.

16. Save your scene.

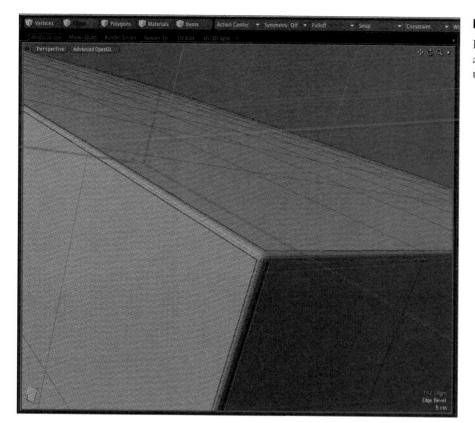

Figure 5.8

Bevel the edges of the cube, and also add a little rounding to them.

Note

If you look at the name of your model in the Item List at the right of the interface, you might notice a little asterisk after it. When this appears, it means that a change has happened, such as a move, bevel, and so on. When you save your work, the asterisk will go away. It's a good idea to keep your eye on this to make sure you're saving often. That is, of course, if you're the forgetful type.

---

17. Now if you press the Tab key to turn on subdivison surfaces, the model holds its shape, but the edges have a very slight but smooth rounding. By beveling the edges, you've added more geometry to those specific areas, and when the subdivision surfaces are applied (Tab key) you have greater control over the shape.

    The toy block you're building doesn't have round edges, but if you were to look at almost any object in the real world, the edges are rarely straight lines. They have smoothness, and it's this edge detail that will help give your models realism.

18. Choose Polygons mode from the top of the modo interface, and select four polygons on the top of the model, at the left corner. However, make the selection one row in from the each edge, as shown in Figure 5.9.

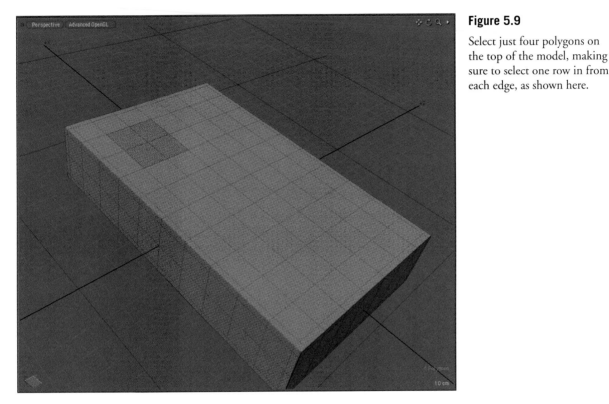

Figure 5.9

Select just four polygons on the top of the model, making sure to select one row in from each edge, as shown here.

19. Press Shift+A to fit the selection to view.

20. Press Shift+T to triangulate the selected polygons. This command activates the Triple function found in the Polygon vertical menu listing.

21. If your model looks like Figure 5.10, you have subdivisional surfaces on. For now, you don't want this because it will complicate the mesh, even though it will give it a better appearance. If it is on, deselect these polygons by left-clicking on them. When the polygons are no longer selected, press the Tab key to turn off the subdivisions. Then, select the four polygons (now eight with subdivisions) again. Your selection should look like Figure 5.11.

Note

Remember that you can just left-click into an empty workspace to deselect vertices, edges, or polygons.

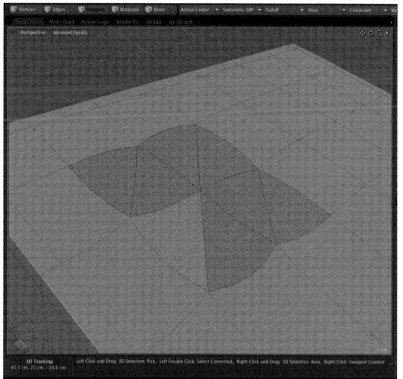

Figure 5.10

If you select and triple these four polygons and the mesh looks distorted, you're in subdivisional surface mode.

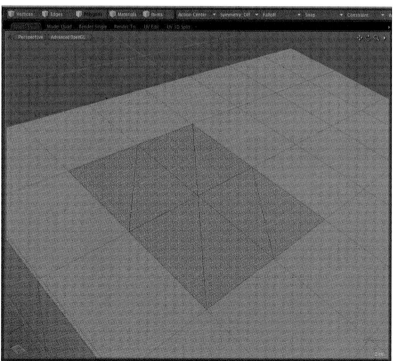

Figure 5.11

Without subdivisional surfaces turned on for this model, the selected and tripled polygons remain squared.

22. Now select Edges mode from the top of the modo interface and then, holding the Shift key, select the two separate edges that run parallel to the two contiguous edges, as shown in Figure 5.12.

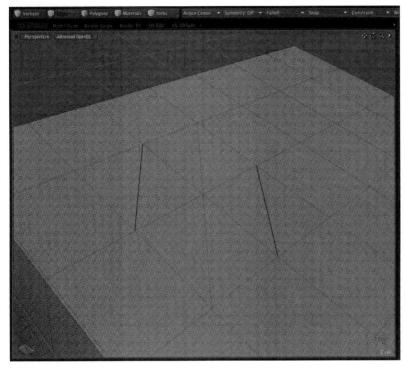

Figure 5.12

Select the two edges that are parallel to the contiguous edges, as shown here.

23. When the edges are selected, press the **v** key to spin them. This command is also found in the Edges tab of the modo Tools form within the Tool Bar tab. Figure 5.13 shows the result.

24. After you've spun the edges so they are contiguous, hold the Shift key and run the mouse around the edges that make up the inside of the initial four polygons, as shown in Figure 5.14.

25. With this star-like ring of edges selected, press the **b** key to activate the Bevel tool. Make sure that in the Tool Properties for the Bevel tool, the Mode is set to Inset, the Value is set to 0 m, Use Material is unchecked, and Round Level is set to 0. The Round Level might have a value from the last time you used it, so be sure to clear it out to 0; otherwise, you'll have odd results.

Note

A great way to work is to press Ctrl+d to reset the tool to its default state.

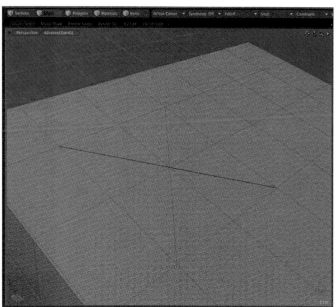

Figure 5.13

Pressing the **v** key activates the Spin Edges command.

26. When you're ready, simply click and drag in the viewport to bevel the selected edges to about 8 cm. You can see the value in the Tool Properties changing as you bevel. You don't want the beveled edges to cross over each other. Figure 5.15 shows the operation. If it looks as if there's an error with the model, don't worry. All you have to do is drop the tool (press **q**) and deselect all by clicking into an empty workspace. Then, go to Polygons mode and press the **f** key twice to refresh everything.

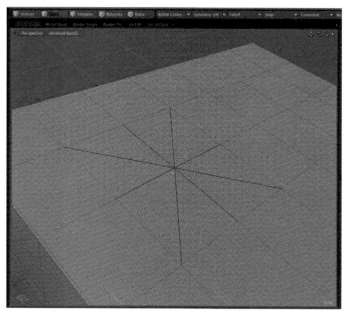

Figure 5.14

Once the edges are spun, select all of the edges that make up the four polygons.

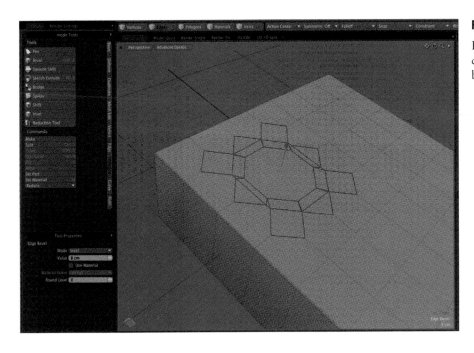

Figure 5.15

Bevel the selected edges, being careful not to overlap them by beveling too much.

27. Once the bevel is complete, press **q** to turn off the Bevel tool.

28. Next, change to Polygons mode at the top of the modo interface, then click to select the center eight-sided disc, as shown in Figure 5.16.

29. Save your model!

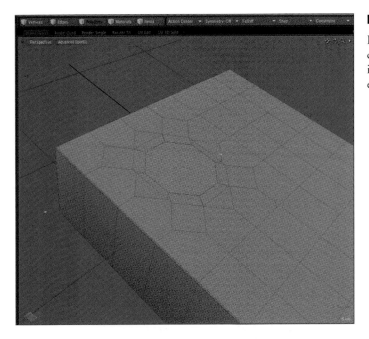

Figure 5.16

In Polygons mode, select the center eight-sided disc, which is the result of the beveled edges.

The process you've done so far is nothing glamorous, but what you're doing is working with simple edges and cubes to create complex shapes. The next few steps will start adding detail to the building block and will show you a way to simplify the process.

Automating with Macros

From this point, you'll be creating the six large tubes that stand out from the base of the building block. And while you could easily repeat the steps shown earlier or attempt to perform them at the same time, this next section of the project will make it easier. Using macros is a way to automate repetitive tasks for all kinds of modeling jobs. You'll use macros here to record your bevel operations so that every tube you need to create will be identical. You can use this process for creating things such as windows or doors as well.

1. With the same eight-sided polygon selected from the previous exercise, select Record Macro from the System menu at the top of the modo interface, as shown in Figure 5.17.

2. At this point, modo's Macro function is recording your steps. With the same eight-sided polygon still selected, press the **b** key to activate the Bevel tool. Click on the polygon, and you'll see the red and blue bevel handles. Click and drag the red handle to inset the bevel about 5 mm. You can see the value in the Tool Properties panel on the left side of the interface. Then, click and drag the blue handle up a little, to shift the bevel about 5 mm as well. These values don't have to be exact, so any approximation is fine. Figure 5.18 shows this first operation.

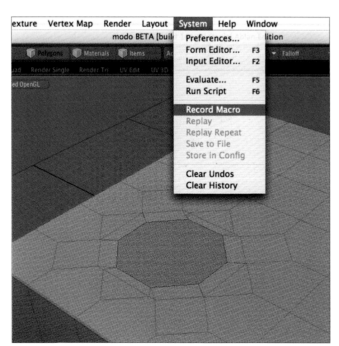

Figure 5.17

To start creating a macro, select Record Macro from the System menu.

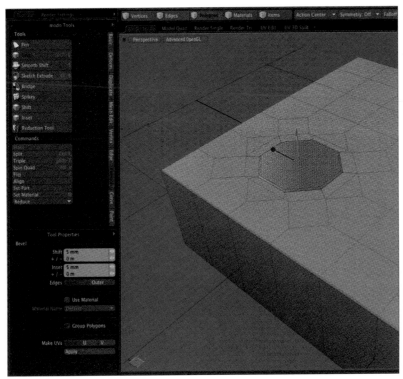

Figure 5.18

Inset and shift the selected polygon about 5 mm.

3. Because the polygon is still selected, you can bevel again to create more detail. The best way to do this is to hold the Shift key, then click on the polygon one time. When you do this, you effectively reset the Bevel tool, and you can confirm this by noticing that the values in the Tool Properties panel area have zeroed out.

4. Now bevel again, with an inset of about 5 mm and a shift of 16 cm. Figure 5.19 shows the operation.

5. Hold the Shift key and click on the selected polygon to reset the Bevel tool. Then, bevel again with an inset of about 6 mm for both the Shift and Inset values. Figure 5.20 shows the result.

6. Finally, hold the Shift key, click on the polygon to reset the Bevel tool, and bevel just one more time with an Inset value of only about 3 cm.

7. After this last bevel, press **q** to drop the tool, then go back up to the System menu at the top of the screen and select the Record Macro function, which now has a checkmark next to it and reads "Recording Macro," as shown in Figure 5.21.

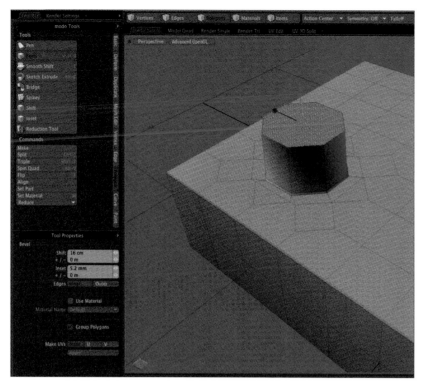

Figure 5.19

Inset and shift the selected polygon to extend it up and away from the block.

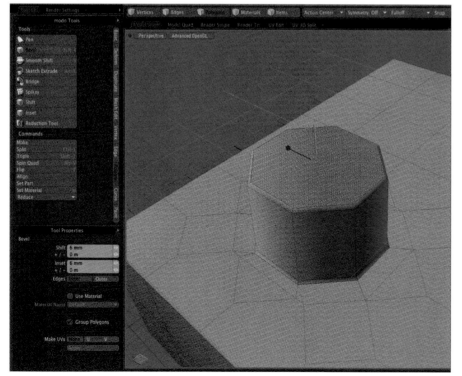

Figure 5.20

Bevel the selected polygon again, but this time to about 6 mm for both the Inset and Shift values.

8. You can save this macro for use any time in the future. It will work now without saving because it's sitting in modo's memory. However, should you quit the program for any crazy reason, the recorded macro is lost forever. So, back in the System menu, select Save to File. Then, give your recorded macro a sweet little name and a place to live. You'll come back to this shortly.

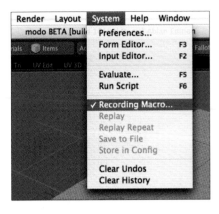

Figure 5.21

Once you've finished your bevel operations, press **q** to drop the tool, then turn off the Record Macro function.

9. Back in the viewport, press the **q** key to turn off the Bevel tool. Then click off of the model to deselect the geometry.

10. Save your work! Use Apple+s on a Mac or Ctrl+s on a PC.

11. Now press the **m** key to assign a material to this block.

12. In the panel that appears, give your model a slick name, add a little color, and up the specularity a bit for maximum visual impact. Okay, it won't be anything to write home about, but it'll help make it shine! Figure 5.22 shows the Polygon Set Material dialog box.

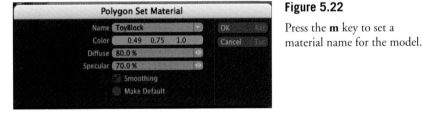

Figure 5.22

Press the **m** key to set a material name for the model.

Note

Remember this rule: If nothing is selected, what you do applies to everything. In the case of setting a material, nothing is selected, so by pressing **m** to call up the Polygon Set Material dialog box, you're applying a surface name to the entire model. You are creating a material group for every polygon in the Mesh Item.

13. Click OK to set the material and close the Polygon Set Material dialog box.

14. Back in the main viewport, press the Tab key to activate subdivision surfaces. Notice how the tube, although extending out of the base model, is cleverly attached? It has a smooth edge, which was the goal of all those little bevels. The bevels are what pick up the light and add that nice detail every model should have. Figure 5.23 shows the detail.

15. Save your work! Tired of hearing that? Good. Then you're getting it.

It's important to point out that what you've created—a round tube blending smoothly out of a box—is not normally an easy task in most modeling programs. By working with edges, spinning and beveling them as needed, you've created an initial polygonal shape that when subdivided (as shown in Figure 5.23) is round and smooth.

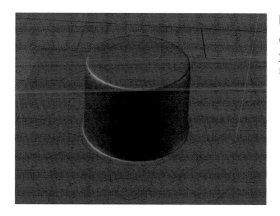

Figure 5.23

Once the Tab key is pressed, you can see how the bevels add necessary detail to the model.

More Automating with Macros

Creating the identical tubes throughout the rest of the model is not quite as arduous of a task as the previous one. Follow along now to see how to use your marvelous macro on the rest of the model.

1. Press the Tab key to turn off the subdivision surfaces. Then, one row over from the first tube you've created, select four polygons, as shown in Figure 5.24.

2. You'll repeat the same steps you performed earlier in the chapter, first pressing Shift+T to triple the selected polygons.

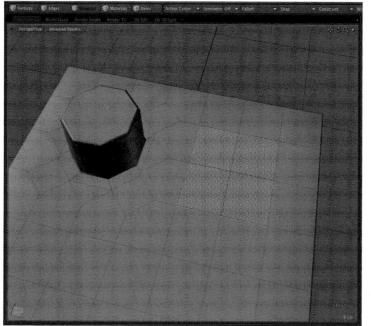

Figure 5.24

To begin creating additional tubes out of your block, select the four polygons opposite the original.

3. Once tripled, switch to Edges mode at the top of the modo interface. Then select the two parallel edges, as shown in Figure 5.25.

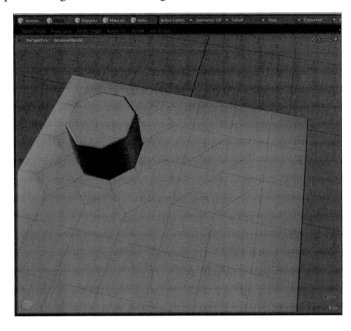

Figure 5.25

Once the four polygons are tripled, switch to Edges mode and select the two noncontiguous edges.

4. With the two edges selected, press the **v** key to spin them so they face in toward the center of the four polygons.

5. Hold the Shift key and run the mouse around all of the other edges within the four polygons, as shown in Figure 5.26.

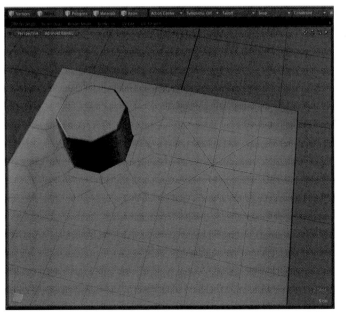

Figure 5.26

After the two edges are spun, select all of the edges within the four polygons.

6. With the edges selected, press the **b** key to activate the Bevel tool. Click and drag in the layout to bevel the selected edges. The first bevel was set to 8 cm. Bevel this selection to about 7.75 cm, being careful not to overlap the polygons.

7. Once you've beveled the edges, press **q** to turn off the Bevel tool.

8. Press the spacebar to jump to Polygons mode. Then, click on the center eight-sided polygon, which is the result of the beveled edges, as shown in Figure 5.27.

9. Save your work.

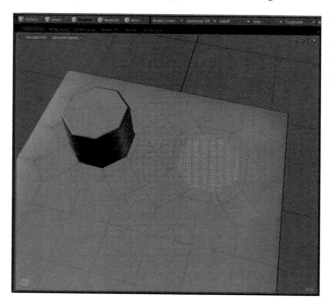

Figure 5.27

After the edges are beveled, switch to Polygons selection mode and select the eight-sided polygon.

10. Now the fun part! From the System menu, select Run Script.

11. Select the Macro script you saved earlier. Remember, you're doing this with the polygon selected first. After you select Run Script, all of the bevel operations you applied to the first tube will be instantly applied to this selected polygon, as shown in Figure 5.28. Pretty cool!

Note

The macro you've recorded does not need to be applied to the same number of polygons. You can use this macro on one polygon, two, or as many as you want. And, there is a macro available on the book's DVD for you, in the Chapter 5 folder.

---

12. Press **q** to turn off the active tool, then click away from the model in the viewport to deselect the polygon.

13. Press the Tab key to see how the model looks in subdivision surface mode. Figure 5.29 shows the model thus far.

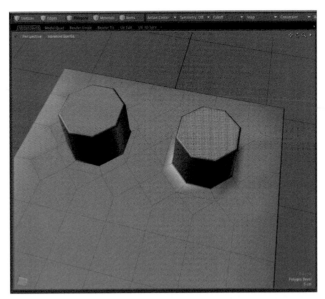

Figure 5.28

By applying the saved Macro function to the selected polygon, the bevel operations from the first beveled tube are instantly applied to the second.

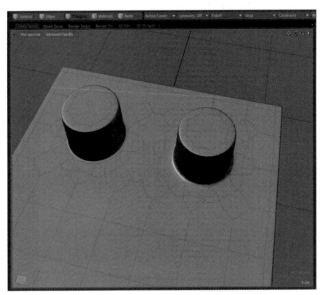

Figure 5.29

After the Macro function is applied and any polygons are deselected and when the Tab key is pressed, the model turns into a smooth, subdivided model.

14. Save your work!

Note

There is a video on the book's DVD that will show you firsthand how to record this macro, and even take a different approach to the process.

15. Repeat the process of selecting four polygons, tripling, spinning the edges, beveling the edges, and then running the macro script on the resulting polygon. Figure 5.30 shows the final six tubes extended from the original cube.

Figure 5.30

The steps described in this chapter are performed again on other sections of the cube, and the recorded macro is applied.

Editing the Shape

You can see that without a huge amount of work, you can create some good-looking models, even on the simplest level. But what if you've built your toy block, and all of a sudden you realize that the tubes are just a little too small? Do you start over? How do you size just the tubes without affecting the rest of the object? This section will show you how to edit the size of the tubes without disrupting the base of the model.

1. First and foremost, make sure your model is saved. And, it's a good idea to make a secondary copy of the model as backup. You can choose Save As from the File menu and give your object a new name or even just add a version number to it.

2. Make sure you're in Polygons selection mode, found at the top of the modo interface, and click on two polygons around the top edge of one of the tubes, as shown in Figure 5.31.

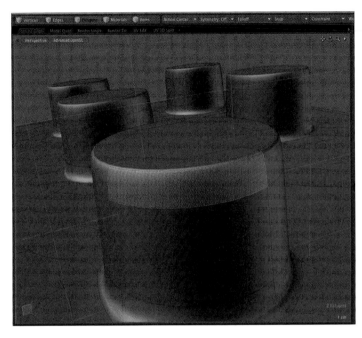

Figure 5.31

To begin adjusting the size of the tubes, select two polygons in order on one of the tubes.

3. Press the **L** key to select the entire loop of polygons. Figure 5.32 shows the full selection.

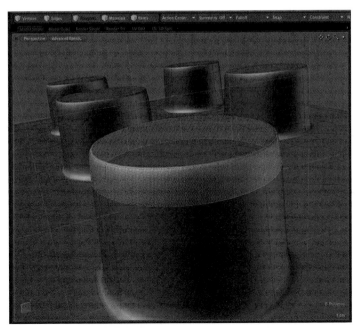

Figure 5.32

Press the up arrow multiple times to select the loop of polygons around the edge of the tube.

4. Repeat the process around the rest of the tube. You can hold the Shift key and push the up arrow on your keyboard three times to expand your selection to include the entire tube, as shown in Figure 5.33. You should have 41 polygons. Remember to make sure you've selected the small beveled-edge polygons as well.

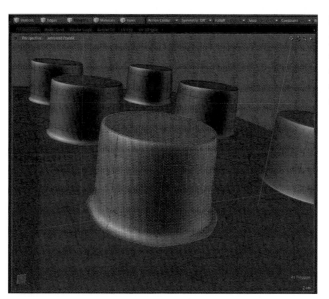

Figure 5.33

Repeat the selection process for the polygons around the rest of the tube, remembering to select the polygons on the top of the tube as well.

Note

You can also switch to a Side view, then use your middle mouse button to lasso-select all the tops of the tubes. Hold the Shift key, then press the up arrow three times to expand the selections.

5. Before you do anything else, assign a selection set to these polygons. You can do this from the Select menu at the top of the interface; choose Assign Selection Set, as shown in Figure 5.34. In the panel that pops up after you choose Assign Selection Set, give the polygons a name and choose Add, then click OK. Then, when you need to reselect these polygons, you can choose Use Selection Set from the same Select menu. You can also access the selection set from the Info & Statistics tab at the bottom-right of the interface.

The advantage of a selection set is that you won't have to reselect these polygons if you accidentally deselect them or you want to continue working later. On a larger scale, a selection set works well for more complex objects when you are creating morph maps, or when there are areas of a complex model you need to edit often.

6. Holding the Shift key, select the rest of the tubes throughout the model. Figure 5.35 shows the full selection. Feel free to create a selection set for these polygons as well—you'll use them later.

7. Because you have multiple polygons selected, sizing them normally would result in them being sized as one unit. That means they would push away from the center origin. Instead, you want each selected tube to size upon itself. No problem for modo! From the Action Center menu at the top of the interface, select Local.

8. In the viewport, press the **r** button on your keyboard to activate the Stretch 3D tool. Then click and drag the center light-blue square to size the selections equally. Paying attention to the Tool Properties on the left side of the interface, scale the selections up with a factor of about 130%, as shown in Figure 5.36.

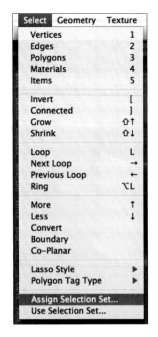

Figure 5.34

Assign a selection set to the selected polygons.

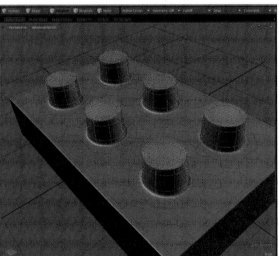

Figure 5.35

Select all of the polygons that make up the tubes throughout the model.

Note

Remember, to add to your existing selection—be it polygons, edges, or vertices—hold the Shift key, and then click the new selection. If you accidentally click a new polygon and deselect something you've already selected, simply undo by pressing Ctrl+z on the PC or Apple+z on the Mac. And, if you accidentally select a polygon you don't want, remember to hold the Ctrl key, and then click on the unwanted polygon to deselect it.

Note

It's important to note that the light-blue square will size the selections equally on all axes. If you wanted to control the scale on the X and Y axes only, simply click and drag on the blue circle (the 2D handle).

Figure 5.36

With Action Center set to Local, you can size each selection upon itself.

9. Press the **q** key to drop the Stretch 3D tool.

10. You can see that because the selections scaled upon themselves, they stayed in place. This is good for the most part, but they pushed themselves into the base of the cube a bit. No worries! Simply press the **w** key to activate the Move tool, and then click and drag the vertical handle to move the selections up about 4 cm. Because the Action Center is set to Local, the axis will read as Z, and the handle will be blue. Normally the Y axis is up and the handle is green. Figure 5.37 shows the move.

Note

Depending on how much you scale your selections, polygons at the base of the tubes might pinch a bit with neighboring geometry. You can scale the polygons less or, after you've scaled them to the desired amount, press the **t** key to activate the Element Move tool, and click and drag the pinched edges to fix them. Additionally, you can select desired edges and use the Slide (edge slide) tool from the Geometry drop-down menu.

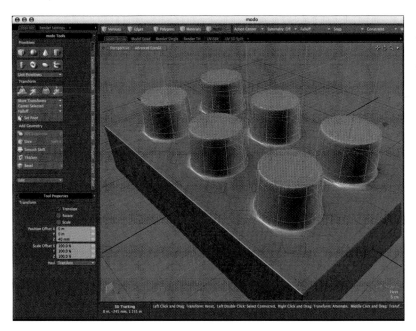

Figure 5.37

Using the Move tool, move the selection up away from the base of the model.

11. Save your work! Then press the **q** key to turn off any active tools.

The toolset within modo makes it easy to create almost anything you can think of. And although the model in this chapter was simple, you used some powerful tools and techniques that can be applied to any model you create. Read on to take your model a step further.

Cutting the Shape

Your model is now looking much better, and there's only one thing left to do. If you hold the Alt key and click and drag in the viewport, you can rotate around to look at the base of your model. The bottom is solid, so if these were real building blocks, they wouldn't be able to stack. Therefore, you need to cut the bottom to match the top. This is easy to do with a Boolean function, but first you need a copy of the model.

1. With your model saved, move over to the Item List on the right side of the interface. Right-click on the model name and choose Duplicate. You'll see a copy of your model added to the Item List, as shown in Figure 5.38.

2. In the main viewport, you'll still see your colored model, but you'll also see a dark outline appear. This is the additional object in the background. The first thing you want to do is size one of the objects down slightly. Make sure all of the tubes are selected by choosing Use Selection Set from the Select menu at the top of the screen. Choose the selection set you created for the selected tube polygons.

3. Once the tubes are selected, press Shift+R to to set a uniform scale by a factor of 90%. Figure 5.39 shows the setting. Just enter the value in the numeric window after activating the tool (Shift+R), and then click Apply. The selected tubes will equally size down.

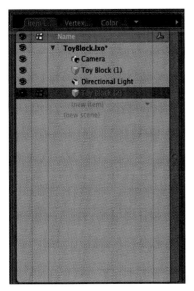

Figure 5.38

Right-click the mesh in the Item List and choose Duplicate. You'll see another copy of your object added to the list.

Figure 5.39

To uniformly scale the selected tubes, press Shift+R and enter a value of 90% in the Tool Properties panel.

4. Before you deselect the tubes, press the left bracket key ([) to invert the selection. Invert is also found in the Select menu at the top of the interface.

5. Press the **q** key to turn off the Scale tool, and then press Shift+R to reactivate the tool. Turning the tool off and on again resets its values as well. Scale the selected geometry to about 95% this time. Press the **q** key to turn off the tool, and then click off of the model in the viewport to deselect the geometry. Figure 5.40 shows the fully scaled model.

Note

You can also click and drag the blue circle for the Scale tool, and then use the Transform command (press **y**) to move the model on the Y axis. The choice is yours!

Figure 5.40

By uniformly scaling the entire model, one copy is now smaller than the other.

6. Save your work.

7. Press the **w** key and move the scaled-down copy of the object about –2 cm on the Y axis. Move it down enough so the bottom hangs out beneath the original version, visible as a background layer.

Note

You should be able to see your background layer by default. If you don't, first select the main item you're working with from the Item List. Then, make sure that the small eyeball icon on the left of the item listing is checked for the background object—in this case, the duplicate copy. Also, you can change your background view style by clicking the Render Style button at the top of the viewport (which probably reads Shaded or Advanced OpenGL right now), then going to Shade Options, then Background Item. You can choose Wireframe, Flat Shade, or Same as Active Layer.

8. Press the single-quote key (') to invert the item selection, putting the smaller, adjusted block in the background and the larger original in the foreground.

9. From the Geometry menu at the top of the interface, select Boolean, and then Boolean again, as shown in Figure 5.41. In the Boolean CSG dialog box that appears, choose Subtract, and click OK. The background layer will be used to effectively cut away the foreground layer. Figure 5.42 shows the result—a holllowed-out building block.

Note

CSG stands for *Constructive Solids Geometry.*

---

10. Right-click on the smaller block layer in the Item List, and select Delete. Save your model.

11. Pressing the Tab key turns on subdivision surfaces (if they're not already on), and the result is a smooth object, as shown in Figure 5.43. But look closely at the edges underneath the object after the Boolean operation. The corners have been rounded. This is because there's not enough geometry there. Press the Tab key again to turn off the subdivision.

Figure 5.41

The Boolean CSG function allows you to use one Mesh Item to cut away another Mesh Item.

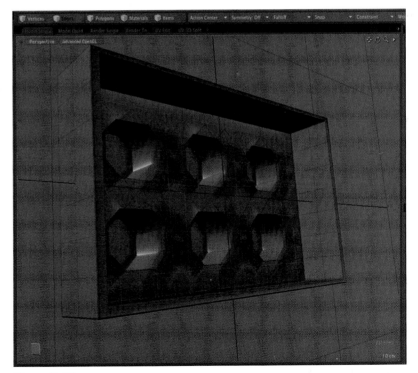

Figure 5.42

After the Boolean function is performed, the smaller block is used to cut out the inside of the larger block, resulting in a hollow shape.

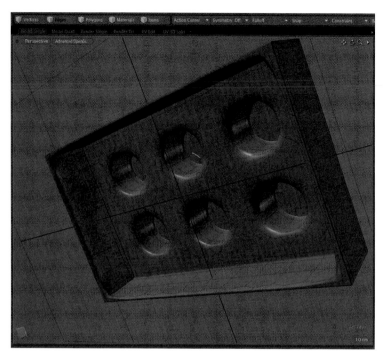

Figure 5.43

When the Tab key is pressed to activate subdivisional surfaces, the object becomes smooth. But there's some trouble in the corners!

12. In Polygons selection mode, select the polygons that make up the bottom half of the entire model, as shown in Figure 5.44. Then, press the left bracket key ([) to reverse the selection.

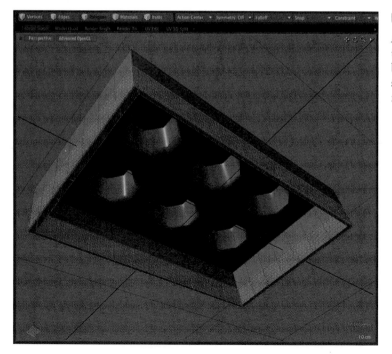

Figure 5.44

Although you could select just the top half of the model, the bottom half is a little easier to select. Then, you can just reverse the selection.

Tip

You can change your viewport (at the top-left of the view) to a Left or Front view to make selections easier.

Tip

Remember, you can use the right mouse button to lasso-select the geometry. And if you want to select in an orthogonal view, such as the Front or Side view, change to a Wireframe shade to make sure you're selecting all the way through the model.

13. When your polygons are selected, press the Tab key again to subdivide on the top half of the model. Because of modo's n-gon capability (the ability to subdivide polygons made up of more than four or five vertices), portions of your model can be subdivided while others aren't. Figure 5.45 shows the model.

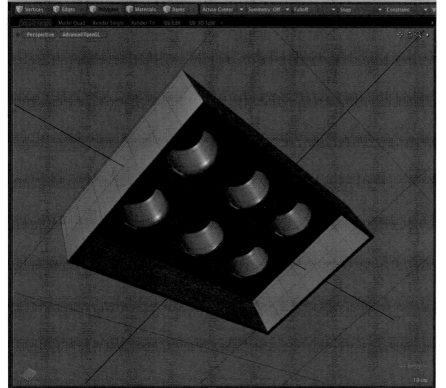

Figure 5.45

The n-gons subdivision capability in modo 201/202 allows you to have some of your model in subdivision mode and some of it not.

Note

An *n-gon* is a polygon made up of any number of vertices. The *n* represents the number. Some programs require geometry to meet two, three, or four vertices, which limits certain functions. The use of n-gons expands the functionality of the program.

Note

There is an alternative method to using the Boolean operation. Take a look at the videos on the DVD for Chapter 5, and you'll learn even more. Again, the choice is yours!

So there you have it. Basic building blocks—literally. Although the chapter didn't show you how to model anything outrageous or super cool-looking, it did show you the basics of general modeling and how modo handles each task. This foundation is crucial to everything you do in modo, so keep in mind what you've done here for the next chapter.

6

Working with Mesh Items

Chapter 5 introduced you to more modeling tools and also might have piqued your interest in the Item List and the elements within. This chapter will outline how mesh items work with a cool project. Later in the book, you'll texture and render the scene you build in this chapter.

The Item List is powerful for a number of reasons. First and foremost, it's a way to work on scenes that encompass multiple elements. For example, in Chapter 5 you built a single toy block. If you wanted to create a scene with many of these objects and perhaps a toy truck to go along with the block, you'd create the truck as a new mesh. The advantage here is that you can build the second object without disrupting the original model. If you've ever used Photoshop, you've worked with layers and used each layer for separate parts of the image. The idea is the same in modo, and the number of mesh items you can use is unlimited.

You can also use different mesh items for creating shapes with functions such as Boolean subtracts. One mesh is used to cut away another. A mesh item is like a container for elements in your scene. Read on to learn more.

Item List Navigation

The Item List is located at the top-right of the interface, as you have already seen throughout the book. But there is more to this handy little panel than meets the eye. Figure 6.1 shows the Item List upon startup.

Note

Your Item List grouping on the right side of the interface might be shortened depending on your screen size. Be sure to place your mouse on the left edge of the panel, then click and drag with the left mouse button to widen the panel and view it in all of its glory.

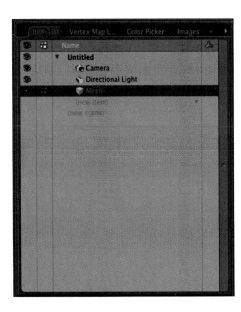

Figure 6.1

The Item List is home to all of your scene elements, from objects to cameras, lights, and more.

By default, a mesh listing is selected in the Item List. The name is simply "Mesh." You'll also see listings for Camera and Directional Lights. These are the default items in modo. You might not actually see a light and a camera in the layout, depending on how you've set up your interface. You can make the camera and lights visible by clicking the drop-down view style (typically listed as Texture) at the top-left of the layout. Then go to the Visibility Options listing and choose Show Cameras and Show Lights, as shown in Figure 6.2.

Note

You've seen that the visibility options are accessible from directly within the viewport, but there's even a quicker way. Press the **o** key on your keyboard (*o* as in *oh*—not as in zero), and the Visibility panel will open. Move the mouse off the panel to close it.

The Item List is easy to navigate and understand, but it's crucial to your workflow, and you have to remember it's there. You use it to select items in the modo layout. You also use it to rename and group items, and even to create instances or duplicates of your 3D objects. But another key feature to remember about the Item List is that it will allow you to work with items in your scene in a similar fashion to working with layers in Adobe Photoshop. Rather than discussing every aspect of the Item List, you can gain a more thorough understanding of it by working through a project using it.

Building in Layers

Normally when someone mentions working in layers, people think of programs such as Adobe Photoshop or something similar. Each layer contains an element of the current project. In modo, you need to think of the Item List the same way. As you create a 3D object, you can build up the layers for it in the same way you would for a Photoshop document. In this project, you'll create a message board that contains many elements, such as a thumbtack, Post-it notes, and newspaper clippings.

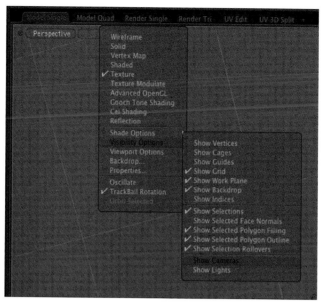

Figure 6.2

The Item List default items include a camera, a directional light, and a mesh listing. You can make the camera and lights visible by choosing these options from the render style drop-down list at the top of the modo layout.

In the following chapter, you'll be introduced to the Shader Tree and you'll learn how to apply image maps to the objects you create in this chapter. The Item List will help you not only create the scene setup with objects and lights, but it will help you organize as well. To begin creating this scene, think of what you'll need to complete it. You're creating a message board, such as a corkboard used in a college dorm room, kitchen, or perhaps an office. The message board will hang on a wall. On the corkboard are clippings, stickers, and thumbtacks holding notes. What do you create first? Truly, it doesn't matter. But to help you with workflow, build from the back forward. You'll start by creating the corkboard, and from there add the notes and other elements.

1. Begin this project with a default modo layout. If you have a project you've been working on, now is a good time to save it. You can then go to the File menu at the top of the interface and select Reset to return to a default modo workspace.

Note

Unlike Adobe's Photoshop or modo's Shader Tree, the order of the layers in the Item List does not matter. You can build a 3D object, and it can be listed above or below another object in the Item List. This will have no effect on its visibility in your final render.

2. Make sure your main view in the modo layout is set to Perspective. You can set this from the top-left of the modo viewport. Better yet, with the mouse in the viewport, press the **o** key to call up the viewport options (as shown in Figure 6.3).

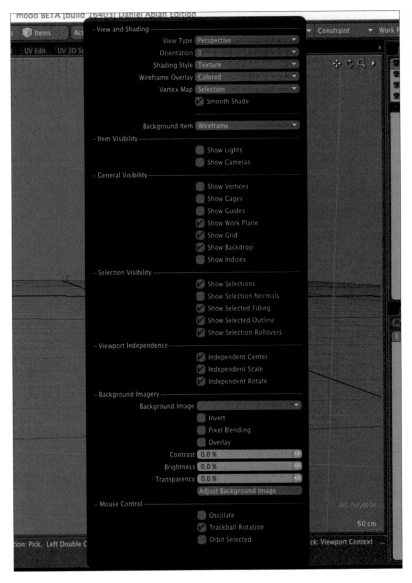

Figure 6.3

You can press the **o** key on your keyboard to open the viewport options.

Note

When you press **o** for viewport options, simply moving the mouse off of the options panel will remove it. To call it back up, press the **o** key again.

3. In the viewport options, set the View Type value (at the top of the panel) to Perspective. Move the mouse away from the options panel, and it will close. Conversely, you can press the Ctrl key and spacebar at the same time to change viewports through a pie menu.

4. Hold down the Alt/Option key and use your left mouse button to rotate the view until the Work Plane snaps to the XY axes. You can look at the icon in the lower-left corner and see the white plane move between X, Y, and Z, which indicates which two axes the Work Plane is aligned to. Figure 6.4 shows the icon.

Figure 6.4

To begin making the corkboard, set the dominant axis to XY.

5. From the Basic tab on the left of the interface and from the modo Tools panel, select the Cube primitive. Then, in the Perspective view, draw out a flat box to fill the majority of the view, about 3×2 meters in size, as shown in Figure 6.5.

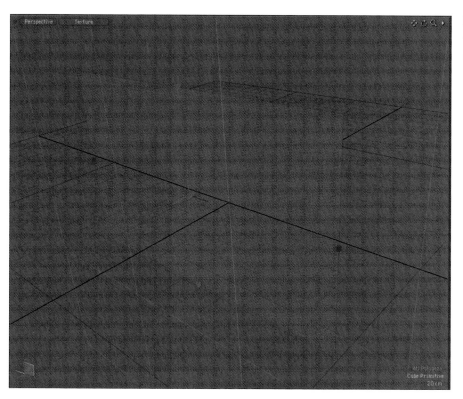

Figure 6.5

You can start the corkboard with a Cube primitive.

6. Before you turn off the Cube Primitive tool, click the blue handle in the middle of the object you've started to create and pull it forward to give the box some depth. Pull it about 20 cm, as shown in Figure 6.6.

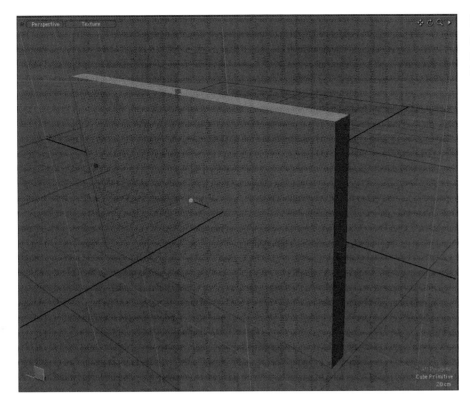

Figure 6.6

Give your corkboard some depth on the Z axis, about 20 cm.

7. Press the **q** key to turn off the Cube Primitive tool, and then save your object as Corkboard.

Note

Remember that you can see the specific measurements of your tools in the Tool Properties panel, which appears at the bottom-left of the modo interface within the Tool Bar tab when a tool is selected.

8. Making sure you're in Polygons mode at the top of the modo interface, select just the front-facing polygon on the corkboard.

9. Press the **b** key on your keyboard to turn on the Bevel tool. Then, click on the selection to activate the tool. At this point, the control handles will appear.

10. Grab the red handle for inset and drag it in about 10 cm, as shown in Figure 6.7.

11. Hold the Shift key and click on the selection to reset the bevel. Then, drag the blue handle in toward the object to shift the selection about –5 cm. Figure 6.8 shows the operation.

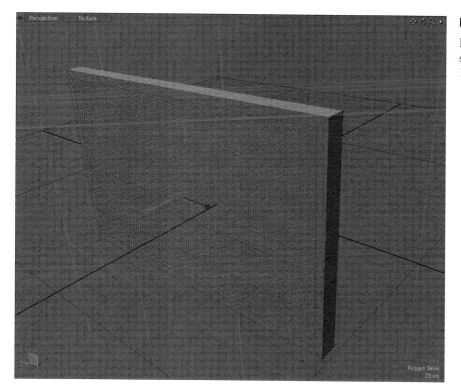

Figure 6.7

Bevel just the inset of the selected front polygon about 10 cm.

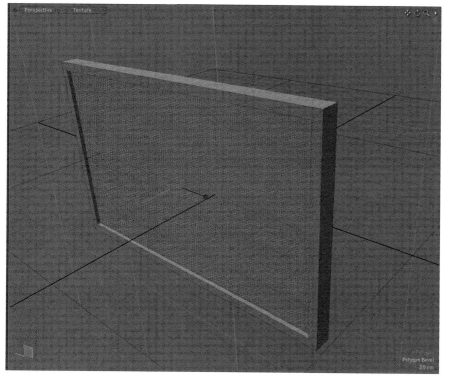

Figure 6.8

Bevel the Shift value by clicking and dragging the blue handle to bring the selected polygon in about –5 cm.

12. Press the **q** key to turn off the Bevel tool, and then click off of the model to deselect the polygon. Conversely, you can just press **b** again to turn off the tool.

13. Take a look over at the Item List on the right side of the interface. If you've saved your scene, the name you chose will appear in bold at the top of the list. Beneath that you'll see a listing for Camera, Directional Light, and Mesh. The mesh is your object. Right-click on it and select Rename from the pop-up that appears. Remember that if you're on a Mac, hold the Apple key and click.

14. Rename the mesh "Board" and click OK. Figure 6.9 shows the panel.

Item Name
Name **Board**   OK   Ret
Cancel   Esc

Figure 6.9

Right-click on a mesh in the Item List to rename it. You can do the same for cameras and lights.

15. Now is as good a time as any to save your work.

16. Most message boards aren't as basic-looking as the one you've built here. They have some roundness to them, which is easy to do in modo. With the existing corkboard in your viewport, choose Edges selection mode at the top of the modo interface to tell the program you want to work with edges.

17. Double-click on the outer front edge of the corkboard to select the entire edge loop, as shown in Figure 6.10.

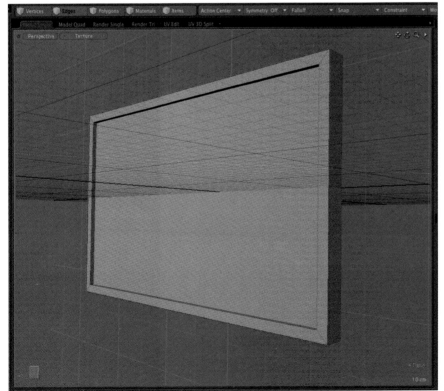

Figure 6.10

Double-click the outer front edge to select the edge loop.

18. When the edge is selected, press the **b** key to call up the Bevel tool.

19. In the Tool Properties panel at the bottom-left of the interface (within the Tool Bar tab), set the Round Level to 3. Then click and drag in the viewport to bevel the selected edge roughly 5 cm. You can see the bevel value in the Tool Properties panel. Feel free to zoom in closer after you bevel to see the detail by pressing the period key on your keyboard. Hold the Alt/Option key and click and drag in the view to rotate it to get a closer look. Figure 6.11 shows the rounded edge.

Figure 6.11

Bevel the selected edge with an added Round Level value to smooth it out.

20. Press **b** again to turn off the Bevel tool, and then click away from the object to deselect the edges. Save as necessary.

21. Now you need to bevel the inside edge using the exact method you used for the outer edge. Double-click the edge to select the entire loop, press **b** for bevel, and bevel it out about 4 cm. Figure 6.12 shows the inside edge nicely beveled.

Of course, you can vary this beveling to suit your taste, but doesn't modo do an excellent job beveling these edges? You can use this technique in almost every model you build. Go ahead and save your model. It's time to create some things to hang on it!

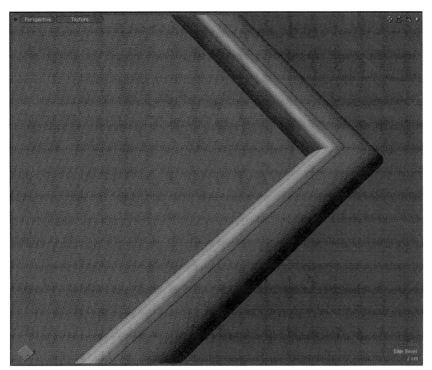

Figure 6.12

Bevel the inside edge of the corkboard to match the roundness of the outside edge.

Adding Mesh Layers

By this point, you've seen that creating a simple primitive shape automatically creates a new mesh in the Item List. But what if you wanted to create more elements in the scene? Would you build them with the same mesh item? Or should you create a new mesh? Truth be told, it really depends on the project at hand; however, you can't go wrong with building each object as a new mesh item, which is what this chapter is all about. So let's take that approach. You see, building each object as a separate mesh allows you to just select that mesh item, move, rotate, and so on. If all objects were built within the same mesh item, you'd need to specifically select certain polygons to change or edit. Your final scene will be the same either way, but working with separate mesh items offers more control and faster workflow.

1. With the corkboard scene saved, head over to the Item List on the right side of the interface and click New Item. This is beneath the current items of Camera, Directional Light, and your Corkboard mesh. It's slightly greyed out.

Note

Clicking New Item in the Item List is easy, but here's one better: Just press the **n** key on your keyboard to create a new mesh item.

2. When you click New Item, modo will give you an option to choose between a new mesh, new light, new camera, and so on. Choose Mesh, as shown in Figure 6.13.

3. If you're working with a default modo layout, the existing corkboard will become a black wireframe, signifying that it's in the background. You don't have to keep it this way for long. Press the **a** key to fit the mesh to view.

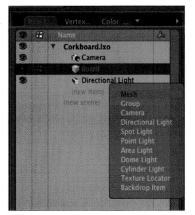

Figure 6.13

To add additional mesh items to your scene, click New Item in the Item List and choose Mesh. Or, press the **n** key on your keyboard.

4. From the Tool Bar tab on the left side of the interface, hold the Shift key and click the Plane primitive, as shown in Figure 6.14. Note that this primitive does not show up until you hold the Shift key.

You'll notice now in your Item List that the new mesh is automatically named for you. This is a handy little feature in modo when you are creating unit primitives with the Shift key pressed. But also notice that the new mesh you created is still blank! The new Plane primitive was created as a new mesh item—yet another handy feature. You'll go back to the empty layer in a moment. First, adjust the new Plane primitive shape.

Figure 6.14

Hold the Shift key to view the alternate primitives, and then select the Plane.

5. Taking a look at Figure 6.15, you can see that the Plane primitive is a flat square mesh centered in the viewport. First, making sure you're in Items selection mode at the top of the modo interface, press Alt/Option and the **a** key to set modo to Auto-Action Center and Action Axis Auto. Then, press the **y** key to activate the Transform tool, and click and drag on the red ring to rotate the plane upward, as shown in Figure 6.16.

Note

Using the Transform tool by pressing the **y** key is sort of a one-stop shop for transforming your object. This one tool allows you to control position, rotation, and scale. Note that position, rotation, and scale are also available on their own. It is a very effective tool, especially when working in Items selection mode. Also, you can view your transform values in the Render Properties tab on the bottom-left of the interface.

Figure 6.15

Creating a Plane primitive creates a flat mesh in the middle of the viewport.

6. Press the spacebar to switch to Polygons selection mode. This first flat plane will be a Post-it note. You'll use the Bend tool to shape it and make it curl out from the corkboard. But in order to bend it, it needs to be subdivided to be more pliable. Press Shift+D to call up the Subdivide Polygons command. Choose Faceted for the Subdivision Method. Other methods are Smooth and Subdivision Surface, or SDS. Because this is not a subdivided object, Faceted is fine. Leave the other settings at 0 and click OK. Your flat plane will be subdivided, and you'll now have four polygons instead of one (two on each axis).

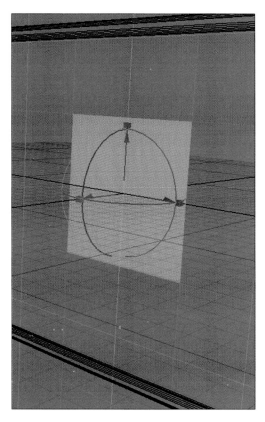

Figure 6.16

Using the Transform tool, click and drag the red handle to rotate the Plane primitive.

7. Repeat the previous step to subdivide one more time.

8. Select the Bend tool from the Deform tab within the modo Tools panel in the Tool Bar tab.

9. When the Bend tool is on, click at the top of the Post-it note in the viewport. When you do, you'll see a control handle—a blue ring. You'll also see a thin line extending out with a square on the end. Click and drag that square to the bottom of the Post-it note object. This sets the falloff for the Bend tool. Set the Action Axis to X in the Tool Properties panel on the left of the interface.

10. Now, click and drag the handle to bend the note. Did you notice that just the bottom of the object bends, not the entire thing? It bends from the point at which you clicked to set the Bend tool. Figure 6.17 shows the operation and settings.

11. Press the **q** key to turn off the tool.

12. Now select the Twist tool. You're going to give a little imperfection to the object.

13. Click at the top of the object, similar to where you did with the Bend tool. You'll see two falloff handles. Before you mess with those, click and drag the blue ring (control handle) to twist the object. Figure 6.18 shows the effect.

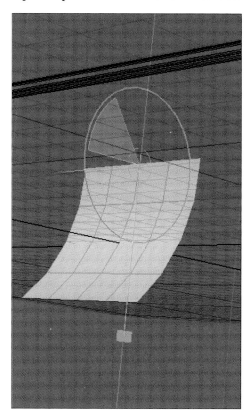

Figure 6.17

Using the Bend tool with a falloff, the Post-it note quickly curls.

14. The falloff of the Twist tool applies the effect more at the fat end of the falloff and less at the narrow end. The result is a curl in the Post-it note object. Before you turn off the tool, feel free to move the falloff around to see the various results. Just click and drag the control handles around either of those light-blue squares—they'll become yellow when selected. When you are finished, press the **q** key to turn off the tool.

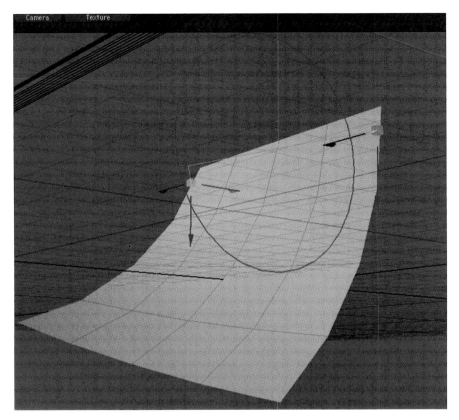

Figure 6.18

With the falloff of the Twist tool, you can bend or curl up just one corner of the object.

Note

Take some time and play with the Bend tool to get a feel for it. You can modify the effect with the tool still active, just like you can with many of modo's tools. You can also drag the small blue crosshair inside the circle and move it around to change the Bend tool's axis. This is the point at which the bend occurs. What's more, the Twist tool is just the axis Rotate tool with a linear falloff. If you take a look at the Tool Pipe tab at the bottom-right of the viewport, you can see what comprises each tool.

15. Save your work.

16. Once you have the shape the way you like it, subdivide it one more time by pressing Shift+D. But this time instead of Faceted, choose Smooth.

17. After the subdivision, press **m** on your keyboard to set the Polygon Material. Give the item a name, such as Post-it Note, and change the color to a pale yellow or something else you might like. Save your work.

Using Background Layers as Reference

So far what you've done is fairly straightforward. You haven't modeled anything outrageous or award-winning. But what you *have* done is build separate mesh items, which is a key operation for almost anything you do in modo. Each mesh item is part of an overall scene, and that means you'll need to reference the other mesh items to line things up for the final render. This section will quickly show you how to work with multiple layers as reference.

1. With the Post-it note object selected in the Item List, your background object should be the original corkboard object. It most likely appears as a black outline. Instead, change it to a solid by pressing the **o** key while your mouse hovers in the viewport.

2. Pressing **o** (not zero) calls up the viewport shading options. Toward the top of the panel is an option for Background Item. Change it from Wireframe to Same as Active Item, as shown in Figure 6.19.

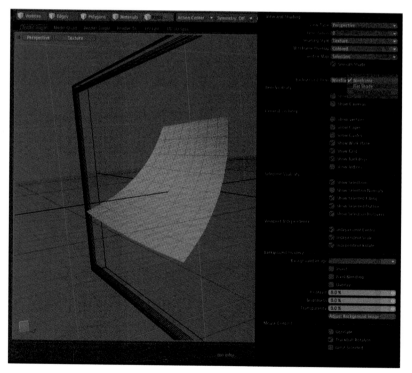

Figure 6.19

Changing the viewport options to see the background as a solid versus a wireframe will help you align objects.

Note

To keep organized, right-click on the mesh listing in the Item List to rename it. Instead of Plane, rename the object PostIt Note.

3. Now that background objects are solid shaded, you'll have an easier time aligning other objects in the scene. From the Item List on the right of the interface, select the Post-it note.

Note

It's often good to set up a scene with multiple mesh items in Items selection mode. If you're in Items selection mode, you can quickly click on the desired item in the viewport without needing to first select it in the Item List. Another thing to mention if you're working with large scenes and many mesh items is Auto Visibility. Right-click on the Item List tab, then go to Viewport Settings; you can choose Auto Visibility. With this active, as you select one mesh in the Item List, all others are deselected.

4. Press **y** on the keyboard to select the Transform tool. Then click the various control handles to rotate and position the Post-it note on the corkboard. Place it so that the top end (which would be the sticky part of the note) is touching the corkboard. Figure 6.20 shows a similar setup.

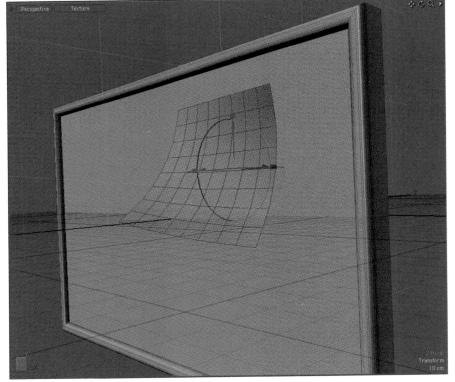

Figure 6.20

Using the Transform tool is a great way to position objects.

Note

To add a little more precise positioning, use the Element Move tool. Press the **t** key to activate the tool. Make sure you're in Polygons selection mode (top of the interface), and also remember to right-click and drag to set the size of the Element Tool influence. Then, click and drag on any point, polygon, or edge to adjust it. Be sure to view the Element Move video on the book's DVD to learn more.

5. You might want to scale the Post-it note a bit. Press the **r** key and then click on the center light-blue square and drag to scale evenly. Also, press the **w** key to select the Move tool and move it over to one edge of the corkboard. Figure 6.21 shows the model at this point.

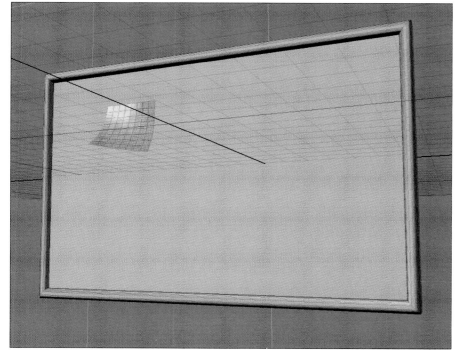

Figure 6.21

The Post-it note on the corkboard, positioned and scaled.

6. Finally, repeat these steps to create new Post-it notes, or simply right-click on the object in the Item List and select Duplicate. Position them throughout the corkboard and bend them, scale them, and rotate them as needed for variation. Remember that for each copy you create, select it and press **m** for material and create a polygon material group. Feel free to use the Element Move tool by pressing **t** on the keyboard to shape the object. You'll be working with materials for these mesh items next in Chapter 7, "Shader Tree Fundamentals." Save your work.

7. Now you'll add a few other interesting things to the corkboard. First, a simple photograph. Create a new mesh layer in the Item List by clicking New Item directly in the list.

8. With the new mesh layer selected, rotate the view so the Work Plane snaps to the XY axes. Remember that this is identified by the small white square between the axis markings in the bottom-left corner of the viewport, as shown in Figure 6.22.

Figure 6.22

The dominant axis is set by holding the Alt/Option key, then clicking and dragging in the viewport to rotate. When rotating, watch this icon in the bottom-left of the viewport to see where the white square lines up.

9. Draw out a flat cube in the shape of a standard photograph, as shown in Figure 6.23. Remember that as you draw it out, if you can't see it, you can click and drag directly on the blue and red handles to position the object.

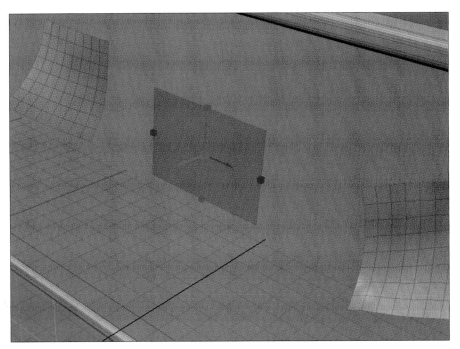

Figure 6.23

When drawing out a Cube primitive, remember to click and drag on the control handles to position it wherever you like.

10. When the object is made, press the **q** to turn off the tool.

11. Press **m** on your keyboard to call up the Set Polygon Material option, and give this new mesh a material name of Photo or something similar.

Make sure you save your work at this point. Go ahead and make other copies of objects if you wish, or simply continue on to the next section. However, if you do build more objects on your own, just remember to press **m** on your keyboard to give each new object its own material group name.

Adding Scenes to the Item List

By now you should see your message board forming. Adding a few Post-it notes and a photograph is getting you close to the final render. As mentioned previously, you'll be texturing and image-mapping all of these objects in the next chapter. There is one thing missing from this message board, and that's thumbtacks! Although Post-it notes have their own adhesive, photographs need to be pinned up. This section will show you how to build a thumbtack and apply it to the existing scene.

1. In this section, rather than building a new mesh item, you'll start an entirely new scene. The reason for this is to show you that you can work on multiple scenes at the same time in modo. From the File menu at the top of the screen, select New. Take a look at the Item List on the right side of the interface. You'll see a new untitled object, along with a blank mesh layer, a camera, and a directional light. Figure 6.24 shows modo after the operation.

   This is a new scene. But if you look at the top of the Item List, you'll see that your original Corkboard object is still there. You can select it, and it will appear in the viewport.

2. With the new scene, select the empty mesh item, and then in the Tool Bar tab on the left of the interface, while holding the Ctrl key on the keyboard, click the Cylinder primitive. You'll see that modo creates a unit cylinder to the current mesh item, as shown in Figure 6.25.

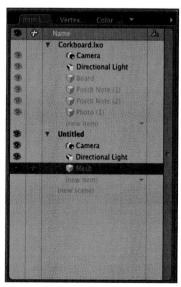

Figure 6.24

Selecting New from the File menu creates a new scene, clearing out the viewport, but still leaves your existing scene intact.

Figure 6.25

Holding the Ctrl key while selecting a primitive, such as the Cylinder, creates a unit primitive.

Note

If you look at a sphere or cube, for example, when creating a unit primitive, you'll notice that the diameter of the sphere or length of an edge on the cube is exactly one meter. This is what modo means by the term *unit*.

3. Holding the Ctrl key, select the Scale tool, as shown in Figure 6.26. At this time, you can also right-click on the mesh listing in the Item List to rename it to Thumbtack.

4. Next, from the top of the interface, select Linear from the Falloff drop-down menu, as shown in Figure 6.27.

5. You'll see a triangular outline appear within the object, as shown in Figure 6.28. When the falloff is turned on, you'll see additional controls appear within the Tool Properties for the Scale tool. Change the Auto Size value from X to Y.

Figure 6.26

To select the Scale tool, hold the Ctrl key on your keyboard and select it.

6. Press Alt/Option and the a key to set Auto Action Center. Then, in the Tool Properties, drag the Factor for Scale down to 60%. You'll see the cylinder bend inward, but only toward the larger end of the Falloff tool. Figure 6.29 shows the result.

7. Now press the spacebar until your selection mode is set to Polygons, visible at the top of the modo interface.

Figure 6.27

Set a linear falloff from the top of the modo interface.

8. Hold the Alt/Option key on your keyboard, and then click and drag in the viewport to rotate around to see the top of the object. Click on it once to select it.

9. Press the **b** key on your keyboard to activate the Bevel tool. Click on the polygon to bring up the Bevel tool handles.

Note

If you want, click and drag the falloff handles to see how their effect changes the shape of the model. Also, view the Falloffs movie on the book's DVD to get a better feel for this powerful control.

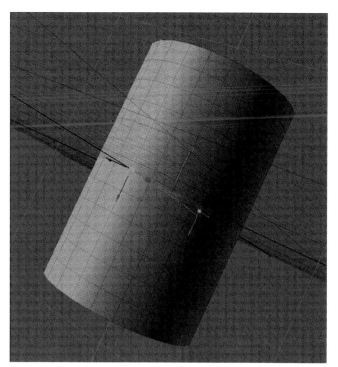

Figure 6.28

When you apply a linear falloff to the object, you'll see the representational outlines appear in the view.

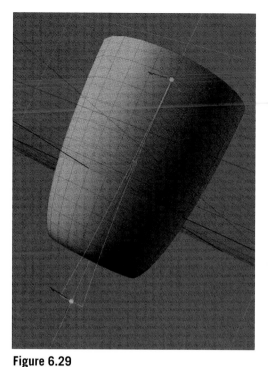

Figure 6.29

Using a linear falloff along with the Scale tool will taper the effect of the tool toward the fat end of the falloff.

10. Click and drag the red handle to bevel the inset to about –10 cm, as shown in Figure 6.30.

11. Hold the Shift key and click on the beveled polygon to reset the Bevel tool. Then, click and drag the blue handle up about 13 cm for the Shift value.

Figure 6.30

Begin shaping the thumbtack by beveling the top polygon of the cylinder.

12. Hold the Shift key and click the selected polygon again to reset. Bevel the inset back in about −10cm by dragging the red handle. Figure 6.31 shows the results.

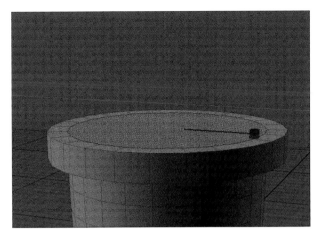

Figure 6.31

Holding the Shift key and clicking once on the selected polygon resets the Bevel tool.

13. Continue beveling the selected polygon a few more times, similar to the previous steps, until you have another wedge in the object. Figure 6.32 shows the result.

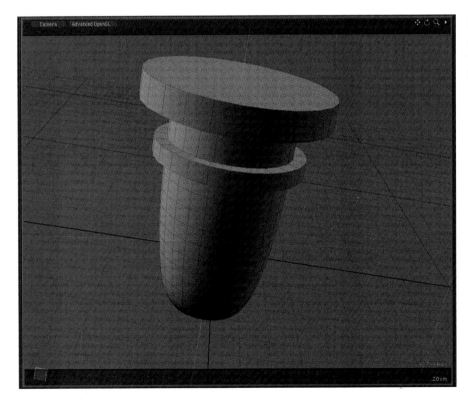

Figure 6.32

Continue beveling the polygon to create an additional wedge for the top of the thumbtack.

14. For the bottom of the thumbtack, select the base polygon on the rounded edge. Figure 6.33 shows the selection.

15. Now bevel the selected polygon to create another wedge in the thumbtack, similar to the way you created the top portion. This time, set the inset to about –25 cm.

16. Bevel again and shift the polygon down, then bevel once more to set the inset to about 40 cm. Figure 6.34 shows the idea.

Figure 6.33

Select the bottom rounded polygon, similar to the top polygon selection method performed earlier.

Figure 6.34

Bevel out the bottom of the thumbtack similar to the top, but set the inset a bit smaller this time.

17. Finally, bevel one more time, but this time extend the Shift value about 1 m and bring the Inset value down to sharpen out the pin, similar to Figure 6.35.

18. Save your work! Press the **q** key to turn off the Bevel tool. Press the Tab key.

When you press the Tab key to activate subdivisional surfaces, you can see that the thumbtack smoothes out—perhaps a little too much, as shown in Figure 6.36. You can fix this with a few edge adjustments.

19. Press the Tab key to turn off subdivision mode. This is not necessary to perform the next steps, but it makes selection a bit easier in this case. Making sure you're in Edges selection mode at the top of the modo interface, select the edges that revolve around the Y axis, including the very small pin tip and the edges underneath each wedge, as shown in Figure 6.37.

Figure 6.35

Bevel again, but this time use both the inset and shift to create the pin of the thumbtack.

Figure 6.36

Pressing the Tab key to activate subdivisional surfaces smoothes out the object, but a little too much.

Figure 6.37

Select all of the horizontal edges of the object, from top to bottom. These are the circular edges created from the bevel operations.

Note

Remember, when selecting in modo, you can double-click on an edge to select the entire edge loop. To add to the selection, hold the Shift key. To deselect an unwanted selected edge without deselecting everything, hold the Ctrl key and click on that edge.

20. With the edges selected, go ahead and bevel them.

21. After a slight bevel on the edges, this added geometry will help hold the shape of the object when subdivided. Press the **q** key to turn off the Bevel tool, then click off of the object to deselect the edges. Then, press the Tab key to see the change beveling the edges has made to the object when subdivided. Figure 6.38 shows the result. You can also apply an edge weight here. First, select the subdivision weight under Weight Maps in the Vertex Map tab. Then go to the Weight (Shift+W or under the Vertex Map menu) and tighten up those edges. Change to Vertex Map mode in your viewport to see the weight.

22. Feel free to undo and tweak the edges and their shape if you want. The goal here is to round out the edges a bit and to show you how a few bevels to a cylinder's polygons and edges can create a cool object.

23. Making sure you're in Polygons selection mode at the top of the modo interface, select the polygons that make up just the pin area of the thumbtack.

24. Press **m** on your keyboard to set the material to Thumbtack Metal or similar.

25. Instead of deselecting, simply press the left bracket key ([) on your keyboard. It's located to the right of the P key. This will invert your selection, and because the remaining polygons are just the plastic portion of the thumbtack, press **m** again and set a material name to these selected polygons of Thumbtack Plastic.

26. Deselect the polygons by clicking an empty area of the viewport, and then save your work. Figure 6.39 shows the final thumbtack.

Figure 6.38

After the edges of the object have been beveled, more geometry is added. When subdivided by pressing the Tab key, you can see that the shape is clean and sharp without being too smooth.

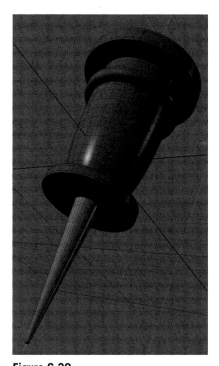

Figure 6.39

After the thumbtack has had its edges beveled, the polygons are given unique material names.

Merging Scenes in the Item List

The previous exercises have given you a lesson or two in working with the Item List, building simple objects, and using the key tools to do so. You've also learned how to add a new scene to the Item List to build new objects. But what if you want that new object in an existing scene?

Figure 6.40 shows the Item List with the corkboard scene and the thumbtack scene loaded into modo.

Because there are two scenes, you need to combine parts of one into the other. In many cases, you will already have set up your lighting and your environment in a particular scene. With the corkboard and thumbtack here, neither scene has had any work done to the lighting. But because the corkboard scene contains four objects, it will be easier to move the thumbtack into it than the other way around.

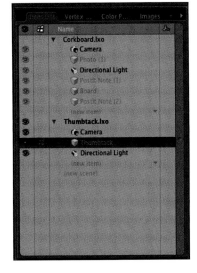

Figure 6.40

Two scenes loaded into modo are visible in the Item List.

1. Select the thumbtack object listing in the Item List. Click and drag it up into the corkboard scene. You can drop it anywhere you want at this point, as shown in Figure 6.41.

2. As soon as you drag and drop the object from one scene to the other, a dialog box pops up, asking you whether you'd like to import children (child objects), shaders, and if you'd like to move the layer. By default these are all checked on, so you can click OK to import the thumbtack object into the corkboard scene.

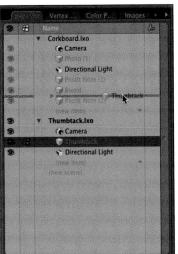

Figure 6.41

To bring an object from one scene into another, simply drag it from one to the other.

3. You'll notice in Figure 6.42 that the thumbtack is significantly larger than the corkboard. No problem! Press the **r** key on your keyboard and then click on the light-blue square in the center of the control handles. Click and drag to size the thumbtack down to about 6% of the original size, as shown in Figure 6.43.

4. Press the **q** key to turn off the Stretch 3D tool.

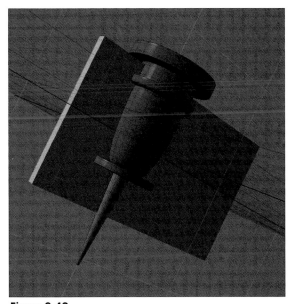

Figure 6.42

Bringing the thumbtack object into the corkboard scene was easy. But it's too big!

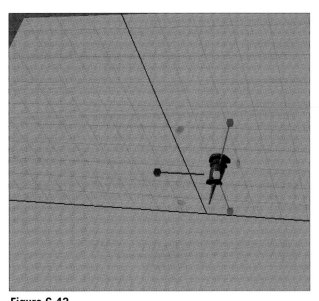

Figure 6.43

Using the Stretch 3D command (the **r** key), it's easy to scale down the object to fit the scene.

5. Rotate the view around to see the front of the corkboard. You can do this by holding the Alt/Option key on your keyboard and then clicking and dragging in the view. You can also use the controls in the upper-right of the viewport—just click on one of the icons, hold your mouse down, and drag.

6. Making sure the thumbtack object is still selected in the Item List, press the **w** key on your keyboard to select the Move 3D tool.

7. Click and drag the handles to move the object to the front of the corkboard. Note, however, that depending on where your model is, you might need to move it in toward the corkboard, rather than pulling it from the back. Either way, use the Move tool to position the thumbtack over the photograph object you created earlier. Figure 6.44 shows the position.

Figure 6.44

Use the Move 3D tool to position the thumbtack.

8. When you've moved the thumbtack into position over the photo object, press the **e** key to select the Rotate tool. Grab the red handle (depending on your setup) and rotate the thumbtack so its sharp end is sticking into the photo on the corkboard. Also, rotate it on the heading a bit—most thumbtacks in the real world are not pushed in completely straight, so angle yours a bit for a better look. You might need to press **w** again to use the Move tool to align it more after you rotate it. Figure 6.45 shows the final thumbtack position.

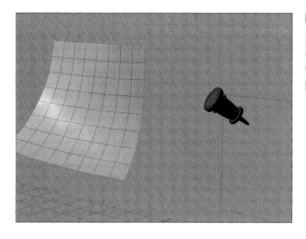

Figure 6.45

Finally, use the Rotate tool (the **e** key) to rotate the thumbtack into a natural position.

9. Save your work! Use Ctrl+s to save!

So there you have it! You've navigated your way through the Item List, making new objects and new scenes, and adding objects from one scene to another. These simple operations are the same no matter what you're making in modo, be it something as simple as a corkboard or as complex as a jet airliner.

You're encouraged to add more notes and items to your corkboard. The objects you've made in this chapter should give you a really good idea of how the process works and how to use the tools. Other object ideas are pendants from colleges. Simply make an elongated triangle, adding a little thickness to it. Or how about a flat, round disc, slightly beveled with a hole cut out in the center to create a CD? Copy your thumbtack object to look as if it's holding up the CD on the corkboard. Use your imagination and have fun with what you build.

When you're ready, move on to the next chapter, where you'll learn about the Shader Tree and use everything you built here as the ingredients to cook up a full textured scene.

7

Shader Tree Fundamentals

In Chapter 6, you modeled something a little untraditional. Although most projects work through modeling a full 3D object, it's a good idea to think beyond the norm. The Chapter 6 project was a lesson in working with the Item List, but it was also designed to trigger your thought process. While most of us head into a 3D modeling program to create cars, character heads, or telephones, the project in Chapter 6 was a little less conventional, but a cool project just the same. The corkboard idea came from talented modonaut Greg Leuenberger, and we'll put our own twist on it here.

In the previous chapter, you learned how to build objects and work with the Item List. You learned how to rename objects in the Item List and how to create materials. You also learned that if you press the Shift key and click on a primitive shape (such as a cube) you get a new item called Cube. By pressing **m** and naming the surface of this geometry Cube, the result in the Item List is Cube(1). From there, you'll see Cube(2) in the Shader Tree, which brings us to this chapter.

The Cube(1) listing is for the item, whereas Cube(2) is for the group mask in the Shader Tree. But this naming convention can get quite confusing. It's something Maya does, but you might want to work around it. By pressing **m** for a selected group of polygons and naming it differently, the group layer name in the Shader Tree is derived from the named polygons. You can always rename in the Shader Tree down the road as you see fit.

Keep in mind that the Item List covered in Chapter 6 gets precedence when it comes to naming. If you name an item "material" in the Item List, it will result in a material(1) name. That material then appears as material(2) in the Shader Tree.

With that said, try not to over-think this process. Those numbers are one of the first things you'll see, and they can be confusing. But what's more important right now is selecting the right material and learning how to apply the right effects.

Note

If your mesh is named Cube, it's a good idea to name the polygon material group Cube_sg (for shading group). Once you get in the habit of appending a short suffix (for shading group, selection set, or whatever), you will unconsciously do it every time and never get names mixed up.

Introducing the Shader Tree

You've worked with the Tool Bar tab quite a bit up until this point, visible at the top-left of the modo interface. If you look to the right of that tabbed viewport, you'll see another tab labeled Render Settings, as shown in Figure 7.1.

When you click the Render Settings tab, you're presented with a viewport entitled Shader Tree. You'll see selections for Filter and Add Layer at the top. You'll come back to these later. In the main Shader Tree window, you'll see three default listings—Render, Environment, and Directional light—as shown in Figure 7.2.

Figure 7.1

The Render Settings tabbed viewport is visible at the top-left of the modo interface.

Figure 7.2

The default Shader Tree within the Render Settings tab is your home for all surfacing and render control.

To the left of each of those three listings is a small triangle. Click the triangle next to the Render listing to expand it. You'll see two things—Base Shader and Base Material, as shown in Figure 7.3.

Figure 7.3

Expanding the Render command in the Shader Tree shows the default material and shader.

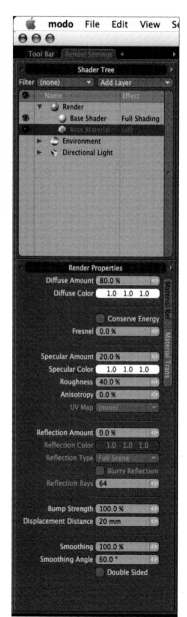

> ## Note
>
> To introduce you to the Shader Tree, work with a default modo interface with no geometry loaded. The best way to set this is to make sure modo is closed, then restart it. Or, if you have modo already running, from the File menu, choose Reset to clear the viewports. Make sure you save any work first.

The base material in the Shader Tree drives everything above it. The material feeds information into the shader, and the shader then takes that information and feeds it into the renderer, taking with it color values. The renderer then adds the appropriate settings you apply. This might sound a bit confusing at first, but don't worry. This chapter will break it down, and then you'll see first-hand how this clever little panel works.

Click the listing Base Material. You'll see a slew of controls appear beneath the Shader Tree. By selecting a name in the Shader Tree list, you activate the controls for that listing. Attributes for the items in the Shader Tree will appear in the Render Properties panel, much like tool attributes and how they will appear in the Tool Properties panel. Now even though there is no geometry in modo, you still see the Base Material settings, such as Diffuse Color, Specular Amount, and so on, as shown in Figure 7.4.

> ## Note
>
> Be sure to check out the Shader Tree video on the book's DVD to get a quick overview of the process.

Figure 7.4

By selecting any listing in the Shader Tree, you activate the controls for that listing. Here, the Base Material listing is selected, and the Render Properties appear below.

As you build objects and add surface materials similar to the project in Chapter 6, the material names you specify will appear here in the Shader Tree. But there's more to this area than meets the eye. This next project will show you how to work with a few settings in the Shader Tree. From there, you'll texture the objects you created in Chapter 6.

1. In the Shader Tree, click the Render listing. You'll see the Render Properties appear beneath the Shader Tree, as shown in Figure 7.5.

Take a close look at the Render Settings tab; on the right of the panel, you'll see a vertical listing. The top selection is Frame, as shown in Figure 7.5. Here you can set the Resolution Unit in pixels or inches. You can also change the size of your render, the default being a 640×480 resolution. The other settings apply to how modo renders, which you'll learn more about later in the book. For now, leave all of these settings at their defaults. The other vertical category listings include controls for anti-aliasing settings, subdivision rates, and displacement rates. You'll also see a category for Global Illumination, a powerful way to render your scenes with added realism. Take a look at these areas to familiarize yourself with them, but leave the settings at their defaults for now. The Render item has many properties that are broken up into relevant tabs on the Render Properties panel. There are tabs for displaying the rendered frame's properties, anti-aliasing for cleaner renders, geometry settings, and global illumination.

2. Back up in the Shader Tree, expand the Environment listing. When this is selected, you'll see a few options below in the Render Properties, such as Visible to Camera, Visible to Reflection Rays, and so on. These are all checked on by default.

Figure 7.5

By selecting the Render listing in the Shader Tree, you gain access to all of the render controls, such as resolution, render settings, and more.

3. With the expanded Environment listing in the Shader Tree, you'll see Environment Material. Select this, and you'll gain access to the colors of the modo render environment, as shown in Figure 7.6.

4. Taking a closer look at the Render Properties for the Environment Material, you can see that the Environment Type is set to 4 Color Gradient by default. Press **F9** on your keyboard to render a frame. Figure 7.7 shows the result with the default render settings. Notice how the render shows the same color gradient structure as listed in the Environment Material.

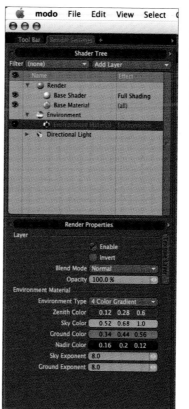

Figure 7.6

The Environment Material within the Environment setting of the Shader Tree is where you can control the color of the modo background for renders.

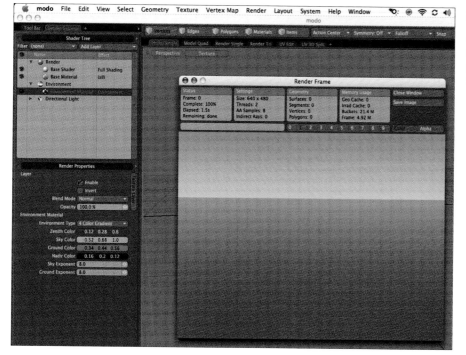

Figure 7.7

A quick render of a default modo scene shows the result of the Environment Material settings.

5. Change the Environment Type to 2 Color Gradient. Change the Nadir Color setting to pale orange and the Zenith Color setting to a deep blue. Do this by simply clicking on the color swatch to call up your system's color palette. Alternatively, you can click and drag on the numer RGB values. When you are finished, press **F9** again to render the scene. Figure 7.8 shows the result.

Note

At any point, feel free to press **F8** and open a floating preview of your scene.

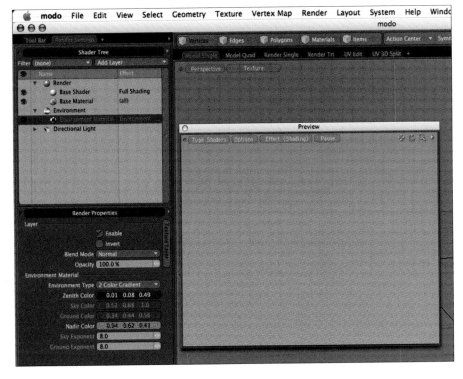

Figure 7.8

Choosing 2 Color Gradient removes the horizon line in the rendered scene, giving you a smooth two-color gradient, as set by the Environment Type. **F8** was pressed to open a preview window.

6. Click the triangle next to Directional Light in the Shader Tree listing. You'll see that there is a Light Material setting for the default light, as shown in Figure 7.9.

7. Now select the Directional Light listing itself in the Shader Tree. You'll see the Render Properties change to some basic but important light settings, as shown in Figure 7.10.

   The settings here allow you to change the light intensity (Radiant Exitance), the Shadow Type, position, and so on.

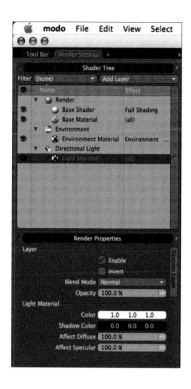

Figure 7.9

A default light in modo also has a default light material.

Figure 7.10

Selecting Directional Light in the Shader Tree rather than Light Material calls up basic but important light settings in the Render Properties panel.

It's important to note that if you select a light, such as the Directional Light in the Item List, you will see that this action also selects the Directional Light item in the Shader Tree and vice versa. The Directional Light item is visible in the Item List and the Shader Tree because it has relevant render properties and acts as a container for light materials and textures. This is similar to an Item Mask, but for lights. These are just a few steps to get you familiar with the basic information in the Shader Tree. Although you haven't created anything yet, you can see how to access the various properties for items in the Shader Tree. Select the item, and the properties for that item will appear below the Shader Tree in the Render Properties panel. Within the Render Properties panel, there can also be Form tab category listings. These are the tabs listed vertically on the right side of the panel. Remember this as you're setting variables for textures, camera render settings, and so on. Now move forward to see the Shader Tree in action by applying textures and image maps to the corkboard model you created in the previous chapter.

Using the Shader Tree

There are still many areas of the Shader Tree yet to be explored. But in order to do that, you'll need to have some geometry to work with. This geometry of course will need to have materials set. But wait! You did that already in Chapter 6. This next project will get you going with applying both image maps and computer-generated textures to your scene.

1. Load up the corkboard object you created in Chapter 6. Or if you want, use the one on the book's DVD. Figure 7.11 shows the model. Note that a few more items have been created for this model since the end of Chapter 6. A large flat plane was created to become a newspaper clipping, and a disc was added to become a CD-ROM. The thumbtack you created was copied a few additional times to hang up the new items on the corkboard.

Figure 7.11

The corkboard object from Chapter 6 with two additional items added to populate it.

2. With the corkboard scene loaded, click the Render Settings tab. Then, expand the Render listing by clicking the triangle icon.

3. Unlike earlier in this chapter, when all you saw were the Base Material and Base Shader settings in the Shader Tree, you now see all of the materials created in Chapter 6 for the objects you built. Remember, you pressed the **m** key after you built the Post-it note and set a polygon material name. This name is what you now see in the Shader Tree. Figure 7.12 shows the tree.

Take a closer look at Figure 7.12, and you can see the materials created. The column on the left shows a little eyeball. This is the material visibility. Clicking this eyeball toggles the material on or off. Next is the name of the material. This is set when you create the material. As a refresher, you can do this by selecting the geometry you want to surface, pressing the **m** key on your keyboard, and giving that geometry a name. That name then appears here in the Shader Tree.

Note

If you drag an object such as the tack from another project into the current scene, it brings its materials along for the ride. It's also going to bring a duplicate base shader and base material. It might throw you off, but don't let it. Just right-click to delete unwanted materials in the Shader Tree.

The last column in the Shader Tree is the Effect listing. Right now, the Base Shader setting at the top of the Shader Tree reads Full Shading. Remember that this shader feeds the renderer; therefore, having it set to Full Shading allows all of the shading options to be applied. But what other types of effects are there? If you right-click (Command-click on a Mac), you'll see the other shading options, such as Diffuse Shading, Luminous Shading, Reflection Shading, and more. You'll use these various

Figure 7.12

The materials created in Chapter 6 are visible in the Shader Tree by expanding the Render listing.

shadings throughout the book. The rest of the materials' Effect listings read (all). If you right-click (Command-click on a Mac), you'll see that all of these materials can be set to any type of effect you want, from a bump, to displacement, to even a mask. You'll learn how and when to use these different effects shortly.

But what if you don't see your material in the Shader Tree? Perhaps you forgot to set a material surface to some geometry in your scene. Can it still be added? Absolutely.

4. To see how easy it is to add a material to the Shader Tree, set your selection mode to Polygons at the top of the modo interface.

5. Next, select the corkboard mesh from the Item List.

6. Then, click on the center polygon of the corkboard to select it.

7. Press the **m** key and set the material name to Corkboard. Give it a slight orange color and click OK. You'll see the material instantly added to the Shader Tree, as shown in Figure 7.13.

Figure 7.13

Materials can be added to the Shader Tree at any time. Assigning a material group to the selected polygons instantly adds it to the tree.

> **Note**
>
> Remember that when you assign a material group to selected polygons, modo does two things. It adds a group item (also called a *material mask*) with a polygon tag type of material and a polygon tag of the name of the material group you've just created. Then, modo adds a material item inside of that material mask.

8. Press the left bracket ([) key just to the right of the P key to reverse the selection. This will select the frame of the corkboard.

9. Press the **m** key and set the material name for these selected polygons to Corkboard Frame or something similar. You'll see this material now added to the Shader Tree as well.

You can see that it's easy to get materials into the Shader Tree, whether they are imported with an existing object or created on the fly. But what do you do with these materials once they're available in the tree?

Setting Materials

Now that the Shader Tree is fully populated with the materials' names, how about actually setting those material surfaces? Because you built the corkboard first, how about starting there? You'll work your way up from there, applying computer-generated surface and image maps.

You might also notice that there are small icons to the left of the material names. Here's how it breaks down. The green dot with a red dot is the mask. This is just a group layer set to mask items or polygon selections. A group layer will have the same icon with the red dot mask whether or not there's a material in there. This section will help explain things further.

1. In the Shader Tree, select the Corkboard material group, as shown in Figure 7.14.

2. It's important to understand the difference between the group layer and the material itself. When you're selecting the Corkboard name (the group layer) in the Shader Tree, you'll see that just a few render properties appear below the tree. This texture layer allows you to set the opacity and apply any grouping. For now you don't need to create a grouping for the texture layer, so with the Corkboard material group expanded in the Shader Tree, select the material for it. This is also represented by a green dot, and the Material listing will be indented, showing that it belongs to the group layer just above it. You'll see the crucial settings appear for this material in the Render Properties panel, as shown in Figure 7.15.

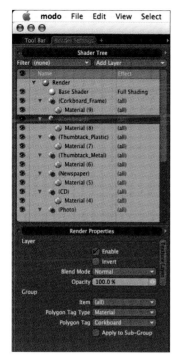

Figure 7.14

Select the Corkboard material group in the Shader Tree.

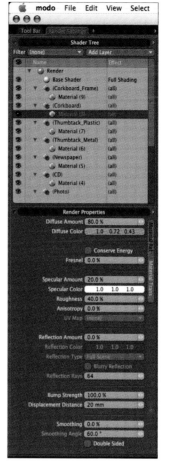

Figure 7.15

Selecting the material for the Corkboard texture layer displays the most crucial surfacing attributes in the Render Properties panel.

3. You'll see that in the Render Properties panel with the material selected, there are two additional tabs on the right side of the panel. The top is the Material Reference, which contains all of the key color and shading. The second is the Material Trans, where you can set transparent, subsurface, and luminous values.

4. But for now, in the Material Ref category of the Render Properties, make sure the Diffuse value default is at 80% and leave it at that for now. The Diffuse Color should be a pale orange or light-brown color, something similar to a corkboard color.

5. The Conserve Energy option for now should be unchecked. This handy little tool's purpose is to provide physically based shading, given realistic input values. This is especially true for surfaces that have both diffuse and reflective values applied. Shading with conserve energy turned on is a bit slower to compute, and if you're just tweaking appearances by eye you probably don't need it. Pure diffuse or pure reflective surfaces don't need it either. So for now, leave it off.

6. The rest of the settings should be left at their defaults right now. They allow you to control the specularity, amount of gloss (roughness), and more.

7. Back up in the Shader Tree, with the Material listing selected underneath the Corkboard texture, choose Add Layer from the top of the Shader Tree and select the Cellular texture, as shown in Figure 7.16.

8. Change your viewport to the Render Tri view. You can do this by selecting the preset tab at the top of the viewport. This will change your view to a three-panel viewport, one panel of which is a preview window. For quick previews of your textures, lighting, and even shadows, use the preview window in a Render-Tri tabbed viewport. You can also press **F8** for a floating pop-up preview window. Figure 7.17 shows the texture layer added and the view changed.

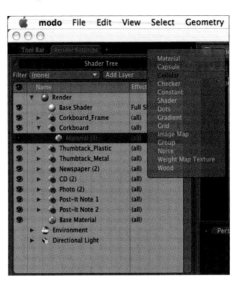

Figure 7.16

Add a layer to the Corkboard material by choosing it from the Add Layer list at the top of the panel.

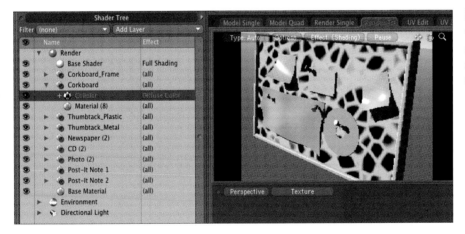

Figure 7.17

When a computer-generated texture layer is added to the material, you can view it with a preview window.

9. Notice that in the Shader Tree, the Cellular texture is added on top of the material for the corkboard. If it were located below the material, you would not see it in the preview window. You'll also see that this added layer has a black-and-white checkered icon. In the Render Properties panel, click the Texture Locator tab. This will present you with the size and mapping settings for the Cellular texture.

10. The texture initially is a little too large, so you'll want to size it down. But instead of randomly guessing a value for the XYZ size settings, you can do some math right in the panel. After the Size X listing, type **/4** to tell modo to divide the value by four, as shown in Figure 7.18.

11. Do the same for Y and Z, and your values will be equally divided. You can see how the Cellular texture is now smaller in the preview window, as shown in Figure 7.19.

12. Right now the texture is black and white because its effect in the Shader Tree is set to Diffuse Color. Right-click (Command-click on a Mac) the Effect listing and change it to Diffuse Amount. You'll see the same Cellular texture now diffused, or blended with the material for the corkboard, as shown in Figure 7.20.

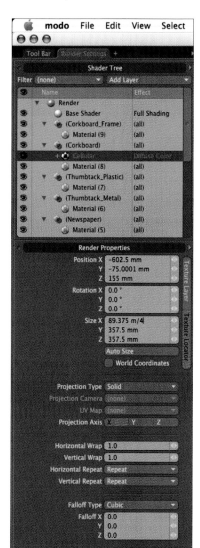

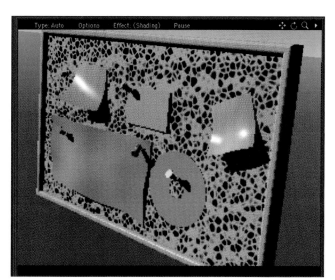

Figure 7.18

You can let modo calculate some math for you; just add a / for divide and the amount you'd like to set. Here, the X value for Size is set to divide by four. Who needs a calculator?

Figure 7.19

The scaled-down Cellular texture is viewable in the preview window.

Note

The diffuse channel controls the strength of the light on the material. For example, with a low diffuse value, the material is lit less. It takes less light from the scene.

Figure 7.20

Setting the Cellular texture effect to Diffuse Amount blends the layer with the base material.

13. Are you wondering whether maybe you can take this texture to another level? Sure you can! Right-click (Command-click on the Mac) on the Cellular listing—not the effect, but the name itself in the Shader Tree. In the pop-up that appears, select Instance to create an instance of the Cellular texture. An instance is not so much a duplicate as it is a carbon copy of the original. It simply references the original, saving you memory and processing power. An instance will appear italicized. And, an instance will update when changes are made in the master (original) layer.

14. For the effect of the instanced Cellular texture, right-click (or Command-click) on the Diffuse Amount listing and change it to Bump. You'll see the Cellular texture in the preview window appear to have depth, as shown in Figure 7.21.

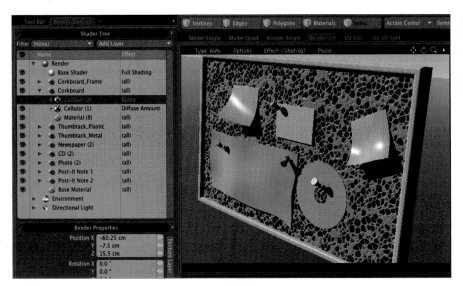

Figure 7.21

With an instance created for the Cellular texture in the Shader Tree and with its Effect setting as Bump, the material now has more depth.

15. This new bump doesn't quite make the surface look like a corkboard, so select the first Cellular texture layer. In the Render Properties panel, change the Cell Value to 60% and the Filler Value to 80%. This will take away some of the heavy contrast by coloring within the cell holes.

16. Back up in the Shader Tree, select the Cellular instance set for Bump.

17. In the Render Properties panel, check Invert to reverse the bump map. Change the Opacity setting to 80%. Figure 7.22 shows the difference.

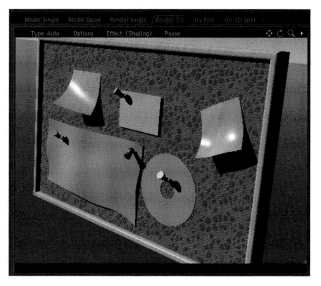

Figure 7.22

The instanced bump texture is leveled off a bit by changing the original Cellular texture and decreasing the bump opacity.

18. Feel free to play with the size and color (Cell and Filler Value) of the Cellular texture to make it your own. Maybe you want to see how the texture looks even smaller? Perhaps more or less bump? Play around with the settings, and you can get some cool results. Try one more setting: Select the Cellular(2) layer—the one with Bump applied. In the Render Properties panel, uncheck the Invert button in the Texture Layer vertical category.

19. In the Texture Locator vertical category, divide the XYZ values for Size by 3. This equals a cellular size of about 2.9 cm. You can simply enter this size as well if you want. Figure 7.23 shows the result in the corkboard.

20. When you're ready, save your work.

Note

Although the default bump settings work well for this corkboard, there are times when you might want more or less bump. The way to do that is with the Bump Strength setting. You can find this in the material properties for the selected group.

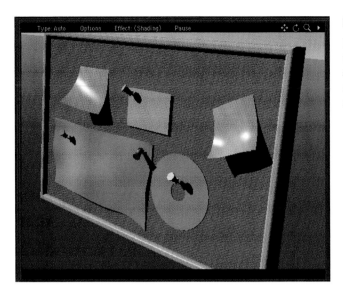

Figure 7.23

By adjusting the Cellular texture to a smaller size and adjusting the Bump layer, the resulting texture more closely resembles a corkboard.

You can see that by adding a procedural texture, making an instance of it, you can quickly create some great-looking organic textures. However, trying to create a Post-it note is not as easy with computer-generated images. Although modo is pretty powerful, it can't quite mimic a handwritten note—at least not yet. So that leaves you with the task of importing existing image maps.

Setting Image Materials

The subject of modo texturing would fill a book all on its own, so this chapter is only here to get you started with the tools. There are many areas and effects you can try, many of which we'll employ in upcoming tutorials in this book. The previous section guided you through adding a procedural texture layer to create the corkboard. This section will take you a step further by showing you how to add images as textures.

1. Continuing from the previous exercise, working with the Post-It Note 1 texture layer, choose its mask and expand it. Choose its Material layer.

Note

A quick and cool way to select specific materials is to switch to Materials selection mode in modo at the top of the interface. Then, simply move your mouse over your scene items. You'll see materials highlight as you mouse over, and then just click to select.

2. If you take a look at the Render Properties panel, either in the Material Ref vertical category or the Material Trans category, there's no setting for mapping an image. What gives? You need to add an image layer to the Post-It Note group. Make sure the material is selected for the Post-It Note 1 group layer in the Shader Tree.

3. At the top of the Shader Tree, select Add Layer and choose Image Map, as shown in Figure 7.24.

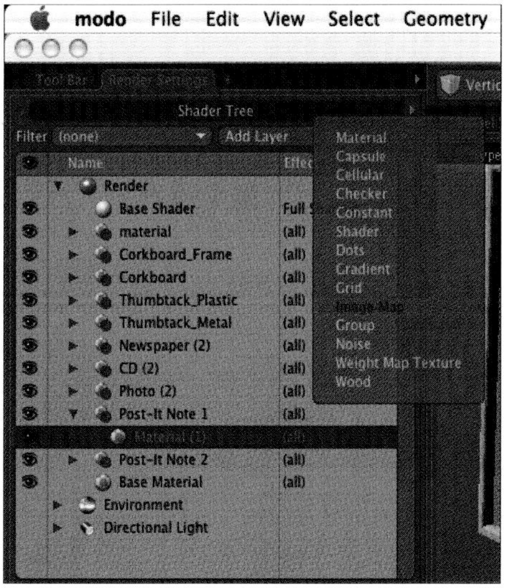

Figure 7.24

Adding an Image Map layer to a material is easy by selecting Add Layer from the drop-down list.

4. When you select Add Layer and choose Image Map, a dialog box will open, allowing you to choose an image. Point to the book's project folder on the DVD, and in the Chapter 7 folder, choose the Note1.png image.

5. When you select the image, the Image Map layer will be created in the Post-It Note group layer, with its effect set to Diffuse Color. This is fine for now. With the Image Map layer selected in the Shader Tree, select the Texture Locator tab in the Render Properties panel.

6. Change the Projection Type setting from UV Map to Planar, as shown in Figure 7.25.

7. After you've set a Planar Projection Type, set Project Axis to Z. Then, click Auto Size. Then, scale down the size on the Y axis so the image map doesn't run off the geometry. And at the bottom of the Render Properties panel, change the Vertical Repeat to Reset. Rotate your view in the viewport to get a closer look at the first Post-it note, now image-mapped, as shown in Figure 7.26.

8. You might notice that this Post-it note could use a little something more. No problem! First, save your work by choosing Save from the File menu.

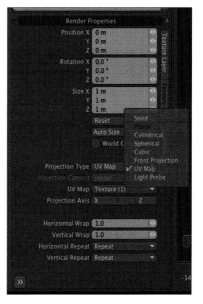

Figure 7.25

Change the Projection Type setting from UV Map to Planar for the image map.

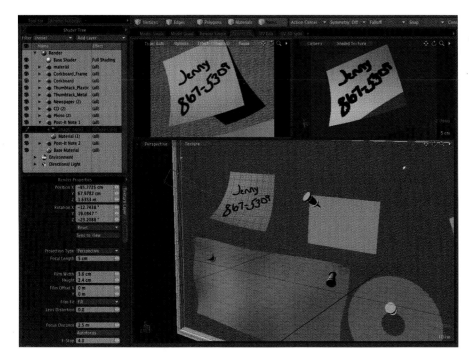

Figure 7.26

The first object has an image map applied.

9. Select the Material layer for the Post-It Note group, just under the Image Map layer. This is the base material for this particular group. When you select it, you can see the basic properties in the Render Properties panel. And because the image you just mapped on the mesh was a 32-bit image, the area around the handwritten text is transparent. This means these base settings will show through.

10. Bring the Specular Amount to 10%. The Specular Color setting can remain at white. Set Roughness to 70%. Because there aren't any reflections, you don't need to set a value there, and this surface doesn't need a bump, so you're all set. Figure 7.27 shows the settings.

11. Save your work! There's another great way to apply an image map. First, head over to the Item List and drag it open a bit to see the Images tab. There you'll see the existing image map you loaded through the Shader Tree. But if you look closely in this image list, you can click the Load Image listing. Click it and select the trees.jpg image from this chapter's project folder on the book's DVD.

12. When loaded, the preview shows just the image, but you can also see the image thumbnail in the Images list, as shown in Figure 7.28.

13. In the viewport, click on the photo mesh on the corkboard. You should be in Items selection mode at the top of the modo interface. Then, click and drag the thumbnail of the tree image from the Images tab and drop it on the photo object.

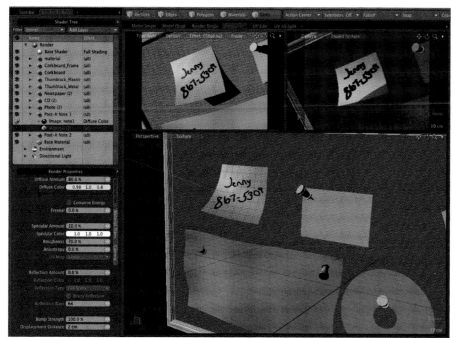

Figure 7.27

By setting a few basic properties, the Post-it note is now textured.

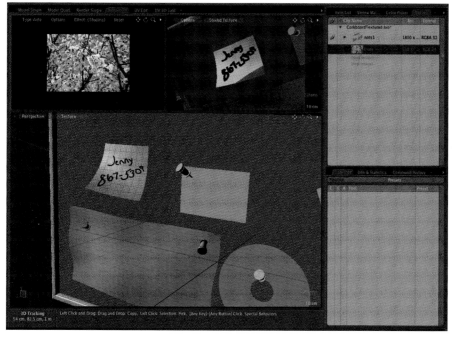

Figure 7.28

Rather than loading an image in the Shader Tree, you can load it directly in the Images tab.

14. In the Shader Tree, look at the Photo group. Expand it if you have to. You'll see an Image Map layer, just like the one you added to the Post-it note. Figure 7.29 shows the Shader Tree with the image applied.

15. Similar to the Post-it note, change the Projection Type from UV Map to Planar on the Z axis for the tree image in the Render Properties panel. Remember that this is under the Texture Locator tab. Also remember to click Auto Size. You'll see the image applied to the photo mesh, as shown in Figure 7.30.

16. Save your work.

The Shader Tree can be confusing, with groups, layers, materials, and masks, but it's easier than you might think. You've already accomplished a lot with the lessons in this chapter, but as always, there's more you can do! The next project will take the texturing capabilities a step further and introduce you to more masking techniques.

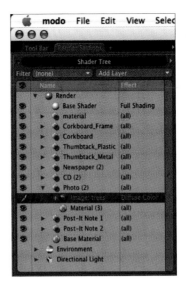

Figure 7.29

When an image is applied to a material, it also shows as a layer in the Material Group within the Shader Tree.

Figure 7.30

Applying the tree image as a planar map on the Z axis with an auto size perfectly maps it onto the mesh.

Masking Effects

The term "mask" will be used a lot when it comes to modo and the Shader Tree. This section will use an image to mask out another. It's a great way to shape a mesh without actually modeling it.

1. Continuing from the previous exercise and your corkboard object, select the newspaper mesh on the board. You can choose Items mode at the top of the modo interface, and then click in the viewport to select the mesh.

Note

A quick way to jump to Items mode is to press the Shift and spacebar keys at the same time.

2. At the top-right of the interface, click over to the Images tabbed viewport, to the right of the Item List.

3. Select Load Image and, from the book's DVD, choose the newspaper clipping.jpg image.

4. When the image loads, drag and drop it onto the newspaper mesh. Figure 7.31 shows the setup.

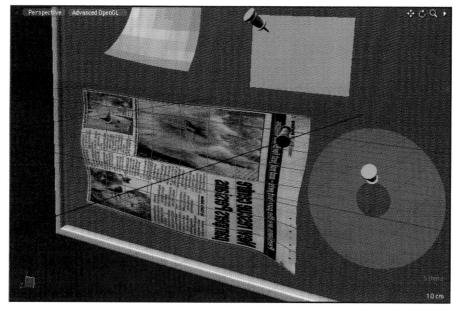

Figure 7.31

Applying a newspaper clipping mesh is easy by loading it in the Images tab, then dragging and dropping it onto the mesh.

5. Expand the Render group in the Shader Tree.

6. Expand the Newspaper group, and then select the image layer that was added by dragging and dropping the newspaper clipping image onto the mesh.

7. In the Render Properties panel, click to the Texture Locator tab listing.

8. Change Projection Type from UV Map to Planar.

9. Set the Projection Axis to Z.

10. Click the Auto Size button. The newspaper clipping is now mapped, as shown in Figure 7.32.

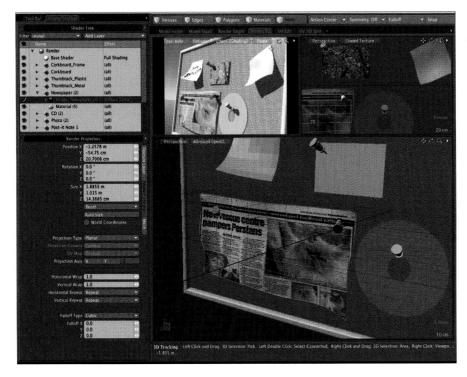

Figure 7.32

Adjusting the newspaper clipping settings in the Texture Locator category of the Render Properties panel maps the clipping onto the mesh perfectly.

11. Now, you know as well as anyone that newspaper clippings hanging on a corkboard need a ripped edge, right? No one cuts out clippings perfectly. Well, some do, but in this exercise we want it ripped! In the Images tab, load the papermask.png image. This is a 32-bit image with a Photoshop-painted rough edge.

12. When the image is loaded, drag and drop it onto the newspaper mesh. It won't look quite right, as shown in Figure 7.33.

13. Similar to how you mapped the newspaper image, you'll do the same for the paper mask. Select the new image within the Newspaper group in the Shader Tree.

14. From the Render Properties panel, select the Texture Locator category. Change Projection Type to Planar. Projection Axis should be set to Z. Then click Auto Size. You'll see the paper mask align better, but it's not quite right yet, as shown in Figure 7.34.

15. Still in the Texture Locator controls of the Render Properties panel, change the Vertical Repeat to Reset.

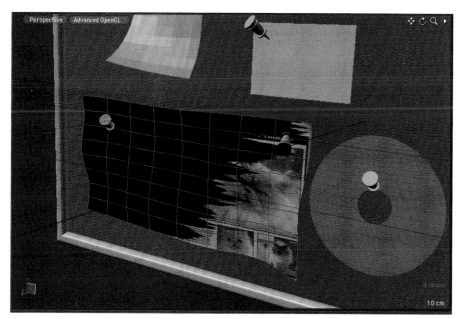

Figure 7.33

Dragging and dropping the papermask.png image onto the newspaper mesh doesn't look quite right yet.

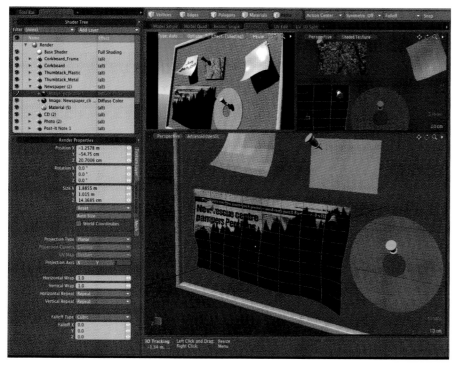

Figure 7.34

Setting auto size and planar image mapping for the newspaper mesh aligns the image.

16. Then, change the size of the image on the Y axis to about 34 cm. By turning off the Vertical Repeat, you won't see a duplicate image as you size the paper mask.

17. Next, move the image down on the Y axis to about −86 cm. Simply click and drag the sliders in the number controls. Figure 7.35 shows the newly placed image and the values in the Render Properties panel.

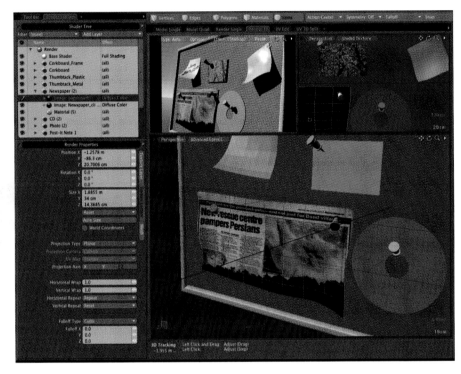

Figure 7.35

Sizing the image in the Render Properties panel, along with moving it down on the Y axis, properly places it on the mesh.

18. You're going to make a few more changes, and then you'll see how this all comes together. Select the papermask image in the Shader Tree within the Newspaper layer group. Notice that its effect is set to Diffuse Color. This is fine for the actual newspaper clipping image, but the 32-bit papermask image is going to be used to cut away the mesh.

19. Change the effect by right-clicking (Command-click on the Mac) on it and selecting Transparent Amount.

20. After the effect value is set to Transparent Amount, you might not see the result. Why? The papermask image is black on a transparent background. To effectively clip the mesh and utilize the transparency, open the Texture Layer category in the Render Properties and click Invert.

21. Making sure you have a preview window open, you can see the instant result. Use the Render-Tri view tab to quickly call up a preview. Figure 7.36 shows the setup.

22. Save your work!

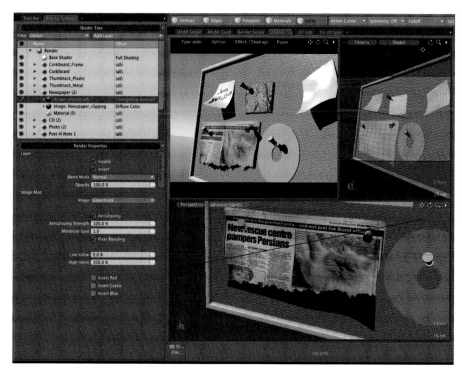

Figure 7.36

Changing the effect of the papermask to Transparent Amount and inverting the image allows you to clip away part of the mesh.

Take a look at Figure 7.37. This is how the Newspaper layer group currently looks. Let's break this down so you see what's happening. The two images are now mapped on the newspaper mesh. In the Shader Tree, within the Newspaper material group, there is a base material. It is home to the base values, such as opacity, specularity, roughness, and so on. Changing any of these values filters up to the images to which they are applied. The effect in the Shader Tree is set to (all), meaning that all values are applied to each effect, the effects being Diffuse, Transparency, Luminosity, and so on. You can also expand the texture layer by clicking the plus sign at the left of the listing in the Shader Tree. Once it is expanded, you'll see the images applied, as in Figure 7.38. You can select the image layers and make adjustments to position, rotation, size, and so on.

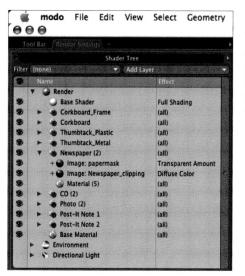

Figure 7.37

The Shader Tree, although simple in appearance, is quite powerful. Here, the newspaper mesh is turned into a clipping on a corkboard with a few texture layers.

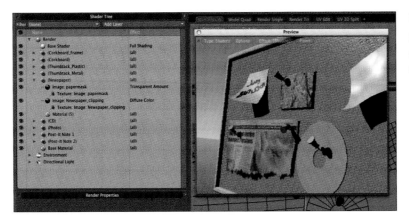

Figure 7.38

In the Shader Tree, you can expand the texture layers to access the image maps applied.

Just above the base material for the Newspaper group is the newspaper clipping. It's a full texture map, so its effect is set to Diffuse Amount. This effect tells modo to apply the full value of the image, allowing other properties in the scene, including light and color, to be diffused or accepted by this texture layer. On top of that layer is the papermask image. This is a 32-bit image, so a portion of it is transparent, and modo reads this data. By setting this image layer's effect to Transparent Amount, you're telling the Shader Tree to use the transparent data. You'll come back to the corkboard scene later to set up the environment and render for it. This is also an important aspect of setting up textures as they work hand in hand to create the final look.

Your Next Few Steps

By no means are you finished using the Shader Tree. Actually, you're just getting started! But you can see that with these few simple actions, your corkboard model is already taking shape and looking good. You've added a procedural computer-generated texture layer. You've mapped images and applied different effects. So what more could you do? On your own, map the other items on the corkboard. Try experimenting with different types of images—just remember that if you create something in Photoshop or another paint package, do so on a transparent background. Save that image as a PNG to retain the 32-bit alpha data that modo will read. Perhaps you can tear off a small piece of the second Post-it note using the same effect as you did for the newspaper. Maybe you have a corkboard in your office or home. Take a photo of it and apply that image to the board rather than using a computer-generated texture.

From here, you'll dive even deeper into the Shader Tree in Chapter 8, "Inside the Shader Tree." There's much more to this than meets the eye, but you'll soon find that out. Later in the book, as you get into more advanced modeling, you'll also learn how to use modo's powerful painting features to create your own unique textures. But first, turn to Chapter 8 to learn about deeper functions of the Shader Tree.

8

Inside the Shader Tree

Chapter 7 gave you a good basis for working with the Shader Tree and helped you identify group layers and materials. It gave you a broad overview of working with the Shader Tree using images and basic materials. However, the real power of the Shader Tree comes from adding layers and masks. What you've done so far is just the first step to this killer addition to modo. In fact, the Shader Tree is one of the most powerful features of any 3D application on the market. This chapter will take you through the Shader Tree to further introduce layers, masks, gradients, and UV texturing.

Masks

A good majority of the work you'll do in modo 201/202 might not be more than projects similar to those in Chapter 7. But it's important to be aware of and understand the tools available to you under the hood. You never know when a project might creep up that requires the use of these controls and settings. Beyond that, you might just find that you like experimenting to create stunning pieces of art.

Item Masks

Item masks are a mechanism that enables you to segment your scene to determine how various materials will be applied to certain elements. There are many ways to set masks in modo, from items to polygons, vertex maps, and more. Item masks begin at the highest level, which is where this chapter starts. From there, you'll work down to polygon materials.

1. Taking a closer look at the Shader Tree, you'll want to open up modo and select Reset from the File menu. This will bring modo back to a default setup.

2. Rather than modeling in this chapter, you'll work with some preexisting scenes created for you. You can find these project files on this book's DVD, in the Chapter 8 projects folder. Load up the Key.lxo scene. Press the **a** key to fit the model to view. Hold the Alt/Option key and then click and drag in the viewport to see both keys. Figure 8.1 shows the key loaded in a Perspective viewport.

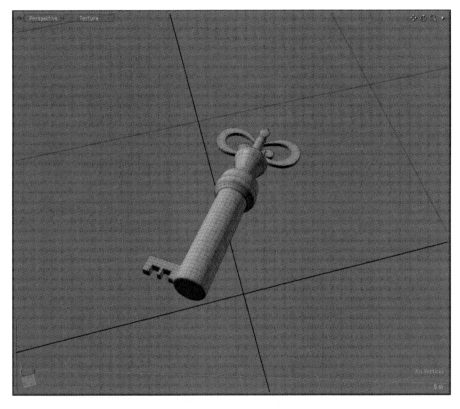

Figure 8.1

The key is loaded in a Perspective viewport.

3. On the left side of the screen, click over to the Render Settings tab to expose the Shader Tree.

4. Click the small triangle to the left of the Render listing to expand its contents. Figure 8.2 shows what's there.

Tip

To learn how to model this key, view the video tutorials labeled KeyTutorial on the book's DVD.

5. Looking at Figure 8.2, there's a base material and a base shader. Make another copy of this key by right-clicking (Command-click on the Mac) on the mesh name in the Item List on the right side of the interface and selecting Duplicate.

6. You'll now see Key(1) and Key(2) in the Item List. In the main viewport, press the **y** key on your keyboard and move the duplicate key from the original position. Feel free to rotate it some. Don't worry about positioning it just yet; you only need to be able to see both keys. Save the new setup as BlankKey or something similar. Figure 8.3 shows the operation.

Figure 8.2

The Shader Tree shows the default settings for the key model.

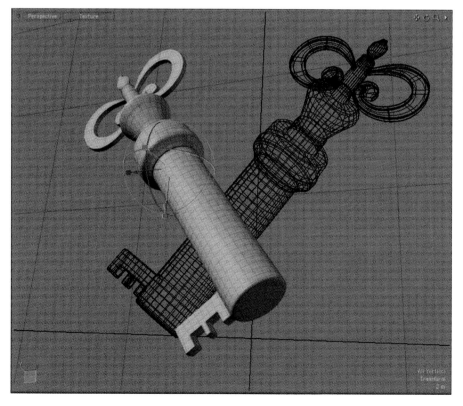

Figure 8.3

A duplicate key is made by right-clicking and selecting Duplicate in the Item List, then positioning it in the viewport.

7. Back over in the Shader Tree, notice that you still only have one base material and one base shader. This is because the original key was duplicated and neither has a mask applied. That means if you change the base material, it will affect both models. First, press the **o** key on your keyboard (not the zero) to call up the viewport options. Set the Background Layer option to Same as Active Layer.

8. Both keys, although in different layers in the Item List, will be visible as shaded models. Select the Base Material in the Shader Tree, and then change the Diffuse Color in the Render Properties to an off-white, soft brown color.

9. Any other value you change for the base material will affect both keys. This includes transparencies, reflections, and so on. In the Item List, right-click (Command-click on the Mac) on the duplicate key and select Create Item Mask, as shown in Figure 8.4.

10. You'll see that the color you applied to the base material in Step 8 is now only applied to one key. And, if you look in the Shader Tree, a new item mask is listed, as well as an additional material, as shown in Figure 8.5.

Note

The viewport options panel that appears when you press **o** on your keyboard looks slightly different on a Mac and a PC. The PC version is more solid; the Mac is darker and a little more transparent. Both are identical in function, however.

Figure 8.4

You can right-click on the key mesh layer in the Item List to easily create an item mask.

Figure 8.5

Adding an item mask to the duplicate key adds new properties in the Shader Tree.

11. This new item mask you've created allows you to set unique surfaces for the key for which you created it. From the Item List, select the original key and create an item mask for it, just as you did in Step 9. Now you'll see another addition to the Shader Tree, as shown in Figure 8.6.

12. Save your scene with a new name, perhaps TwoKeys or something similar. It's a good idea to save your scene in stages so you can always get back to a previous version at any time.

Note

The item mask is actually a group layer that is configured to limit its effect to the item you choose.

13. By adding the second item mask, you can see that both keys are now back to their original blank surfaces. The coloring you applied to the base material initially is now overwritten by the new masked materials. In the Shader Tree, right-click (Command-click on the Mac) on Item:Key(1) and select Rename. Rename it to just Top Key. Do the same for Item:Key(2), naming it Bottom Key. This is only for organization, and you can rename it anything you like. It has no effect on the scene. You can also rename the material listing as well, if you want.

Figure 8.6

Adding an item mask to the original key adds additional settings in the Shader Tree.

14. Now, the original base material is overwritten, but it still holds a place in the scene based on the settings applied in the Shader Tree. Select the material for the Top Key. Change its diffuse color to a soft beige.

15. With the material still selected for the Top Key, increase the specular amount to 50%. This increases the shininess of the object. Bring the roughness to about 80% to spread the shine created by the increased specularity. Figure 8.7 shows the settings.

16. Because you want the base material to be the same for both keys, right-click (Command-click on the Mac) on the Top Key material listing and select Copy. Then, select the Bottom Key material listing and right-click, choosing Paste. You'll see the Bottom Key in the shaded viewport now matches the Top Key. Save the scene!

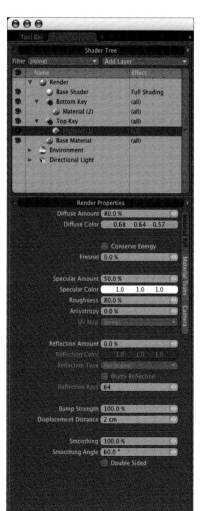

Figure 8.7

With just a few changes to the Top Key materials, the object starts looking better.

Polygon Masks

Similar to an item mask, a polygon mask creates a material mask in the Shader Tree. But rather than creating a mask for the entire object, a polygon mask allows you to set a material for a specific set of polygons. For example, the key object you're using in this scene really only needs one surface, and therefore an item mask is enough. But perhaps you'll need to create a separate surface for one particular part of the key. This is where a polygon mask is used.

1. Switch to Polygons selection mode at the top of the modo interface. Then select the polygons at the end of the key making up the tip, as shown in Figure 8.8. A quick way to select this region is to click once on the end, then hold the Shift key and press the up arrow five times to expand the selection up around the end.

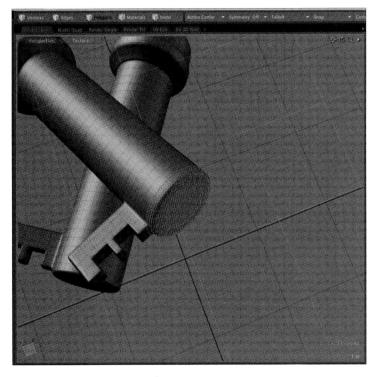

Figure 8.8

The end of the top key's polygons are selected.

2. Press the **m** key on your keyboard to call up the Polygon Set Material dialog box. Set the name of the selected polygons to Top Key Tip and click OK. Figure 8.9 shows the Shader Tree with the polygon mask added.

3. Take a close look at the key in the viewport. Notice that the tip is now a default white color again and does not retain the original surface properties you set. This is because the new polygon mask overrides the original one you created.

The problem now is that even though you have an additional material for a specifically controlled surface, you have a sharp crease between the two. Ideally, you'd want the tip material to blend with the rest of the key material. The goal is to create just enough variance in the texture to make the key look a little worn at the tip. By adding a vertex mask, you can blend the surface of tip of the key.

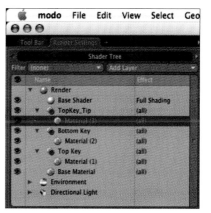

Figure 8.9

When the selected polygons have a mask applied, a new material name appears in the Shader Tree.

Vertex Masks

Taking the masking information down one more level, you come to the vertex mask. This is similar to applying an item mask to the item or a polygon mask to polygons, in that you're applying a mask to the vertex or vertices of the model. This mask will allow you to blend the tip of the key and any surfaces you apply to the rest of the key.

1. In the viewport, switch to Edges selection mode, and then carefully select the edge at the top of the tip selection. Figure 8.10 shows the area.

Figure 8.10

Select the edge around the tip of the key that rests between the two surface materials.

2. Up to the right of the Item List, you'll see the Vertex Map List tab. Select it to view the contents. Expand the Weight Maps listing, and underneath the Subdivision listing, choose New Map. The Create New Vertex Map panel will appear, as shown in Figure 8.11.

3. In the panel that appears, set the Vertex Map Name field to KeyTipWeight. Click OK to close the panel.

Figure 8.11

You can create a new vertex map for selected vertices and edges within the Vertex Map List tab.

4. Change your modo viewport to a Render Tri view by clicking the Render Tri tab from across the top of the viewport. Press Shift+A to fit the selection to view.

5. Then, change the viewport style in either the Perspective view or Camera view to Vertex Map. The items in your scene will appear as a flat green color, as shown in Figure 8.12. This color represents the weight applied, and the flat color refers to a neutral value.

6. The edge is still selected in the viewport, so from the Vertex Map drop-down menu at the top of the interface, select the Weight tool. Or, you can simply press Shift+W to activate it.

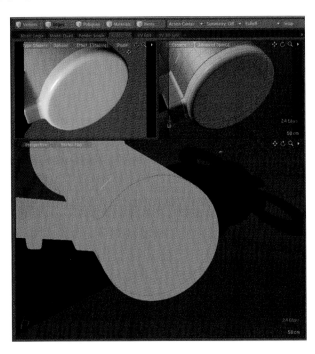

Figure 8.12

Change your viewports to a Render Tri view, and also make one viewport a Vertex Map style for shading.

7. Click and drag to the right in the Vertex Map shaded viewport. You should see the selected edge's surrounding areas become red, as shown in Figure 8.13.

8. A red color means that the weight applied to this edge is a positive value. If you click and drag to the left, the weight turns blue and is a negative value. For now, press the **k** key to call up the numeric entry for the Weight tool, and make sure it's set to 100%.

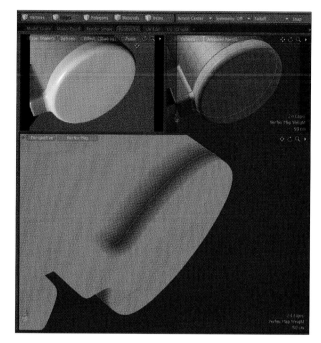

Figure 8.13

Once a Vertex Map is created, the Weight tool can be used to set the value of the weight. Here, the weight is created with a 100% positive value and is signified by red.

9. The preview window in the Render Tri view still shows the white tip with a hard edge to the rest of the key. That's because although you've created a weight map for the selected vertices, you've not applied it anywhere.

10. Over in the Shader Tree, select the TopKeyTip group. Then, from the Add Layer drop-down at the top of the Shader Tree, select Weight Map Texture. Figure 8.14 shows the setup, along with the preview window. Notice how the tip is now black except for the weighted edge, which is white.

Figure 8.14

When a Weight Map Texture is applied in the Shader Tree, the material starts to change but does not yet blend.

11. The new Weight Map Texture doesn't blend into the key just yet because its effect is set to Diffuse Color in the Shader Tree. Right-click (Command-click on the Mac) on this effect listing and change the Weight Map Texture to Group Mask. You'll now see that the tip of the key is the same color as the rest of the key, but the edge between the two sets of materials has a soft white to it. This soft white is the vertex mask. But there's a little more to do. Figure 8.15 shows the change.

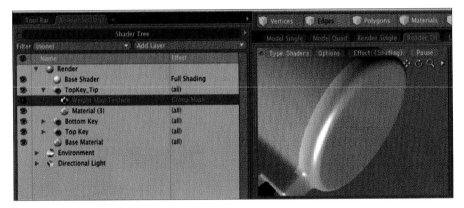

Figure 8.15

As a group mask, the Weight Map Texture applied now uses the vertex mask to blend the materials.

12. Make sure the Weight Map Texture is selected in the Shader Tree. By having this material layer selected, additional materials added will be placed directly above. From the Add Layer drop-down menu in the Shader Tree, select Noise to add a noise layer to the Top Key Tip group. You can see from Figure 8.16 that the noise material layer is concentrated within the edge weight.

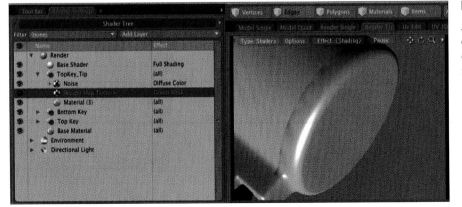

Figure 8.16

An added noise layer doesn't exactly get applied to the tip of the key when applied above the Weight Map Texture.

13. Select the Weight Map Texture, and in the Render Properties panel, making sure you're in the Texture Layer tab, change Value 1 to 100% and Value 2 to 0%. This essentially inverts the values of the Weight Map Texture. And yes, you could have simply clicked the Invert button at the top of the panel.

However, it's important to know what you're inverting first. Figure 8.17 shows the noise channel now applied to the tip of the key, but blended nicely into the main key material.

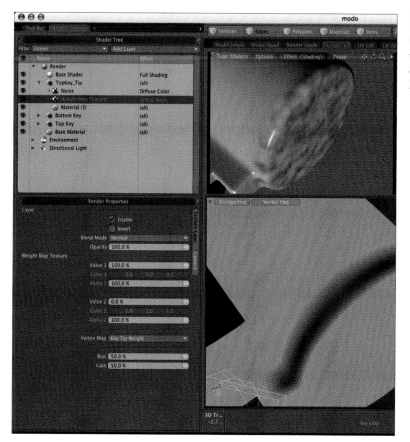

Figure 8.17

Once the Weight Map Texture values are changed, the noise channel blends well with the key materials.

Note

In this particular case, the positions of the group mask and the Noise layers do not make much difference. In other situations, you might want the group mask on top of the Noise layer. It's good practice to keep the layer stacks organized in a similar fashion no matter what scene you're working on.

You might ask why you would create two separate masks for the keys if all you were going to do was copy and paste the material settings. That's a good question! You create separate noise channels for each mask to have great control over the final look. The added noise to the tip of the key blends nicely, but still needs a little adjustment.

Additional Material Layers

You can see that by weighting the vertices and applying a Weight Map Texture in the Shader Tree, two masks are blended together—an item mask and a polygon mask. With this setup, you can add in any additional materials you want, such as the noise layer you've already added. But this is just the beginning.

1. In the TopKeyTip group in the Shader Tree, select the Material listing. Its diffuse color is still at its default state of 1.0, 1.0, 1.0, white. To successfully blend the tip of the key with the rest of the mesh, set this base color to the same beige color you applied earlier for the rest of the key. If you're not sure, select the Material listing for either the top or bottom key. You can also just right-click (Command-click on the Mac) on the top or bottom key Material listing, select Copy, and then select the key tip material, right-click, and select paste.

2. Once the key tip material's diffuse color is set, select the Noise layer. In the Render Properties panel, change the blend mode to Hard Light. Color 1 should be 0,0,0, or just pure black. Set Color 2 to the same color as the material color, the beige.

3. Finally, change the Type setting to Turbulence. Leave the other settings as they are, which should be Frequencies at 4, Frequency Ratio at 2.0, Amplitude Ratio at 0.5, with Bias and Gain both at 50%. Figure 8.18 shows the results. Looks a bit like rust, doesn't it?

4. With the Noise layer values set, save your scene. Then, with the Noise layer still selected, right-click (Command-click on the Mac) on it and choose Create Instance. An instance is like a copy or duplicate, but it doesn't tax your system as much as a copy. An instance references the original item, similar to a clone. It will be italicized.

5. Select the noise instance after it's created, and then right-click on the Effect value in the Shader Tree, changing the diffuse color to Displacement.

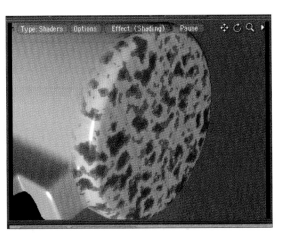

Figure 8.18

Changing a few color values and the blend mode results in swell-looking rust!

Note

Bias will affect the texture to favor the primary color value when setting a positive amount. Setting a negative amount will tell the texture to favor the secondary value. The values here are Value 1 and Value 2, the two colors you just set. Gain, on the other hand, is like a gamma control that affects the falloff between the two values. A 0% value is a soft falloff, whereas a 100% value is a sharp falloff. You can experiment with these values in the Render Tri view (or open a preview window by pressing F8) and see the results.

6. Select the Material listing for the TopKeyTip and change the displacement distance to 4 cm. Because this material is at the bottom of this group, it affects everything above it. And because you now set the noise channel (the instance) to Displacement, this material value will be applied. Figure 8.19 shows the result.

Figure 8.19

Changing the noise channel to displacement, the tip of the key has added dimension.

You can see that once you apply a texture layer, you can quickly copy it by making an instance of it, changing a few values and enhancing the shading on your model even further. Quite honestly, the possibilities are endless. You'll come back to more shading soon, as you move on to more advanced projects. But first, this last section mentioned groups a few times, so read on to learn more.

Note

The advantage of using an instance is that any change you make to the first noise value (the rust texture) will automatically propagate to the second noise value that's driving the displacement, thus saving you the time of having to manually match them up.

Groups

A group in the Shader Tree contains your material masks, such as the TopKeyTip you just finished surfacing. But what would happen if you or your client wanted this same surface applied to the rest of the key, but perhaps with a slight variation? Certainly you can copy and paste all the values, and on many occasions you will. But you can also use groups, which allow you the control to make variations to multiple surfaces at one time while still tweaking individual ones, as well as help to keep you organized. Using a group, you'll be able to apply the same surfacing from the tip of the key to the entire key and make adjustments to each. You're going to create one master group in order to give both keys the same diffuse and reflectivity values.

1. In the Shader Tree, choose Group from the Add Layer drop-down menu.

2. Select the Top Key, Bottom Key, and TopKeyTip material groupings by selecting the first one, holding the Shift key, and selecting the last one. This selects everything between the two.

3. When you have the three selected, click and drag the three groupings into the new group you've just created. A great way to make sure the selections are placed within the new group is to drop them right on top of the group name. Figure 8.20 shows the setup.

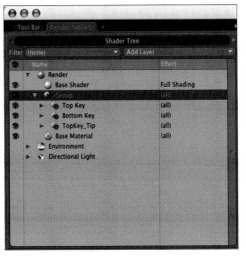

Figure 8.20

Move your three original material groups into a newly created empty group.

4. What you might see at this point as well is that your object's recently applied surfaces to the KeyTip are not visible. If they are not, make sure that the TopKeyTip is the first listing under the new group.

5. Next, expand the TopKeyTip material listing and select the Noise(1) material listing. Right-click (Command-click on the Mac) on it and select Duplicate. This will create a Noise(3) layer (the third Noise layer in the scene) in the Shader Tree.

6. Click and drag the Noise(3) material layer up into the new group. The result is that the rusty noise is now applied not just over the entire key, but to both keys in the scene. This is because both of the material masks you set for the two keys now live within this new group. Each material, however, can still be

varied, such as the key tip—it has a displacement that falls off due to the Vertex Map. Figure 8.21 shows the change. You'll also notice that the main Perspective viewport has had its preview style changed to Advanced OpenGL from Vertex Map.

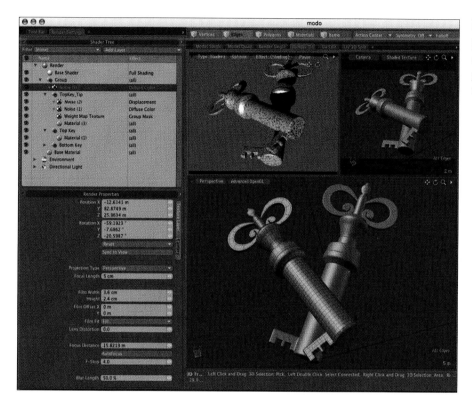

Figure 8.21

By moving the newly copied noise material into the new group, the rust color is applied to both keys in the scene.

Tip

It's always a good idea to name your material layers, especially after you're starting to duplicate them. You can do this by right-clicking (Command-click on the Mac) on them and choosing Rename.

---

7. Because the new noise channel lives above everything else in the group, whatever material you place here blankets the other materials by default. The TopKeyTip material was originally set to Diffuse Color for its Effect value. By copying this noise channel, you've doubled up on the color for the tip. To fix this, change the TopKeyTip Effect value by right-clicking and selecting Diffuse Amount.

8. Now suppose you want to wash some additional values over the entire key. The easy way to do this is to add a new material layer from the drop-down menu in the Shader Tree. Select the Cellular material. Then, move it up to the top of the group. You'll see your original surfaces completely covered by the new material, as shown in Figure 8.22.

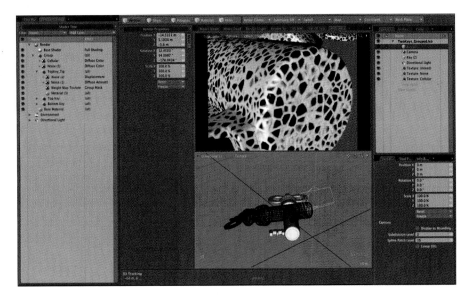

Figure 8.22

A new Cellular material placed at the top of the group overrides every other material! Note that the interface layout has been modified to show a better arrangement. Feel free to arrange your layout as you like.

9. The newly created Cellular texture blankets all other materials because its default Effect value is set to Diffuse Color. The noise channels are doing a good job of mucking up the key, so how about making the Cellular texture just some added dirt? You can do this by changing its Blend Mode value. With the Cellular material selected, change the Blend Mode value to Multiply in the Render Properties panel.

10. Next, change the Cell Color setting to a soft brown, but leave the Filler Color setting as white, its default.

11. Change the Type value to Round for a more dotted appearance. Increase the Cell Width value to about 45% and the Transition Width setting to 92%. Figure 8.23 shows the changes.

12. Click over to the Texture Locator vertical category in the Render Properties panel and change the size to 6 m for each of the X, Y, and Z axes. Figure 8.24 shows the change.

You can see that adding materials to the main group affects everything in it. But you can still go into the group itself and specifically change values for various masks that you have set.

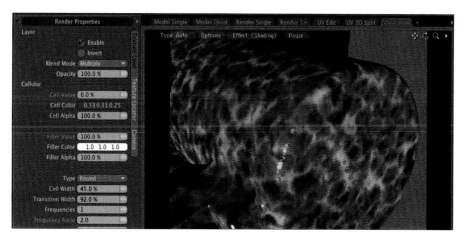

Figure 8.23

A few changes to the Cellular material in the Render Properties panel, and the added stains to the key are beginning to take shape.

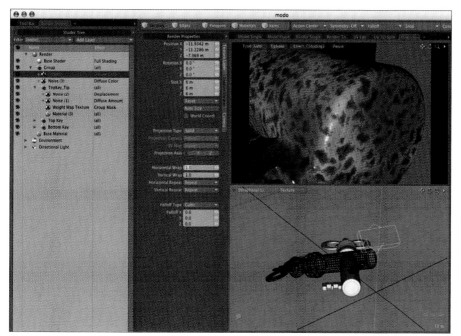

Figure 8.24

By simply increasing the size of the Cellular material, the effect of added dirt is now visible on the keys.

From this point on, you can vary the existing materials for the keys, such as bringing down the opacity for the Noise(3) and Cellular materials in the main group's Render Properties. This will help soften the look. And by all means, play with these settings to come up with something on your own!

Note

It's important to note that there's value in placing the masks within the group. It provides the ability to give the materials the same values for channels such as diffuse value and reflectivity all in one shot, while allowing the other masks to keep their individual color values. This is the importance of creating one master group.

The Next Phase

The information in this chapter gave you a good overview of the types of masking capabilities in modo. The Shader Tree is a powerful element and, although it appears simple, it can be complex. The tutorials you've just read through are effective for many projects you will encounter in your modo career. But alas, there is so much more to learn, grasshopper! The keys in this chapter can be surfaced in a number of ways, and the methods shown here are just one example. These methods were also chosen to demonstrate techniques such as setting up a Vertex Map to blend different masks.

To go even further, there is a 70-minute video tutorial provided for you on the book's DVD, covering modeling, shading, and rendering of the keys used in this chapter. Feel free to watch those when you have some time to learn about some additional techniques.

Now, move on into the third section of the book, where the more serious tutorials begin. First, you'll create a slick still-life scene, inspired by the book's technical editor, Greg Leuenberger. Then, you'll build, texture, and render a realistic traffic light using cool cloning tools and explore modo's powerful modeling system further. From there, the fun really begins when you start painting textures directly onto your models. If you're ready, let's get started.

Part III

Working Projects

9

Still Life

Because modo is a modeling, texturing, and rendering application, there's a tendency for artists to create amazing still-life shots. Later in the book, when you read more about rendering and lighting, you'll see how powerful the modo 201/202 toolset really is. And because there's not animation to worry about, you can feel free to take a little extra time rendering your image using the higher-end setups. Time is not your concern in 201/202, unlike most 3D programs. This allows you to concentrate more on the modeling, texturing, and rendering of your scene.

This chapter will take you to the next level in learning modo 201/202. By utilizing some primary modeling tools and the more advanced texturing capabilities of the Shader Tree, you'll see amazing results. You'll learn about modo's easy UV mapping tools and see how to unwrap an object for texturing. Additionally, this chapter will cover the Image Synth plug-in that came with your modo 201/202 software. This slick little plug-in for Adobe Photoshop will allow you to create seamless textures in minutes.

The tutorial in this chapter is based on a project created by the book's technical editor, Greg Leuenberger. Using his amazing talent and skillset, Greg took a few simple objects and made them look lifelike with the right textures and shading. This chapter will have you do the same.

Creating the Models

By now, you should be comfortable with the modo modeling tools. There are quite a few tools you've yet to use, and a good portion of this book is designed to introduce those tools to you. The models used for this project are simple, and it's how you texture them that will make all the difference. Even so, it's important to start off on the right foot. Figure 9.1 shows the modo 202 interface with the models you'll create.

Figure 9.1

Although the models for this still-life project are simple in form, the right texturing will make them come to life.

To start, you'll use a few more modeling tools, which will help you get the feel of the program even more.

1. Open up modo and head over to the Tool Bar tab. Hold the Shift key and click the Cube primitive. This adds a cube to the scene and instantly puts a layer named (cube) in the Item List.

2. Press the **a** key to fit the model to view. Then, press the **d** key three times to subdivide the cube. Figure 9.2 shows the new pliable mesh.

Note

Remember that pressing the **d** key performs a "subdivision surface" type of subdivision. You can also press Shift+D and choose a faceted or smooth subdivision method. You should also press the Tab key first to turn on subdivisions for your model.

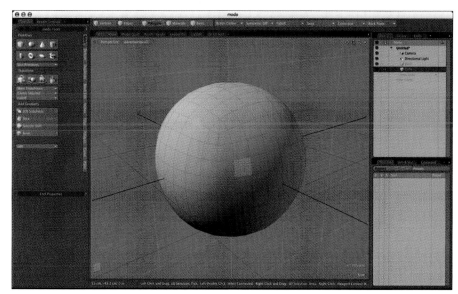

Figure 9.2

Pressing the **d** key a few times on a cube subdivides it, making it more pliable for shaping into a rock.

The reason you subdivided a cube rather than just creating a ball to begin with is that by subdividing a cube, you keep the shape comprised of all even quad polygons—that is, polygon patches made up of four vertices. For the displacement you'll be applying, the results will be cleaner and more on target. That is to say, deforming geometry not made up of an even quad mesh will work, but results may vary. Beyond that, you'll be applying a UV map to this soon-to-be rock, and this subdivided cube shape will lend itself better to this type of texture mapping.

3. To continue, click over to the Deform category by choosing the vertical category listing in the Tool Bar tab.

4. From the Scale Tools category within the Deform tab, click the Sculpt tool. Now, if you take a look at the Tool Pipe tab on the bottom-right of the screen, the Sculpt tool is nothing more than the Push tool with an Airbrush falloff. What does that mean, you ask? The Push tool literally pushes the geometry. If you applied a falloff to that, the push would diminish based on the area of influence you set. Therefore, the Sculpt tool already has the proper tools in place. Click and drag on the model and watch what happens. Nothing!

5. For the Sculpt tool to work, you need to give it some distance. In the Tool Properties for the Sculpt tool, change the value to about 12cm. You should see your cube begin to deform. modo has remembered that you tried applying the tool and you're making live adjustments to it.

6. Now click and drag some more on the object and watch the deforming. Figure 9.3 shows the start.

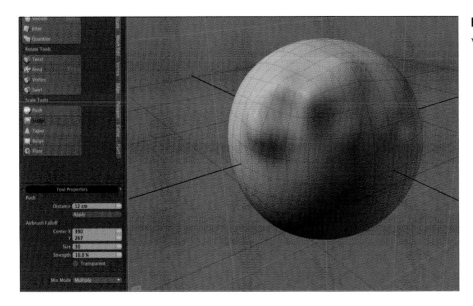

Figure 9.3

Watch the object deform.

Note

If your object looks chunky, you might not have subdivision surfaces applied. If this is the case, simply press the Tab key.

---

7. Right-click (Command-click on the Mac) and drag in the layout on the mesh. This will show a ring, which represents the size of the Sculpt tool. You can also set this in the Tool Properties. Click and drag again with the left mouse button to deform the cube.

8. Now, hold the Ctrl key down as you sculpt. You'll create an opposite distance, essentially denting the object.

9. Deform the cube on all sides. Remember to hold the Alt/Option key, then click and drag to rotate the 3D viewport. Also, be creative and change the distance value and size often. Figure 9.4 shows the full cube with many sculpt deformations.

Note

In addition to using the right mouse button to adjust the sculpt distance, you can also set it numerically in the Tool Properties tab.

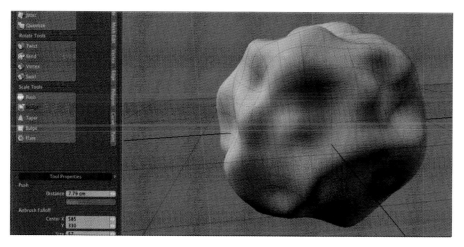

Figure 9.4

Using the Sculpt tool, you can quickly and easily deform the subdivided model.

10. You'll also need to flatten out this rock a bit. When you're finished with the Sculpt tool, press the **q** key to drop the tool. Then, change your viewport to a Front or a Side view. Click to Polygons selection mode at the top of the interface.

11. Using your middle mouse button, lasso-select the bottom half of the rock. By right-clicking and dragging, you "lasso-select." However, with a shaded viewport style, as shown in this chapter, you'll only select what's visible. But, if you use the middle mouse button, you'll select "through." Selecting through will select the geometry entirely through the object when in a shaded view, not just what's visible to you. If you don't have a middle mouse button, you can change your viewport render style to a wireframe, and the right mouse button lasso-select will now select all the way through. Figure 9.5 shows the selection.

12. When the bottom half of the rock is selected, press the **r** key to call up the Stretch 3D command. Click right above the entire selection to set the Action Center. Then, click and drag the green handle to stretch the selection on the Y axis. Figure 9.6 shows the result.

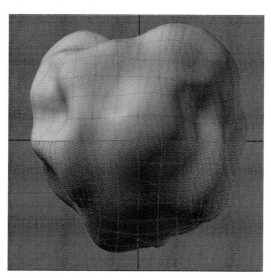

Figure 9.5

Using the middle mouse button to select "through" the visible polygons, select all the polygons encompassing the bottom half of the rock.

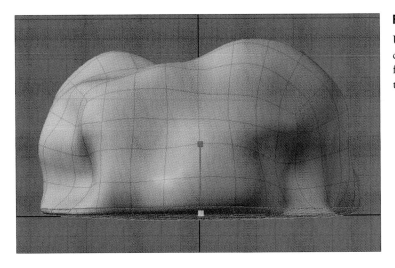

Figure 9.6

Using the Stretch 3D command (**r** key), you can flatten out the bottom of the rock.

13. Press **q** to drop the Stretch 3D tool.

14. Change back to a Perspective view and take a look at the overall shape of the rock. Feel free to sculpt it more, or even use the Element Move tool (press **t**) to shape it with more detail. Figure 9.7 shows a somewhat reasonable-looking rock before textures. If you want, press the **d** key to subdivide the model one more time for added detail.

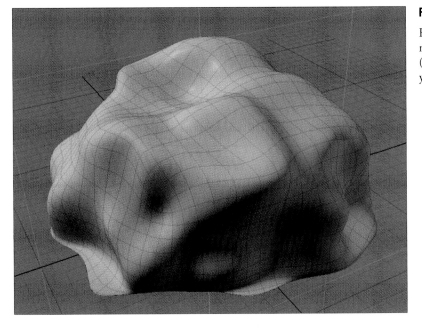

Figure 9.7

Feel free to use the Sculpt tool more, or even Element Move (**t** key) to shape the rock to your liking.

15. Finally, press the **m** key and give the rock a polygon mask to assign surfaces, naming it "rock" or something similar. Save your work.

This next section will guide you through modeling a leaf, which you'll do based on an image map. The image was created from a real leaf, scanned, and cleaned up in Adobe Photoshop CS2. Once you create the leaf, you'll use the Clone tools to generate more of them.

1. Create a new mesh layer in the Item List. Rename this layer "leaf."

2. Change your viewport to a Front view. You can hide the rock if you want, but it's not necessary. Do this by clicking the eyeball icon in the Item List just to the left of the mesh layer listing.

Note

As your scenes grow, a good way to work on different mesh layers is to turn on Auto Visibility. This will automatically make the selected layer visible and the non-selected layers invisible. Do this by right-clicking on the Item List tab itself, then choosing Viewport Settings, then selecting Auto Visibility. To turn Auto Visibility off, select the option again.

3. Click over to the Images tab at the top-right of the viewport, and then click the Load Image listing. Load the Leaf_ref image provided on the book's disc.

4. At the top-left of the viewport, select the Viewport Render Style button (which might say Shaded Texture or Advanced OpenGL) and choose Backdrop.

5. You'll see two dark squares. If you mouse over the first square, it will say "none." This is how you remove an image from the backdrop. If you mouse over the other box, it will show "load image." Click it and load the Leaf_Ref image from the book's disc. You can also add more than one image. For now, the single leaf is fine. Figure 9.8 shows the panel.

Note

Once the image(s) are loaded, you can also press the **o** key for visibility options and remove or change the image as well.

Figure 9.8

To load or remove an image from modo's backdrop, simply do so from the Backdrop option in the Render Viewport Style options.

6. This leaf reference is a crummy scan of a plastic leaf, but you'll see that it will serve this tutorial well. And hey, it'll keep nature lovers happy! The image is a bit large in comparison to the rock. If you can't see your rock in a background layer, make it visible by clicking the eyeball for it in the Item List. You'll need to scale this image a bit. Press **o** for visibility options and select Adjust Backdrop Image. You'll see the Tool properties appear on the left of the interface.

7. In the Tool properties, you can set the contrast, brightness, angle, and more. Note that in the visibility options, you have control over contrast, brightness, and transparency for the image as well. For now, you'll work just with size. But to use these adjustment tools, you need to first click on the image. You'll see it highlight, as shown in Figure 9.9.

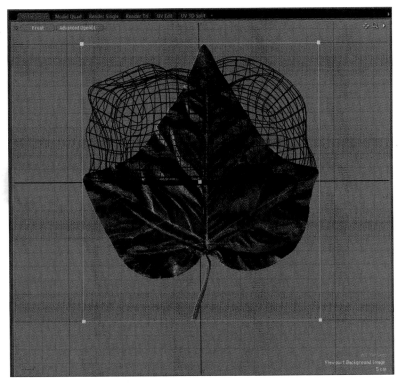

Figure 9.9

To adjust the backdrop image, you must first select it.

8. Clicking and dragging on the center square moves the image around. Clicking and dragging the corners sizes it accordingly. Size the image down to about 50cm or so. You can also set the value numerically in the Tool properties. When the value is set, press the **q** key to drop the Adjustment tool.

9. Go ahead and turn off the visibility for the rock. Make your work easier by concentrating on one item at a time. Also, save your scene at this point.

10. Next, from the Tool Bar tab on the left side of the interface, select the Curve vertical category. Select the Curve tool, and then click around the backdrop image. Essentially, you're tracing the image. Space the points evenly as you click to set them, something like you see in Figure 9.10.

Figure 9.10

By using the Curve tool, you can quickly begin modeling a flat shape based on the backdrop image.

Note

A few cool things to know about the Curve tool. You can also choose to edit or delete points on the curve. Do this by changing the Mode setting in the Tool Properties panel. You can also tell the curve to generate UVs for texturing.

11. Once you've laid down all the points, you can mouse over any desired point until it turns yellow. When it does, click and drag it to adjust the point position. Make sure, however, that you click directly on the point; otherwise, you'll add another point to the entire shape. You can change the mode to Edit, but it's still possible to adjust the points in Add Mode. Just be careful not to click off of a point because you'll generate a new one, changing the shape of your curve all together. Finally, click the Close option in the Tool properties to close the curve.

12. After you've adjusted your points, press **q** to drop the Curve tool, or simply click on the Curve tool button to turn if off.

13. Save your work. Now click over to the Polygon vertical category within the Tool Bar tab and select the Pen tool. This handy tool will allow you to create polygons for all kinds of uses quickly and easily. After you select the Pen tool, make sure that Flip Polygon is off and Make Quads is checked on. These are both in the Tool Properties panes.

14. You're going to use the Curve as a guide to build the geometry for the leaf. To do so, go up to the top-right of the interface and select the Snap drop-down menu. Choose Geometry, as shown in Figure 9.11. This tells modo to snap or attach what you create to the geometry in the scene.

Figure 9.11

Turn on Snap and set it to Geometry to easily place the Pen tool.

Note

In the Tool properties for the Pen tool, you can set the layer for Geometry Snap, either foreground or background. For now, use foreground.

15. With the tools set, click near the top-left of the leaf, on the curve. You'll see a yellow square appear. Move it around slightly until it snaps into place. Then click on the right side of the leaf, and again just below. You'll see a square polygon appear (the quad from Make Quads option), as shown in Figure 9.12.

Figure 9.12

Click once on the left side of the leaf curve, then on the right, and once below to create the quad polygon.

16. After three clicks of the Pen tool with the Make Quads feature active, modo generates a quad shape—that is, a polygon made up of four vertices (or points). Now, with the third point selected, you can create another quad and build up the geometry. The third point is the third point you created in the last step. It is also the point that snapped to the geometry on the right side of the leaf. With that point selected, just click below it, and you'll generate a new quad polygon, as shown in Figure 9.13.

17. Now, before you continue making more quad polygons with the Pen tool, position the existing points. Click and drag the left side of the quad polygons until they snap to the left side of the curve, as shown in Figure 9.14.

18. Depending on where you created the points for the curve on each side, the alignment might not be perfect, but that's okay for now. Select the last point on the right side of the curve, then click beneath it to generate another patch, and again, and so on. Figure 9.15 shows the result.

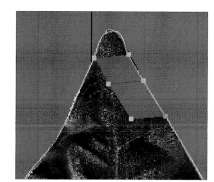

Figure 9.13

When the initial quad-shaped polygon has been created, you can click once to generate an entirely new polygon and begin building up the object.

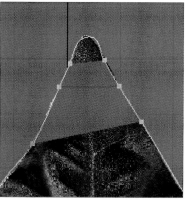

Figure 9.14

Adjust the left side of the quad polygons by clicking and dragging their points to the left side of the leaf curve.

Note

If you inadvertently turn off the Pen tool, you can still adjust points by using the Element Move tool (press **t**). And, snapping to geometry will still be applied.

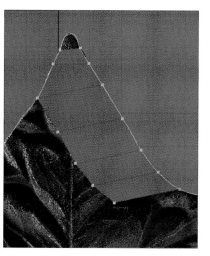

Figure 9.15

By clicking from the last selected point, you can easily add more patches of geometry.

19. As you did in Step 17, click and drag the left side of the points on the new geometry to snap them to the left side of the curve. Figure 9.16 shows the example.

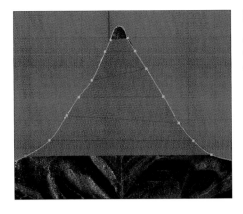

Figure 9.16

Adjust the left side of the quad polygons by clicking and dragging their points to the left side of the leaf curve.

20. Repeat the process of generating more geometry, then snapping the points to the left side of the curve to build the entire leaf shape. Don't worry about it if there are a few odd-looking angles. Also, since the bottom curves down and up, it'll be a little tricky to shape the geometry the way you're doing it. So for now, extend beyond the curve, as shown in Figure 9.17. You'll adjust the shape in the next steps.

21. Save your work at this point. Click over to Polygons selection mode at the top of the modo interface. Select a few polygons you've created.

22. Press Alt+c (Option+c for the Mac) at the same time to call up the Loop Slice command, which is also found under the Mesh Edit vertical category list.

23. Click and drag on the geometry. You might not see any change. In the Tool properties for the Loop Slice command, set the count to 10. This will slice up the geometry to a better-working mesh, as shown in Figure 9.18.

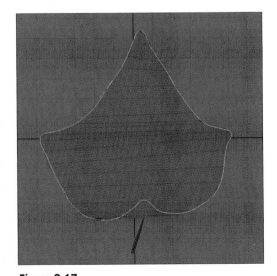

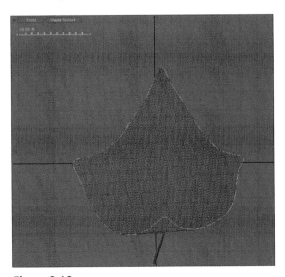

Figure 9.17

Finish creating the geometry with the Pen tool using the Make Quads feature. Extend the points to the opposite side of the leaf curve and go beyond the bottom of the leaf to set the initial model.

Figure 9.18

Using the Loop Slice command, you can slice the geometry into multiple segments to make a better mesh suitable for bending and shaping.

24. Press **q** to drop the Loop Slice tool. Now it's time to fix the extra geometry at the bottom near the stem. Change to Polygons selection mode at the top of the modo interface. Then click directly on the geometry that extends between the two halves of the leaf, as shown in Figure 9.19.

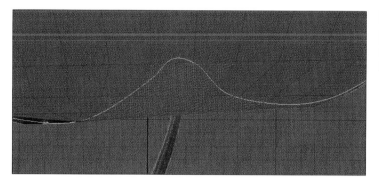

Figure 9.19

Select the polygons that make up the area between the two halves of the leaf.

25. Once they are selected, press the Delete key on your keyboard to remove these polygons.

26. Then, press the Tab key to turn the polygons into subdivisional surfaces. Then press the **t** key to turn on the Element Move tool, and adjust the points and/or edges to shape the geometry to the initial curve. Remember that the Snap to Geometry function is still active, and if you feel you can position the points and edges better without it, turn it off from the Snap menu at the top of the interface. Figure 9.20 shows the adjusted polygons.

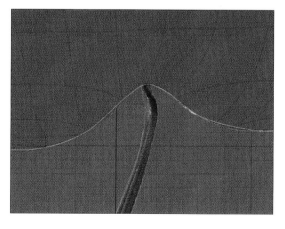

Figure 9.20

Using the Element Move tool (**t** key), adjust the points and edges as needed to clean up the shape of the leaf.

27. Using the Element Move tool, adjust the shape of the entire leaf as needed, making sure to adjust the very top as well. Change your view to a Perspective view. Rotate around by holding the Alt key and then clicking and dragging in the viewport. Select the outer edge of the leaf, which is the initial curve you created. Press Delete, leaving just the polygons.

28. From the View drop-down menu at the top of the modo interface, select Adjust Backdrop Image. Click on the 3D viewport to select the backdrop image. Change the Image listing in the Tool properties to None to remove the image.

29. To shape the leaf, start with a simple bend. Choose Bend from the Deform vertical category listing within the Tool Bar tab. Click in the center of the leaf.

30. In the Tool Properties for Bend, make sure the Action Axis Auto is set to Y. This will bend the leaf around the Y (up and down) axis. Before you bend, however, click the Symmetry drop-down menu at the top of the modo interface and choose X. This will mirror the bend operation.

31. Now, carefully click and drag the blue ring and bend the leaf forward, as shown in Figure 9.21.

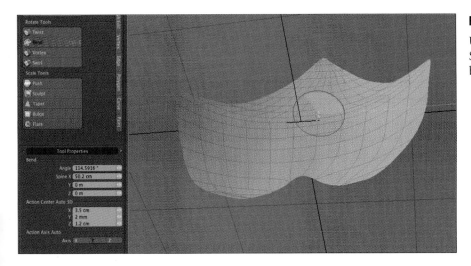

Figure 9.21

Using the Bend tool with Symmetry active, you can bend both sides of the leaf.

32. Press the **q** key to drop the Bend tool. Now try out another tool to shape the leaf. Select Swirl. Click on the leaf. Make sure the Action Axis Auto is set to Y. Then, click and drag out the red square on the tool handles and the blue square to encompass the leaf. Also, drag the green square up toward the top of the leaf. This sets the radial falloff for the tool. Then, click and drag on the blue ring to swirl the geometry. This is simply another way to shape the leaf, and the look is totally up to you. A swirl is a rotation command with a radial falloff. Figure 9.22 shows the tool applied.

33. Bend the leaf one more time. Select the Bend tool, and then click at the base of the leaf to set the axis. Change the Action Axis Auto in the Tool properties to X. Then click and drag the blue ring to bend the leaf back, similar to Figure 9.23.

34. Save your work. At this point, use all of the tools described here to manipulate your leaf further, including Element Move, Bend, Swirl, Vortex, and more. Be creative and experiment. When you are ready, save any changes and move on to the next phase.

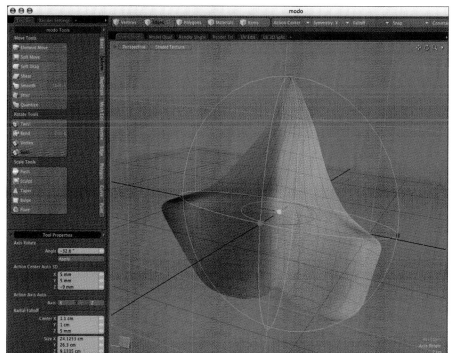

Figure 9.22

Use the Swirl tool to shape the leaf further.

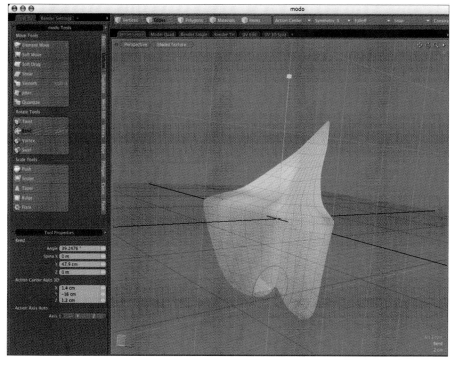

Figure 9.23

Bend and shape the leaf to your liking.

35. With the leaf still visible and selected in the Item List, press the **m** key to set a polygon material mask. Give it a name of "leaf." So original!

36. Save your work.

37. Lastly, in the Tool Bar tab, from the Basic vertical category, hold the Shift key and click the Plane primitive. This will create a flat plane in the scene, which will be placed in its own layer in the Item List.

38. Press the **r** key to call up the Stretch 3D tool, and click and drag on the center light-blue square to scale the entire plane up to about 200%.

39. Press **q** to drop the tool. Then press **m** and give this flat plane the name "Ground." You can also name the layers for your meshes in the Item List by right-clicking on them. It helps to stay organized!

40. With the ground plane selected in the Item List, press the **y** key and position the mesh under the rock. You'll adjust and position the leaf soon enough. If you can't see your rock, remember that you might have Auto Visibility on. You can click the eyeball to the left of the mesh listing in the Item List. Save your work!

You've created three simple objects, but you did so with a number of tools. The goal of this and other tutorials in the book is to help you understand the tools available in modo 201/202. From there, you can springboard to anything! But how about some textures for these objects?

Texturing with imageSynth

One of the most important parts of 3D imaging is texturing. And part of creating textures is making images that map seamlessly onto your objects. Luxology has provided a killer plug-in for Photoshop with every copy of modo 201/202. imageSynth, developed by the Allegorithmic company, allows you to create seamless textures without much effort. This next section will walk you through using the plug-in, which you'll then apply to your still-life scene in modo.

> **Note**
>
> You will need Adobe Photoshop for this section. Please follow the instructions provided by Luxology for properly installing the imageSynth plug-in. It should reside in your Photoshop plug-ins folder.

1. Open Photoshop and create a new, blank image, roughly 800×600 in size, as shown in Figure 9.24.

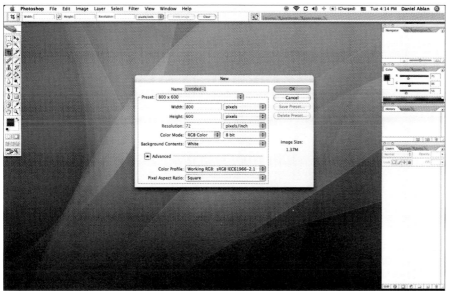

Figure 9.24

Create a new, blank image in Adobe Photoshop.

2. When the image is set, click the Filter drop-down menu at the top of the interface. Then, from the Luxology listing at the bottom, choose imageSynth, as shown in Figure 9.25.

3. When imageSynth opens, you'll see a modo-like interface. imageSynth (stands for *Synthesis*) is a fairly straightforward application. To start, load the rocks.jpg image from this chapter's projects folder on the book's disc. You do this by clicking the Add button on the lower-left side of the interface.

4. You'll see a warning from imageSynth that the image is too large and scaled down, as shown in Figure 9.26. This is normal because imageSynth requires that you work with a smaller image than the one supplied here.

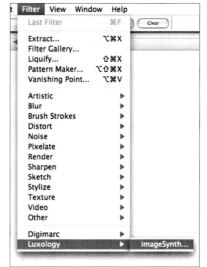

Figure 9.25

The imageSynth plug-in, once placed in the Photoshop plug-ins folder, appears in the Filter menu.

5. imageSynth works with chunks. A chunk is…well…a chunk of an image. imageSynth blends these chunks either automatically or manually to create a seamless image. How big will the image be? Remember Step 1, in which you created the 800×600 blank Photoshop image? That's the size of the final image. If you require a larger final image, start with one set to the desired size. Note, however, that the imageSynth plug-in will take longer to calculate.

Figure 9.26

When the rocks.jpg image is loaded into imageSynth, a warning comes up telling you that it's too large and will be scaled down.

6. With the image loaded, you can see a ghosted copy of the image by moving your mouse over the main workspace, as shown in Figure 9.27.

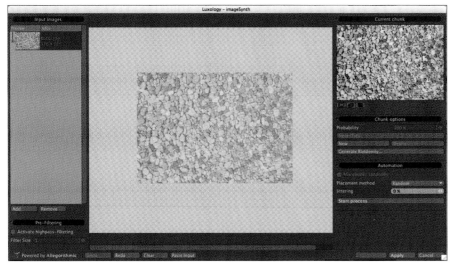

Figure 9.27

Moving the mouse over the main workspace shows a ghosted version of the image.

7. If you click once, you'll see the image stamped down. This is one chunk. Now move the mouse over to the side, perhaps up a little to the right, and click again. imageSynth will calculate, and in a moment you'll see the two images perfectly blended together, as shown in Figure 9.28.

8. imageSynth calculates the two image chunks and blends between them to make a seamless image. Repeat the process of clicking the image in empty spaces, stamping it down to fill the workspace. Remember to overlap and extend toward and beyond the edges. Figure 9.29 shows the full image.

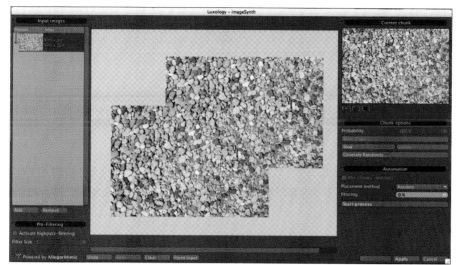

Figure 9.28

Clicking once, then twice blends two images together.

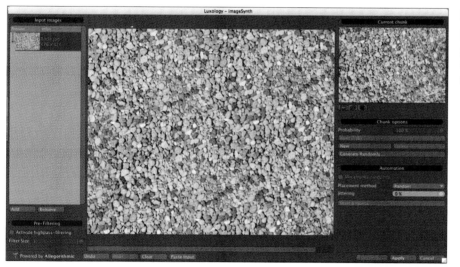

Figure 9.29

Continuing the stamping process, the image is mapped seamlessly within the workspace.

9. You can see that as you move the image toward the edges of the workspace, it repeats on the opposite side. This makes it easy to fill in blank areas.

Note

The imageSynth plug-in has a few more cool features—too many to show here. Therefore, there is a more in-depth training video on the book's disc to explain this nifty plug-in even further.

10. After imageSynth has blended each chunk, click the Apply button at the bottom-right of the interface. This will place the new seamless texture into the blank 800×600 image created in Step 1. Save this image and jump back to modo. Conversely, you can use the rockseamless.jpg image provided on the book's disc.

    Applying the imageSynth results in modo is easy. You'll simply save out the seamless image generated, and then load it into modo.

11. Back in modo, click over to the Render Settings tab on the left of the interface, expand the Ground Mask listing, and select its material listing.

12. With the material selected, you can add this seamless image. Choose Image Map from the Add Layer drop-down menu at the top of the panel, as shown in Figure 9.30.

Note

Another cool way to add an image map is to select the desired mesh in the Item List. Then, click over to the Images tab on the right side of the interface. Load the desired image. Then, drag and drop it right onto your object in the 3D workspace. Even simpler, open a folder on your hard drive, and you can drag the image from any location right into modo. Cool!

Figure 9.30

You can easily add an image map to a material from the Add Layer menu.

13. As soon as the image map loads, you can see it applied to the ground object, as shown in Figure 9.31.

14. The image is a bit large, but no worries! This image was created in imageSynth and is seamless. What does that mean to you? That means you can scale it down and not worry about seeing a repeating texture. Click the Texture Locator vertical category in the Tool Properties panel.

15. First, change the Projection Type to Planar. Then, set the Projection Axis to Y. This will project the image down on the ground.

16. Change the Size to 10cm for the X and 5cm on the Z. Remember that the ground plane was perfectly square. The image created in Photoshop was 800×600. So, it's easy to correct. You can of course create an 800×800 image in Photoshop to keep things consistent. The goal here is to show you that either method is possible and every project will vary. Once scaled, the image fits well on the ground, and it's hard to tell that it's repeated, as shown in Figure 9.32.

Figure 9.31

The image map is applied to the ground object, but initially is too large.

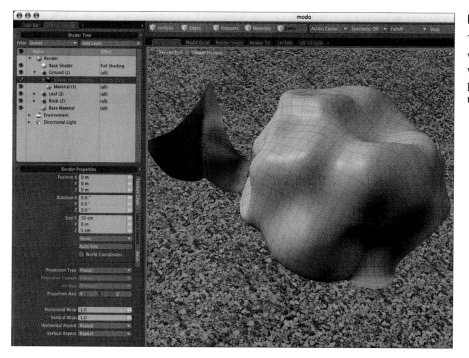

Figure 9.32

The seamless texture created with the imageSynth plug-in works very well on the ground plane, even when repeated up to 10 times.

17. The ground could use a little more work, but you'll get to see that firsthand in the video portion of this chapter.

From here, you'll create another imageSynth texture for the rock. Then, remember the leaf you built? You'll use that texture to surface the leaf. Then you'll see how to light and render it. Additionally, you'll see a video on how to create added details and learn about a few other tools. So when you're ready, pop open the videos for this chapter to continue on. Then, move on to Chapter 10 to learn how to model and texture a realistic traffic light.

10

Hard Surface Modeling

Part of modo's flexibility is the way it handles various tasks, such as hard surface modeling, in addition to organic-type shapes, as demonstrated in Chapter 9. Hard surface modeling is for things such as electronics, spacecrafts, machinery, and so on. This type of modeling may or may not use subdivisional surfaces, but it relies on the use of edge weights and bevels for fine details.

This chapter will guide you through the creation of a realistic traffic light. You'll learn modeling techniques that can be applied to any number of objects you choose to model. In addition, you'll learn to combine the use of instances to build and control the finer details.

Working from References

To begin this project, you'll use references from photographs. Often, 3D artists feel that their work should be unique and that using photos is cheating. Quite the contrary, photographs as reference are the leading way that professional 3D artists build their creations. Does this mean that their work is not unique? Not at all. The photographic reference gives you the basis for your model. As much as you think you know what something should look like, you'll be able to create it better when using a photo reference. The reference image is only the start of your model; it helps you remember detailed aspects as well as proper proportions. From there, the model is all your own. Change the color, the style, and so on. This applies to modeling cars, furniture, or even characters. Whatever you create, make it your own.

Take a look at Figure 10.1. Here, you'll see the stoplight on the left, a real photo. On the right is the 3D version you'll create in this chapter. You can see image details in the glass, the proper curvature of the lens hood for each light, as well as the backside shape. Now, you don't need to model the stoplight exactly like this. In fact, it's good to change the model a bit, which you'll do in this tutorial. As stated, the picture is simply a reference to get started. And hey, speaking of getting started....

Figure 10.1

The 3D stoplight you'll create is on the right. It's based off of the photograph on the left.

Note

In the Projects folder for this chapter on the book's disc, you'll find a few additional stoplight reference images.

1. Open modo and start with a blank scene. You can do this by saving any previous work, then selecting Reset from the File drop-down menu.

2. Hold the Alt/Option key, and then click and drag in the viewport to rotate the view until your dominant axis is Z. Watch the legend in the bottom-left corner of the viewport until a light square is drawn between the X and the Y. This light square represents the Work Plane.

3. Then, from the Tool Bar tab, select the Cube primitive. Drag out a flat cube, roughly 100cm for the X and Y. Don't add any depth on the Z axis.

4. In the Tool properties for the Cube primitive, change the Radius to 5cm. This will round the corners of the cube. Set Radius Segments to 3. Figure 10.2 shows the setup.

5. Because each of the three lights is the same on the model, you can create one and then duplicate it later. Go to Polygons mode at the top of the interface (you can press the spacebar repeatedly to change modes too), and then press the **x** key for Extrude. Click on the object to call up the control handles.

6. Click and drag the blue handle about –7cm, as shown in Figure 10.3.

Figure 10.2

Begin building the stoplight with a simple flat cube.

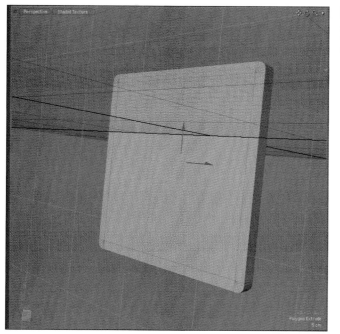

Figure 10.3

Extrude the object on the negative Z axis to give it depth.

7. Press **q** to drop the Extrude tool. Double-click on the edge between the sides and the face. Press **b** for bevel, then click and drag. Bevel the edge to a value of about 5mm. Set the Round Level to 2, as shown in Figure 10.4.

Note

Here's a trick! To select an edge, you can select the large center polygon, then hold the Shift key and press the up arrow on your keyboard to expand the selection. Next, press and hold the Ctrl key, and the Edges selection mode button at the top of the interface will change to Boundary. Click this to convert your polygon selection to a boundary of edges. The same can work for vertices.

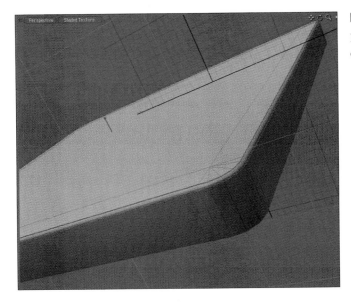

Figure 10.4

Bevel the front edge of the object.

8. Repeat this edge bevel step for the back side of the object as well.

9. Press the **a** key to fit the model to view.

10. Select the front face polygon by clicking on it. Make sure you're in Polygons selection mode. Figure 10.5 shows the initial polygon selection.

11. Hold the Shift key, then click the up arrow once to expand the selection. Now the entire face of the object is selected, as shown in Figure 10.6.

12. With the front face polygons selected, press **b** for bevel and bevel the geometry on the Inset only, about 2.4cm or so, as shown in Figure 10.7.

13. If you press the Tab key to turn the model into a subdivision surface, you won't notice much change. Unlike more organic models, this edge beveling and detail hold the object together in such a way that subdivisions don't change the shape of the model much. However, look very closely at the corners. Figure 10.8 shows a side-by-side comparison of the model without subdivisions on and with subdivision applied.

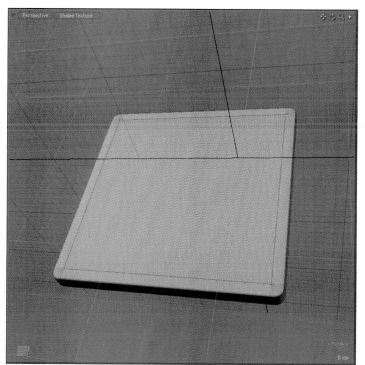

Figure 10.5

Select the large center polygon on the front of the object.

Figure 10.6

Expand the selection by holding the Shift key and clicking the up arrow on the keyboard.

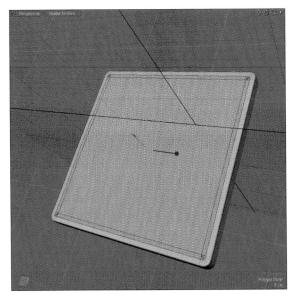

Figure 10.7

Bevel the front face polygon for a little added geometry.

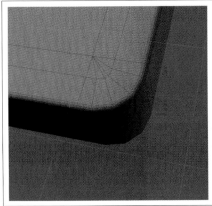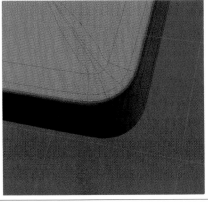

Figure 10.8

By beveling edges with the help of subdivisional surfaces, creating clean, smooth models is made easy. The image on the left is the model without subdivisions applied. The image on the right has subdivisions applied, but other than making the model smoother, the process doesn't change the shape of the model.

14. Now you can add more detail to create the lens. First, save your work to this point. Rename the current mesh layer to something other than "mesh"—perhaps "Base." Then, in a new mesh layer in the Item List, create a flat disc slightly smaller than the flat cube you created earlier. Use the photo presented at the beginning of this chapter as a size reference. Figure 10.9 shows the flat disc.

Note

To help you place the disc evenly, you can center the models. Select the base mesh layer, and from the Basic vertical category in the Tool Bar tab, select Center Selected, then All, as shown in Figure 10.9. Do this again for the disc to center it evenly after it's created.

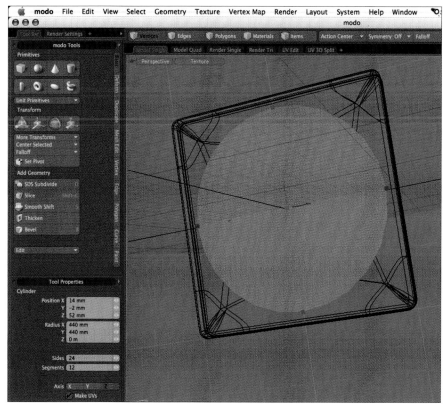

Figure 10.9

Begin creating the housing of the lens with a flat disc.

Note

In this project, the background item visibility is set to Wireframe. Press **o** for viewport options, and change the setting if you'd like.

---

15. Press **w** for the Move 3D tool, then click and drag on the blue handle to position the disc directly on top of the cube. A good trick for doing this is to carefully watch the background layer's wireframes. If the solid object in the foreground active layer is above the background layer, you won't see the wireframes. As you move the flat disc, look for the wireframes coming through the disc. Move the disc very slowly and carefully until the frames are behind it.

16. Select the single flat polygon (make sure you're in Polygons selection mode). Bevel the disc to create two rings. The first bevel should be about 1.5cm for the Shift value. Then, holding the Shift key, click the selection to reset the bevel. Click and drag again to bevel 1.5cm again, but this time just for the Inset value. Figure 10.10 shows the operations. Note that you can grab the blue and red handles of the bevel tool to easily make the adjustments.

17. With the polygon still selected, bevel two more times, just like you did in Step 16.

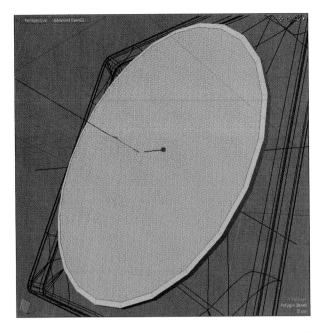

Figure 10.10

Bevel the selected polygon, the flat disc, once for the Shift value and once for the Inset value.

18. When you are finished, press **q** to turn off the Bevel tool, and then click off of the model to deselect the polygons. Then, press the Tab key to view the model with subdivisional surfaces. The shape remains, but it's too smooth. Figure 10.11 shows the situation.

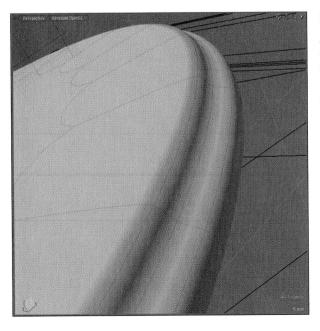

Figure 10.11

After the bevel operations and viewing the model with subdivisional surfaces applied, the object is clean, but too smooth.

19. To sharpen the edges but still leave detail, you'll bevel the edges. Select the four edges that make up the model, starting from the bottom edge. Figure 10.12 shows the selection. Remember to change to Edges selection mode at the top of the interface, then double-click on the edge to select the edge loop. Conversely, you can select one edge, then press the **L** key to select the rest of the edge loop.

Figure 10.12

Select the four edges that make up the sides of the model.

20. Once the edges are selected, bevel them (press **b**) about 2mm or so, with a Round Level of 2. What you'll see is a sharp-edged model, but one that is not too sharp or too smooth. Figure 10.13 shows the result.

21. Select the top polygon and bevel again, but this time with just a Shift value of 64cm. This creates the lens hood for the stoplight.

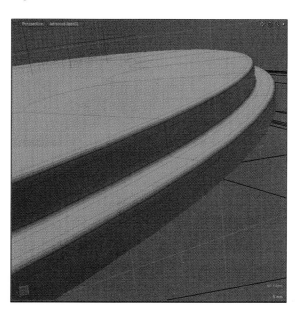

Figure 10.13

Beveling the edges of the disc results in a sharp, but smooth corner.

22. The top end of the bevel will look very rounded and like a shriveled melon. No worries, though—just hold the Shift key and click on the model again to reset the bevel. Figure 10.14 shows the two results.

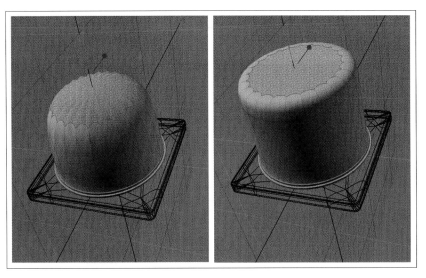

Figure 10.14

When you bevel a subdivisional surface, you might think your hard surface model is losing shape. But with just one additional bevel, the shape tightens up. More control to the edges will sharpen the model even more.

23. As you can see in Figure 10.14, the model takes better shape even with just one added bevel. When you're creating hard surface models, the more control you add to your model's geometry, such as bevels and weights, the sharper it will be. Bevel one more time with just an Inset value of about 14cm. Deselect the polygon and save your work.

24. Now tighten up some other edges before moving on to the finer details. Select the edge at the base of the stoplight lens hood, as shown in Figure 10.15.

25. Although you could bevel this edge, you might want to use an edge weight. Edge weights control the curve in a positive or negative fashion and are especially good when you don't want added geometry. In this spot, you can use either a bevel or an edge weight. But an edge weight will come in really handy for areas such as tight corners. For now, with this edge selected, choose the Edge Weight tool from the Vertex Map drop-down menu, as shown in Figure 10.16.

Figure 10.15

Select the edge at the base of the lens hood.

26. With the Edge Weight tool selected, click and drag in the viewport. You'll see the geometry on either side of the edge change shape. Dragging to the left softens the weight, setting a negative value, while dragging to the right hardens the edge with a positive value. Note that you can turn on Vertex Map Shaded render style at the top of the viewport to see the weight. Red shows that the edge weight is positive, while blue shows a negative value. Figure 10.17 shows the edge weight in both Vertex Map Shaded value and Shaded.

27. Press **q** to drop the Edge Weight tool, and then click a blank area in the viewport to deselect the edge.

28. Head back up to the top of the lens hood and select the polygon. Hold the Shift key, then press the up arrow once to expand the selection. This will select all the polygons that make up the front of the lens hood. You'll want to remove these, and in some cases you can delete them. But the polygons are only one-sided, and modo does not (yet) have a Thicken tool to create the insides. It is not recommended that you use the "double-sided" feature in the surface properties to create inside-facing polygons on the lens hood. So bevel the selection once, with a small inset of about 2cm.

Figure 10.16

Using the Edge Weight tool, you can sharpen the effect of the selected edge.

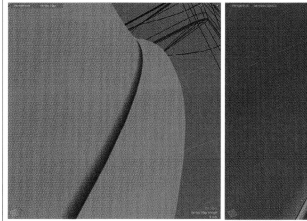

Figure 10.17

Using an edge weight, you can sharpen the effect of a selected edge. Here, the Vertex Map render style shows the positive edge weight in red. The Shaded render style shows the actual geometry shape with an edge weight applied.

29. Hold the Shift key, and then click to reset the bevel. Bevel the shift down inside the lens hood, about –66cm. Figure 10.18 shows the results.

30. Next, bevel one more time, but all you need to do is Shift-click the selected polygon to sharpen it. This inside end will be covered with the lens of the traffic light. Save your work.

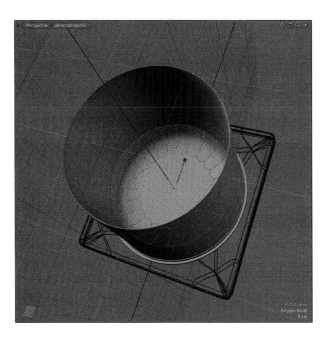

Figure 10.18

Because you need to have an inside to the lens hood, bevel it in and then back down.

31. With a few more steps, the basic housing is complete, and then you'll add the small details such as screws and brackets. Deselect all polygons, and then turn off subdivision surfaces by pressing the Tab key. Click over to the Vertex vertical category in the Tool Bar tab and click the Merge button. A Merge Vertices panel will appear, as shown in Figure 10.19. The default setting is Automatic. Make sure that Keep 1-Vertex Polygons is checked. Click OK, and modo will tell how many vertices are merged, if any. What did this do? Often, when modeling shapes with tight bevels, you can generate points (vertices) that live right on top of each other. This can cause problems later on. Performing an automatic merge fixes that.

Figure 10.19

From the Vertex category in the Tool Bar tab, select Merge to eliminate unwanted points, if any.

32. After the merge, select the bottom polygons inside and out, as shown in Figure 10.20. These are the polygons that make up the bottom curve of the lens hood.

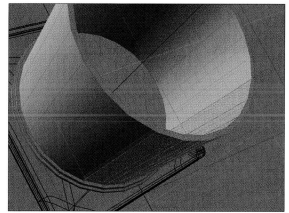

Figure 10.20

Select the polygons that make up the bottom-center polygons of the lens hood.

33. Rotate the view to see the bottom outside edge of the lens hood, and then press the **r** key to activate the Stretch 3D command. Click at the base of the lens hood to set the Action Center, as shown in Figure 10.21.

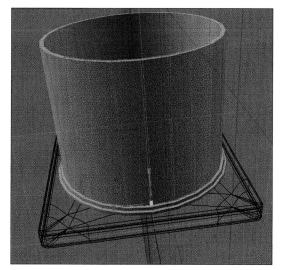

Figure 10.21

Select the Stretch 3D command and click at the base of the selection.

34. Click and drag directly on the blue handle to stretch the selected geometry down on the Z axis. Figure 10.22 show the operation.

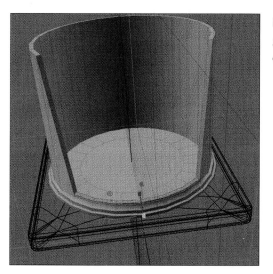

Figure 10.22

Stretch the selected geometry down on the Z axis.

35. Feel free to undo if needed, click to reposition the Stretch 3D command, and grab the blue handle to stretch again. Conversely, after you've stretched the geometry, you can press the **w** key to simply move the selected geometry to sit just above the back of the lens hood.

36. When the stretch is complete, press **q** to drop the tool. Deselect the polygons. Press the Tab key to view the model in subdivisional surfaces, and you should have something like Figure 10.23. Looks good, but it could use a few adjustments.

37. Turn off the subdivision surfaces by pressing the Tab key. Double-click the outside and inside edges of the lens hood, as shown in Figure 10.24.

38. Bevel the selected edges about 4mm with a round level of 2.

39. Deselect the edges, and then press the Tab key to see the model as subdivisional surfaces. Ah, much better. But look at the bottom inside edge of the lens hood (see Figure 10.25). A little weirdness going on there. No problem!

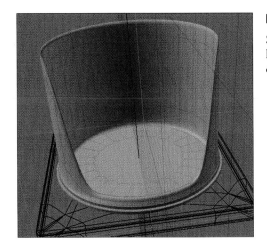

Figure 10.23

Stretching the geometry down looks good, but a little more detail is needed.

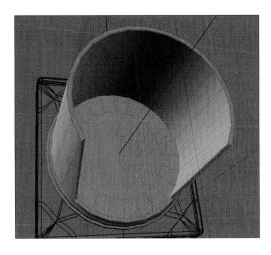

Figure 10.24

Select the outer and inner edges of the lens hood.

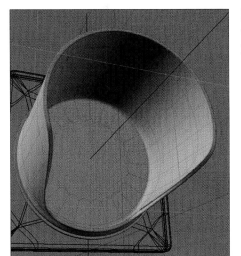

Figure 10.25

With the edges beveled, the lens hood looks much sharper.

40. Click over to the Mesh Edit vertical category within the Tool Bar tab, and choose the Slice command (or press Shift+C). Rotate your view around to see the bottom of the lens hood, then click on the outside of the lens hood and drag across and all the way through the object to slice in added geometry. Figure 10.26 shows what this looks like.

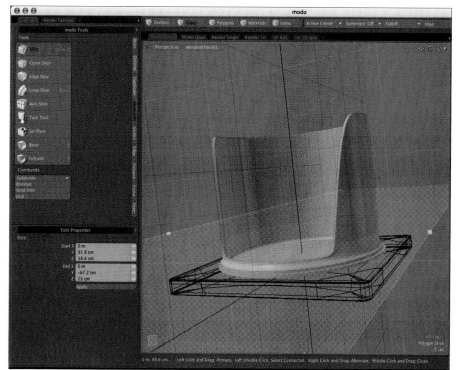

Figure 10.26

Using the Slice tool, you can add geometry to your model in necessary areas.

Note

As mentioned earlier in the chapter, make your model your own, using the initial image only as a reference. In studying traffic lights, there seems to be quite a few varieties. For this 3D model, the lens hood sides angle up. In the image, the opening is straight. Yours can be shaped any way you like!

---

41. The Slice tool is a little odd to get the hang of, but it's simple to use after a few tries. When the slice is through, you can click and drag on the light-blue squares on either side of the slice to position it. Feel free to rotate your view to make sure the slice goes all the way through the model. You want to position the slice slightly above the inset curve of the lens hood, as shown in Figure 10.27.

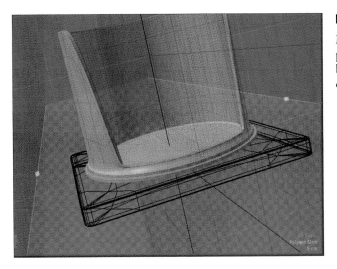

Figure 10.27

Make sure that your slice is positioned just above, not below, the base of the inset curve.

42. When you're finished with the Slice, turn off the tool and save your work.

43. Lastly, press **m** for Polygon Set Material and give the lens hood a polygon mask with a name of LensHood and color of shiny black.

44. Also, select the base model that the lens hood rests on, and give that a polygon mask name of Base or something similar. Name your mesh layers by right-clicking on them, and save your scene.

What you've done here is relatively basic, but you can see with just beveling edges and polygons, using the Stretch, Merge, and Slice commands, you can create detailed shapes. Almost everything you build can benefit from these tools, which is the reason this tutorial is here! But there's much more that can go into this, so read on!

Modeling Details

Details in your models will make them stand out from the rest. The tight beveled edges you created in the previous exercise are just the first step. It's highly important to make sure the edge bevels are included, but it's also the other smaller details that can make or break your final image. This section will get you started making the details of the stoplight, including screws, the lens, and brackets. To begin, you'll finish filling in the lens hood area with the glass lens.

1. Press Ctrl+spacebar to call up the viewport pie menu. Select the Front view. When working with round shapes, sometimes it helps to be straight on. Then, select the polygons that make up the inside back end of the lens hood, as shown in Figure 10.28. Remember to change to Polygons selection mode at the top of the interface (or press Alt/Option and the **q** key to call up the pie menu selection modes).

2. Why create a new disc and worry about shaping it to build the lens? You're halfway there with the existing lens hood! With the polygons selected, press Ctrl+C to copy them. Select a new mesh layer in the Item List, then press Ctrl+V to paste the copied polygons.

3. Press Ctrl+spacebar to call up the pie menu, and switch back to a Perspective view.

Figure 10.28

Select the polygons that make up the back inside end of the lens hood.

4. Select the new mesh layer, and with all of the new disc polygons selected, press **s** for Smooth Shift. This tool is sort of like Bevel, but it allows you to add scale to the multiplied polygon, which is perfect for creating this lens. By the way, this tool is located within the Polygon vertical category in the Tool Bar tab.

5. With Smooth Shift active, click and drag so that you set an Offset of 3cm and a Scale of about 95%. You can click and drag the red and blue handles just as you do with the Bevel tool, or you can enter the value numerically in the Tool Properties panel. Figure 10.29 shows the operation.

6. Hold the Shift key, and then click on the lens to reset the Smooth Shift tool. Smooth Shift again with an Offset of 2.5cm, and this time an 85% Scale.

7. Repeat the process one more time, with an Offset of 4cm or so and a Scale of 80%.

8. Press **q** to turn off the Smooth Shift tool and deselect the polygons. Press the Tab key to activate subdivision surfaces if they're not already applied. Figure 10.30 shows the lens created with Smooth Shift.

9. Press **m** to create a polygon mask for the lens, giving a surface name of Lens. Then, hold the Shift key and select all mesh layers in the Item List to see how your model is coming along. Figure 10.31 shows the model so far. It's getting there!

10. Now finish up the back side of the base of the model. Then it's time for finer details, such as screws to hold it together! Turn off subdivisional surfaces for right now by pressing the Tab key. Select the base mesh layer and rotate the 3D viewport to see the back side.

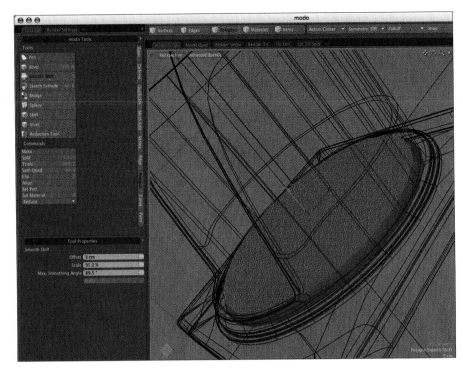

Figure 10.29

Using Smooth Shift, you can create the lens for the stoplight.

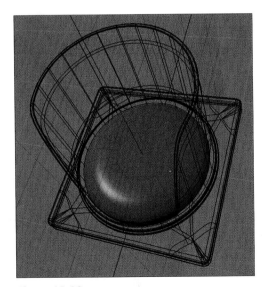

Figure 10.30

The lens is created with Smooth Shift.

Figure 10.31

Taking a look at all the layers together, the stoplight model is starting to resemble something familiar! Note that the surfaces are set to a grey, rather than black, for visibility.

11. Select the polygons that make up just the back side. You can do this by clicking in the center, then holding the Shift key and pressing the up arrow to expand the selection. Figure 10.32 shows the selected polygon.

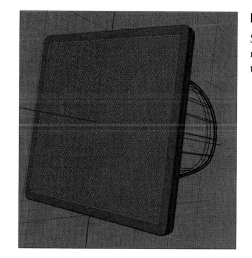

Figure 10.32

Select the polygons that make up the back side of the stoplight base.

12. Press Shift+D to call up the Subdivide Polygons command. The default selection is Faceted, which is for flat geometry, such as you have here. Click OK. The selected single polygon is now four polygons. Repeat the process one more time, and you'll now have 16 polygons occupying the same space, as shown in Figure 10.33.

13. Switch to Edges selection mode at the top of the modo interface. (You can click it, press the spacebar repeatedly, or press the **2** key.) Then, carefully select the inner square of edges, as shown in Figure 10.34.

14. Press the **r** key, and then click and drag on the light-blue square to scale the selection up to about 170%, as shown in Figure 10.35.

Figure 10.33

Subdivide the selected polygon twice to generate 16 polygons.

Figure 10.34

Select the edges in the center of the polygons.

15. Press **q** to drop the Stretch 3D tool, and select the two crossing edges in the center of the polygons, as shown in Figure 10.36.

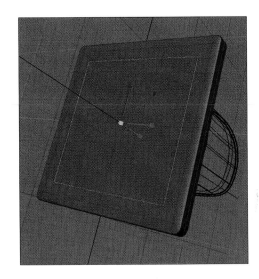

Figure 10.35

Scale up the selected edges.

16. With the edges selected, press the Backspace key on your keyboard to remove them. On a Mac, it's the larger Delete key, next to the = key. Pressing Delete will remove the polygon. At this point, you're probably wondering just what the heck you're doing, right? Don't worry, it'll make sense in a minute. To create a round shape out of this square shape, you're generating additional geometry within the model. The next steps might make this clearer.

17. With the center edges deleted, switch to Polygons selection mode, then select the center polygon. Then, from the Polygon vertical category in the Tool Bar tab, select the Spiky tool. Click and drag slightly on the selected polygon. You should have pie shapes within the geometry, similar to Figure 10.37.

Figure 10.36

Select the edges in the center of the polygons.

18. You see, the subdivisions generated extra geometry so that when it was time to perform the Spiky operation, the tool was able to grab onto the points generated, even though you removed the edges. Cool, eh? But wait. Press **q** to drop the Spiky tool. Switch to Vertices selection mode.

19. Select just the center point, directly in the middle of the model. Then press **b** for bevel, and click and drag. Yes, you can bevel the points of an object too. And because the extra geometry was there with the Spiky tool, you have enough points to generate a round shape. Figure 10.38 shows a 35cm bevel on the center point.

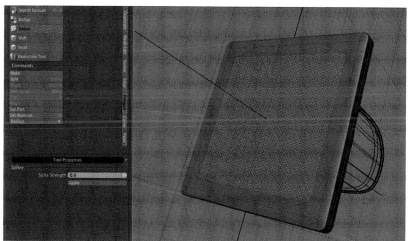

Figure 10.37

Using the Spiky tool, you can subdivide your geometry in a whole different way.

20. Switch back to Polygons selection mode and select the center polygon. You now have a round shape in the center of the square polygon shape. Well, okay, it's not that round yet, so bevel it in about 1.5cm on the Inset. Bevel again with a 40cm Shift, and finally do another bevel with an Inset of 1.5cm.

21. When the three bevel operations are finished, press **q** to drop the Bevel tool, and then deselect the polygon. Press the Tab key to turn on subdivision surfaces, and look! A round shape coming out of a square shape. Cool. Figure 10.39 shows it.

22. Save your work!

Figure 10.38

Select the center point on the back of the model and bevel it.

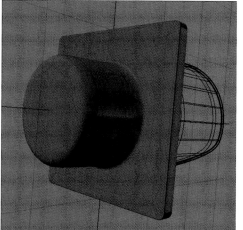

Figure 10.39

With a few bevels and subdivision surfaces applied, the back side of the object, the square base, now has a round shape extruding out of it.

This technique can be used for any number of things, from electronics, to cars, to spacecrafts. Take a look around you, on your desk, in your kitchen, anywhere. You'll often see machine-made objects that have smooth, round shapes molded as part of a more squared shape. And the round shape is not just sitting on top of the square; it's truly part of it, as shown in the previous example. The round shape extruding out of the back of the stoplight might be too small and too long, but by selecting the necessary geometry, you can easily scale and move it as needed.

Hard surfacing modeling and subdivisional modeling (or "sub-d" modeling, as many say) are not as complicated or as separate as you might think. The examples in this chapter have clearly shown that a combination of both methods works well to create sharp, detailed models. By applying subdivisional surfaces, a model does become smooth—often too smooth, as you saw with the lens hood. But by beveling edges, slicing, and simply adding more geometry to control the flow of the model, you can create very specific details.

But wait, there's more! For the next portion of this tutorial, turn to the videos on the book's disc. You'll learn how you can further edit the back end and shape the round lens housing behind the lens hood. You'll also clearly see how to build the screws and brackets, and you'll discover how instancing can help out. And, you'll pick up some other cool tidbits along the way. When you are ready, pop open the book's disc and continue this chapter's projects in the Chapter 10 folder. Then, move on to Chapter 11 to learn how to surface this model with modo's killer paint tools.

11

Creating and Painting Textures

When the new surfacing and painting features were promoted for modo 201 at a SIGGRAPH conference one summer long ago, users rejoiced. When modo 201 finally shipped, the tools were more than users could ask for. Why is that, you say? While many programs have node-based surfacing, the modo team opted for a Shader Tree and a system of masks. This tree-like approach appears quite simple and is actually very easy to use, but powerful at the same time. In addition to this cool modeling application adding the ability to paint color and texture directly on your models, you can also brush in bump maps and displacements, and even use images to paint.

This chapter will first introduce you to additional surface properties for glass and ice. Then, you'll learn about the painting tools, how to use them, and ways they can be altered. From there, you'll work on a project utilizing the painting and bump tools, then you'll take it a step further and apply these techniques to the traffic light you created in Chapter 10. Honestly, these topics can be a book all on their own. However, we've added a few tutorial videos on the book's disc to help you understand the tools covered in this chapter as well as guide you beyond the text.

Understanding the Paint Tools

To begin, it's important to understand a few key tools that make up the powerful painting features in modo. This section will guide you through using and setting up a model for painting. The handsome and talented Philip Lawson has generously provided a cool scene for you to work with in this book. Figure 11.1 shows the model with which you'll be working.

Figure 11.1

Philip Lawson's martini glass model is a perfect launching pad for learning how to create and paint textures.

Because the original scene Philip created is done so well, it's only right that we paint it with graffiti! Well, probably not graffiti, but rather than painting on a ball or donut shape, it might be fun to paint on a cool model. You can load the glassFinal.lxo scene to take a look at Philip's glass settings and lighting. For now, you'll begin with a blank version of the model—that is, one without textures. You'll resurface this model entirely for yourself. But wait! You'll take it a step further by adding painted textures to the scene.

1. Open up modo and load the glassBlank.lxo scene from the book's disc. It's in the Chapter 11 projects folder.

2. When the scene is loaded, click over to the Render Tri tab at the top of the viewport. You should see something like Figure 11.2.

Figure 11.2

Philip Lawson's martini glass model is a little boring without textures and surfaces.

3. To begin, you'll set up the glass surface. You might think this is hard to do, but modo makes it so simple, you'll be surprised by how easy it is to set up.

4. If you take a look at the Item List, you'll see that the object layers are all named. However, looking at the Render Settings tab, there's only one Base Material and one Base Shader. The objects in the scene do not have materials set up. Could this have been done for you? Sure it could have! But really, the next few steps will help reinforce a key aspect of using modo. Select the Glass mesh layer in the Item List.

5. With the Glass mesh layer selected, press **m** on the keyboard to call up the Polygon Set Material dialog box. Enter the name "Glass" and maybe tint the color a bit. Then click OK. Original name, don't you think? Figure 11.3 shows the material now added to the Render Settings tab.

> **Note**
>
> For the projects you've done so far, including the work in this chapter, you'll learn how to light and render these scenes in Part III of this book.

> **Note**
>
> In addition to the polygon masks you've made in this book, you can also create item masks. In the Item List, right-click on a mesh and choose Create Item Mask. This will instantly create a material group for the entire mesh.

Figure 11.3

Setting a polygon material mask adds specific surface controls to the Render Settings tab.

6. Select the mesh layer named Drink, and again, press **m** to set a material name. Enter the name…oh, perhaps, "Drink?" This now adds the material to the Render Settings tab, as shown in Figure 11.4.

Figure 11.4

Create a material mask for the Drink mesh layer, creating surface controls for the liquid in the glass.

7. Repeat the previous steps for the remaining mesh layers. Figure 11.5 shows the Shader Tree with all of the material masks applied.

8. Save your scene, perhaps with a new name so you don't save over the original glassBlank.lxo scene. Choose Save As from the File menu to quickly save the scene with a new name.

Note

If you look at the Shader Tree in Figure 11.5, you'll see that all of the materials have numbers after the names. This is modo's way of organizing names that are the same within the scene. If you rename the mesh layer (or material) to something different, even changing one character to a capital letter, the numbering will be removed. Having your mesh layers named the same as the materials or different really doesn't matter. It's up to you and how you like to organize your scene and objects. What is important is that the materials are applied to the right objects.

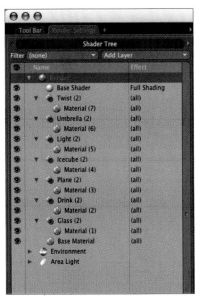

Figure 11.5

Repeat the process of assigning material masks to each of the mesh layers, naming the materials according to their layer names.

9. Now head over to the Render Settings tab. Select the Glass material, and feel free to slide the viewports around to increase the size of the preview window. You can do this by clicking and dragging directly on the borders between the views.

10. For the surface of the glass, you can set this up without much effort in modo 202. With the glass material selected in the Render Settings tab, go down to the Render Properties panel. In the Material Ref vertical category, set Diffuse Amount to 0%. This tells the surface not to accept any light from the scene. What's that? No light? Yes, no light. Glass surfaces benefit more from reflection and refraction (the bending of light).

11. Set the Fresnel (pronounced *Fre-Nel*) to 100%. What this does is tell the surface to be more reflective as the glancing angle changes. What does that mean? Well, you sure have a lot of questions! Consider a car window. If you look at the passenger window of a car from the vantage point (the glancing angle) of the front of the car, the window is hard to see through. This is because at that angle, it's very reflective. But if you walk up to the window and stand directly in front of it, the reflection is very slight and you can now see through it. In the case of the glass surface in this scene, the sides of the glass away from our view will be more reflective. Cool!

12. Next, set Specular Amount to 75% and Roughness to 10%. The Specularity is the amount of shininess on the surface, while the Roughness is how glossy it will be. The specular property emulates the reflection of the lights in the scene and is a shortcut to having to physically model the lights in order for them to reflect in the surface. And, modo calculates faster this way.

13. Set the Reflection Amount to 2%. Add a little bluish tint to the Specular Color. Figure 11.6 shows the setup so far. Right now, the glass looks more metallic.

14. Click to the Material Trans vertical category, and set Transparency to 100%.

15. For glass to look like it should, you need to apply refraction. Set the Refractive index to 1.4. Refraction is what happens to light as it travels through transparent surfaces, such as glass, water, and so on. It essentially bends. Typically, glass has a refraction index of about 1.35, but depending on your model, you can vary this to your liking.

16. Finally, set the Absorption Distance to 5m. This value sets the thickness of the transparency. If you set a Transparent Color, you'll obtain the effect of tinted glass in thicker areas, such as the base of a drinking glass. The Absorption Distance determines how far a ray of light can travel before it completely falls off. Figure 11.7 shows the preview and setup.

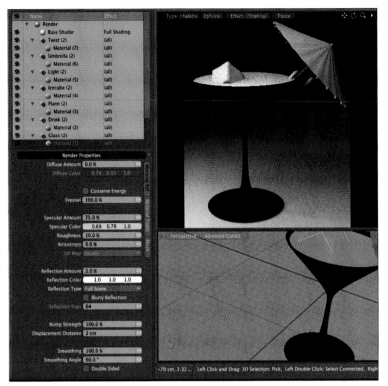

Figure 11.6

A few settings setup for the glass material, and the surface is looking more like a metallic martini glass.

Note

By setting the distance to a value greater than the glass is thick, you are ensuring that the glass is never fully opaque. It will be just slightly opaque and blue.

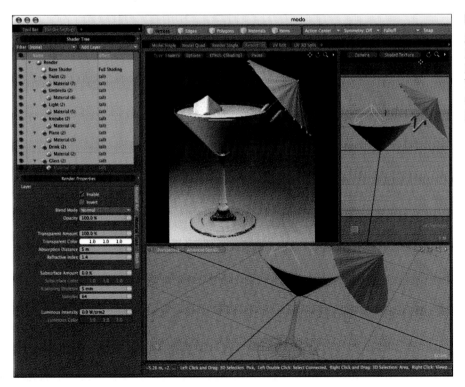

Figure 11.7

Setting a few values in the Material Trans vertical category helps create the glass effect. You can see how the base and stem of the glass look pretty good!

17. Now the scene is still quite dull and doesn't have much color. Change that by going to the Environment Material listing in the Shader Tree within the Render Settings tab. Make sure that the Environment Type is set to 4 Color Gradient, as shown in Figure 11.8.

18. Philip Lawson's original scene used an HDR image to light the environment, but for this setup, you'll use something simple. Later in the book we'll talk about HDR (*high dynamic range imaging*) and other render techniques. For now, select the Render listing at the very top of the Shader Tree. Then click the Global Illumination vertical category down in the Render Properties panel. Click the Enable option. Let your preview window redraw. You might need to nudge it a bit by slightly dragging the border of the window. Ah! Now there's color in the scene, as you can see in Figure 11.9.

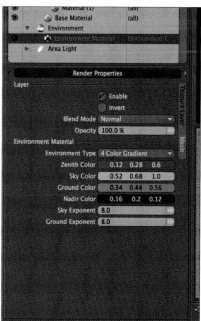

Figure 11.8

Make sure the Environment Material has a four-color gradient applied.

Note

Another way to "nudge" the preview window to update is to click the Pause/Reset button in the top-right of the preview window.

19. Save your work.

20. Now you need to take what you've learned about glass and apply it to the liquid and the ice cubes. First, select the Drink surface in the Shader Tree.

21. In the Render Properties panel, set Diffuse Amount to 0%. Fresnel should be 100%, while Specular Amount is 5%, and Roughness is 40%. Give the Specular Color a slight off-white, perhaps 082, 082, 082 RGB. Set the Reflection amount to just 1%. You only need a little bit of reflection here. Figure 11.10 shows the settings.

Figure 11.9

By simply turning on Global Illumination, modo uses the colored environment as an added light source, enhancing your surfaces.

Note

The colors from the environment are also reflecting in the glass, and you can achieve different looks by changing these values with the Environment Material.

> ### Note
>
> Although this is not a chapter on rendering or lighting, it's important to understand that these areas play a key role in the surfacing of your objects, especially glass. Therefore, you've cheated and used global illumination before it's officially discussed. You'll read more about HDR and global illumination later in this book.

22. Next, click to the Material Trans vertical category. Set Transparent Amount to 100%. Absorption Distance should be only 5cm. This is a small amount to give the drink more transparent thickness. Lastly, set Refractive Index to 1.1.

23. One more setting to go. Change the Transparent Color in the Material Trans vertical category to a very slight green, about 0.9, 1.0, 0.93. Although it might not look like a very strong color, it will be vibrant on the surface of the model because of the low Absorption Distance. If you were to increase the Absorption Distance, the green color would fade as the transparent thickness falls off. Figure 11.11 shows the Material Trans settings along with a preview.

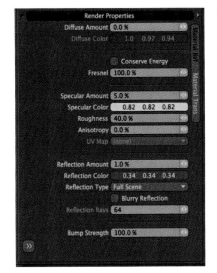

Figure 11.10

The surface settings for the drink liquid are similar to the glass surface, with minor differences.

As you can see, the glass and liquid are starting to look pretty good! Of course, you can vary these settings and watch the results, making the surfaces look any way you want. The idea here is that you get a feel for setting up surfaces, specifically glass surfaces, and of course you understand what needs to be set to see decent results. There are a few other surfaces to apply, specifically the ice cubes.

24. Select Ice Cube material in the Shader Tree, within the Render Settings tab. Then, in the Render Properties panel, you can set up the surfaces in a similar fashion to the glass and liquid.

25. Set the Diffuse Amount to 20%. Diffuse Color should be 1.0, 1.0, 1.0. Click on Conserve Energy. This blends the specular light reflections and diffuse values. It's a filter of sorts that suppresses the diffuse value as the reflection increases. It's a handy feature to help balance the surfaces in your scene.

Figure 11.11

The last thing to change is the Transparent Color amount. With a very slight change to this value, the Absorption Distance carries it through the surface.

26. Set Specular Amount to 45% and Roughness to 20%.

27. In the Material Trans vertical category, set the Transparent Amount to 100%. Then, place Absorption Distance to 10m. Remember, this sets the transparency thickness. For ice, change the Refractive Index to 1.8. This will really help sell the ice look.

28. Change the Subsurface Color to a very pale blue, about 0.87, 0.93, 1.0.

29. Then, set the Subsurface Amount to 50%. The Subsurface Amount adds to the diffuse values of your material. This setting helps balance the diffuse color values in your materials with the Subsurface Scattering amounts. Subsurface Scattering, then, is the effect of light "inside" a surface. A good example of this is human skin or a candle. Light rays travel through or penetrate the visible surface of an object and are scattered, interacting with the material and passing through, illuminating a subsurface. You can see this in a video tutorial on the DVD, showing you how to create a candle with subsurface scattering.

30. Set the Scattering Distance to 10cm. Along with that, set the Samples to 64. This sample rate controls the quality. Simply put, the higher the value, the better the quality. But as with any setting, start low, test your model, and see how it looks. Then increase as needed. Figure 11.12 shows the render properties for the ice cubes.

Note

On the book's disc, be sure to check out the Subsurface Scattering video. This is a major feature, and writing about it here doesn't do it justice. It's best to see it in action, so watch the tutorial video for more information.

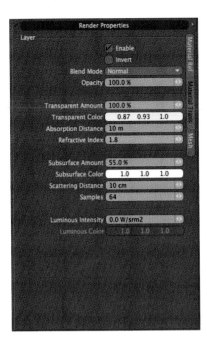

Figure 11.12

You can achieve a good look for the ice cubes by using similar transparent settings for the glass and liquid, and then applying subsurface effects.

31. The ice looks good, but a little bright. And, it could use a little bit more than just shading. Making sure the Ice Cube material is selected in the Shader Tree, add a gradient from the Add Layer drop-down menu at the top of the Shader Tree. This gradient effect will help the surface reflections.

32. For the effect, right-click in the Effect column next to the gradient and set it to Reflection Amount, as shown in Figure 11.13.

33. In the Render Properties panel, make sure the Blend Mode is set to Normal; for the Input Parameter, choose Incidence Angle. The Incidence Angle will allow you to vary the amount of reflection based on the angle of incidence in the angle between the ray and the surface normal.

34. Click the Gradient Editor button. You'll see modo's Gradient Editor appear, as shown in Figure 11.14.

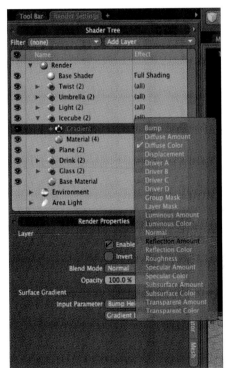

Figure 11.13

Apply a gradient to the Ice Cube material and set its effect to Reflection Amount.

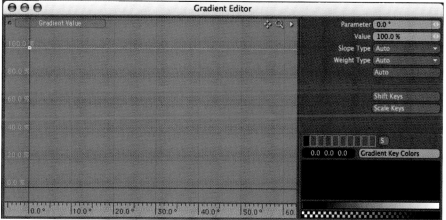

Figure 11.14

When a gradient is applied, you can open the Gradient Editor to set the values.

35. Click and drag the first keyframe down to the bottom-left corner. This is 0% for both the amount and percentage of the input parameter you've chosen— in this case, Incidence Angle. The vertical value is the amount, while the bottom horizontal numbers are the degrees for the angle of incidence. To create an additional key, middle-click in the Gradient Editor. Zoom out to see more degree values by using the Zoom tool in the top-right of the Gradient Editor. Then, drag that key with the left mouse button up to 40% at 90 degrees.

36. You'll see small squares hanging out of the keys. Grab the first handle and drag it up and out from the 0% position. This will ease the value out, as shown in Figure 11.15. They'll turn green when selected.

Note

I've included a Gradient Editor video on the book's disc to help explain this cool feature of modo.

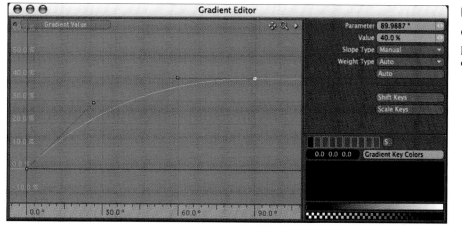

Figure 11.15

Create a key at the 90% point, and adjust the slope of the curve for the 0% key.

37. Close the Gradient Editor and save your work thus far.

38. Back up in the Shader Tree, select the Ice Cube material, then select Add Layer and choose Cellular. Set Effect to Displacement. This will help roughen up the ice a bit.

39. In the Render Properties panel, make sure Blend Mode is set to Normal. Opacity should be 10%. This will create just a slight displacement.

40. The Cell Value should be 0%, while the Filler Value should be 100%.

41. The Type can be set to Angular, with a Cell Width of 60%, and a Transition Width of 30%. These values vary how this computer-generated procedural texture is used. You've already told modo that it's used to displace the object, but now you're telling it how it's applied.

42. Frequencies should be set to 1, and the Bias and Gain can remain at 50%, as shown in Figure 11.16. Most of these values are default, but check them to make sure.

43. Click into the Texture Locator vertical category, and change size to 5mm for each of the X, Y, and Z axes.

44. The Projection Type should be set to Solid. This applies the procedural directly over the entire surface.

45. Save your work. Figure 11.17 shows the scene thus far. You can see that the ice cubes are now looking pretty good!

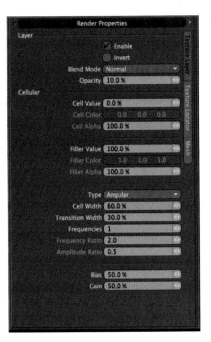

Figure 11.16

The Cellular texture is a cool-looking procedural texture that also works well for random displacements.

At this point, feel free to tweak and play with your scene as you like. Try adding another layer on top of the Cellular texture, perhaps a Noise layer, set also to Displacement. Save your project when finished. Now, it's time to surface the umbrella. But rather than adding a typical material color or a procedural layer, you'll paint the surface!

Note

If your preview window slows down redrawing after you've applied the displacement to the ice cubes, you can click the Options button at the top of the preview window and turn off Displacement. This turns off the displacement preview, but does not change the surface settings.

Figure 11.17

By customizing a few more settings to the ice cube and adding a displacement, the surface looks good.

Painting Surfaces

Painting surfaces is a cool technique from which any 3D modeler can benefit. You do not need to be an artist by any means. This next section will introduce you to the painting tools, showing you how to set them up on a model and how to use them. From there, you'll move onto the book's disc to watch video tutorials taking you further with painting and texturing. You'll use the traffic light model created in the previous chapter and finish what you started. After all, what's a good model without good textures? But before that, read on to learn about this slick modo feature.

1. Open up modo, and click over to the Tool Bar tab. If you have a scene loaded, save it and then select Reset from the File drop-down menu.

2. Click the Paint vertical category, as shown in Figure 11.18.

3. Because your scene has become complex and you want the best resources possible for feedback on your painting, right-click on the Item List tab. From the Viewport Settings, choose Auto Visibility, as shown in Figure 11.19.

Figure 11.18

Open the Paint category from the Tool Bar tab.

4. Select the Umbrella mesh layer. Also, for working with the Paint tools, change back to a Model Single viewport by clicking the first tab above the viewports.

5. Click the Add Blank Image Texture button. A system window will open, asking you where you'd like to save the image, as shown in Figure 11.20.

Figure 11.19

Activate Auto Visibility to isolate the selected mesh.

Figure 11.20

Choosing Add Blank Image Texture from the Paint category first prompts you to specify where to save the image.

6. Give the image the name UmbrellaPaint and save it as a PNG or TGA, or whatever file format you like. PNGs are the images of choice for this book, although you're welcome to use any format you like. Once you click OK, another dialog box will appear, asking you some specifics of the image. For this particular image, choose 1024×1024 for Image Resolution. You can go up to 4000 for the image, but because the umbrella is not completely filling the scene, a 1k image works fine. You can choose RGBA for the Format setting. Figure 11.21 shows the panel. This tells modo you're creating a color image with an alpha channel. Floating Point and Set Color don't need to be checked, but can be if you'd like to set these. This image does not need to be a floating-point image. Essentially, a floating-point image is one that stores

32 bits of data per channel, compared to the typical 8 bits. Therefore, it's capable of displaying a much higher range of values. For color maps

Figure 11.21

Choose the resolution and format for your image.

it's not that important, but it's very useful if you want to paint a map to light the scene with global illumination.

7. Click OK, and you've now set up an image on which to paint. If you look at the Item List, you'll see a Texture Image has been added. But, make sure that in the Shader Tree, you drag the newly created image into the umbrella mask.

8. To begin, fill the umbrella with color. Do this by selecting the Fill tool, which is the paint can icon. When this tool is selected, you can change the FG (foreground color) to a bluish green. Then, click and drag slightly on the umbrella in the viewport. After a moment, your umbrella will be colored, as shown in Figure 11.22.

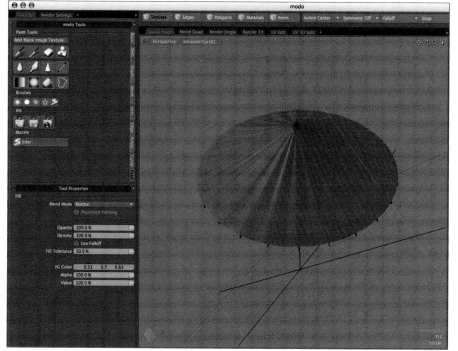

Figure 11.22

Using the Fill tool, you can quickly fill an object with color.

9. Coloring the umbrella is not a big deal—this doesn't look much different than just setting a basic material color. Okay then, take it a step further. Back in the Paint tools, select the first brush icon, the Airbrush.

10. Then, under the Brushes category, select the third brush icon, the Procedural brush. The first brush is the Airbrush, which falls off to a soft edge right from the center. The brush next to it, the Hard brush, is solid, but you can set a soft border in the Tool Properties panel. For now, the Procedural brush will work well, and it allows you to set some procedural noise in your paint.

11. Next, at the bottom of the Tool Properties panel, change the Type to Cellular. Remember that if you can't see the settings, click and drag between the windows to adjust them.

12. You won't use the Ink setting right now. However, this is where you'll be able to set images for painting. You'll do that in the video portion of this chapter on the book's disc.

13. With that all said, right-click on the umbrella and drag. This sets the size of the brush. Set it to about 100, which you can also do numerically in the Tool Properties panel. Figure 11.23 shows the operation.

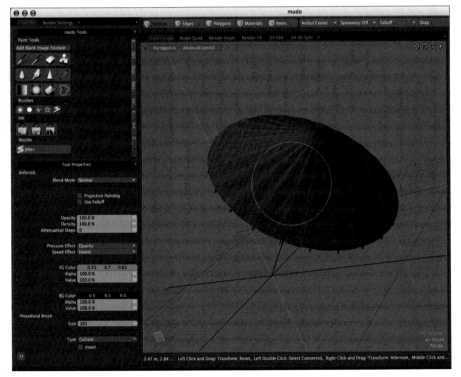

Figure 11.23

Right-click and drag on the model to set the size of the paintbrush.

14. With the size set, click over to the Color Picker tab, which is to the right of the Item List. Pick a bright color, perhaps yellow. Then, using the left mouse button, click and drag on the umbrella. Voila! You're painting on a 3D model! Figure 11.24 shows the result.

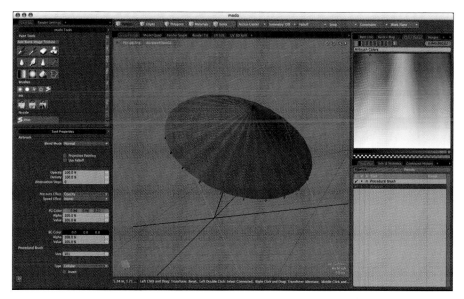

Figure 11.24

By clicking and dragging with the left mouse button, you're now painting on a 3D model.

15. When painting, you'll find that you might want to redo your work often. Press Ctrl+z (PC) or Command+z (Mac) to undo your painting. Hold the Alt key, then click and drag the view around so you're looking more at the top of the umbrella. Then, brush the paint around the entire object, as shown in Figure 11.25.

16. As you can see, it's pretty easy to paint right on your models. But this is only the beginning.

17. At the top of the viewport, click the last tabbed view, the UV 3D Split. Press the **a** key to fit the geometry to view. Figure 11.26 shows the screen.

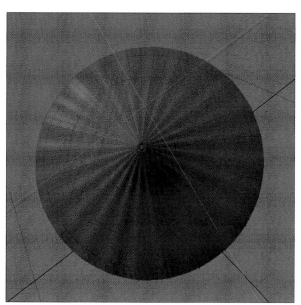

Figure 11.25

Remember that you can undo your paint operation, and then paint again.

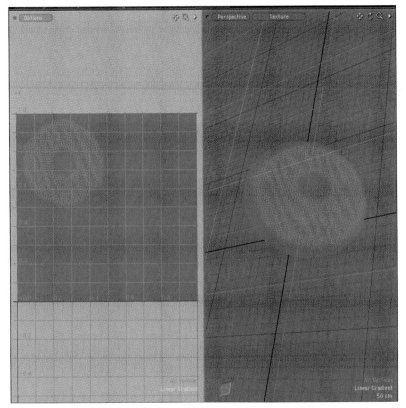

Figure 11.26

Using the UV 3D Split view, you can see the map you're painting.

18. What you're seeing is the object's UV map superimposed on the image map that you created when you clicked Add Blank Image, and subsequently painted on. In the Paint tools, select the Airbrush tool, which is the first icon. Set the FG Color to something other than yellow—red or blue, perhaps. Change the brush to a smooth brush, the first icon under the Brushes category. Paint on the UV map, the left window, in the center of the yellow ring. As you do so, watch the 3D viewport on the right. Figure 11.27 shows some red paint in the center of the model.

19. Continue painting as you like and save your work. You can continually add different brushes and procedurals to make a very stylized umbrella. Perhaps write in your name? Or create bands of color. It's completely up to you.

20. Take a look at the Shader Tree. Your painted image might be above all of the other material layers, if you've not already moved it to the umbrella mask, as shown in Figure 11.28.

21. If this is the case, drag it under the Umbrella mask layer, above the material, as shown in Figure 11.29.

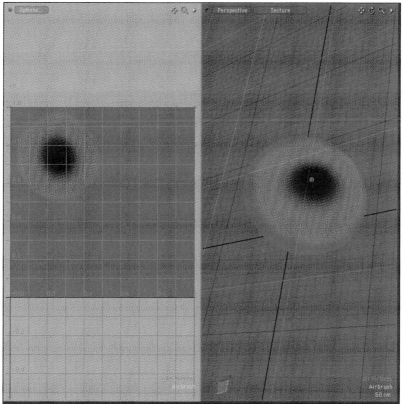

Figure 11.27

In addition to painting on the model directly, you can also paint on the UV map.

Figure 11.28

Your painted texture might end up on top of your other materials. If so, just drag it into the mask layer that it belongs to, in this case, the Umbrella.

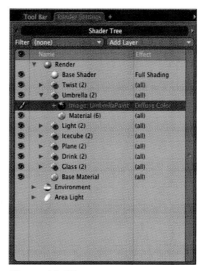

Figure 11.29

Place your painted texture into the layer mask that it belongs to—in this case, the Umbrella.

22. With the painted image now within the Umbrella mask layer in the Shader Tree, right-click on it and select Duplicate. Notice that the first image layer's effect is set to Diffuse Color. That's fine because it allows you to see the color you've painted.

23. Select the duplicate image you just created, and in the Effect column to the right, where it says Diffuse Color, right-click (Command-click on the Mac) to change it to Bump. When you apply a bump, modo will only be looking at the brightness value of each pixel to determine the bump amount, not the depth of each pixel.

24. Click to the Material layer, then down in the Render Properties, change Bump Strength to about 400%. Figure 11.30 shows the painted image, duplicated and applied as a bump map.

Note

To see the bumps in your viewport, make sure you turn on Advanced OpenGL from the top of the viewport window.

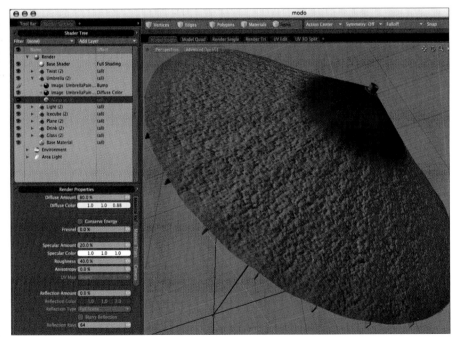

Figure 11.30

By copying the painted texture in the Shader Tree and changing its effect to Bump, you now have an interesting-looking object.

This only scratches the surface of modo's painting tools. To cover them properly, I've included video training tutorials exclusively for this book from 3D Garage.com. Although 3D Garage.com offers a full modo training course, the videos for this chapter have been created to match these projects. Additionally, you'll learn more about the UV maps, such as how to unwrap them, and you'll see how to create additional surfacing techniques using the traffic light model created in the previous chapter.

12

Lighting and Rendering

When modo was introduced, its strong points were, and still are, modeling and productivity. With the release of 201 and 202, lighting and rendering have added to the functionality of modo without complicating the workflow.

This chapter will guide you through the use of lights in modo, and then get you started with its powerful rendering engine. You'll use scenes you created earlier in the book as examples.

Lighting in modo

Before the projects begin, take a brief tour of the lights in modo and how they vary. Figure 12.1 shows a scene with two keys on a flat plane.

As you can see from Figure 12.1, the default light, a directional light, illuminates your scene and applies shadows. There's nothing glamorous about this light, and it's primarily good for outdoor situations, in which you need light from afar, such as a sun or a moon. A directional light's position is not important—only its rotation is. It will emit light from a distance, and this will vary only when you rotate the light, not when you move it. However, although a directional light's shadows are normally hard-edged, you do have the ability to soften them in modo by increasing the spread angle.

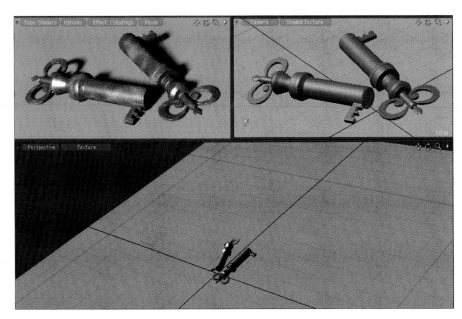

Figure 12.1

The default light, a directional light, has shadows and lights evenly.

Figure 12.2 shows the same scene, but the light has been changed to a point light and moved to the middle of the scene. Can't see much there, can you? That's because the point light emits in an omnidirectional fashion, and a radiant intensity needs to be increased for the light to emit further. A point light's rotation does not matter, only its position does. Think of this light as the opposite of a directional light.

Figure 12.3 shows the same scene with a spot light. With this type of light, your scene can benefit from the light's position and rotation. Light is illuminated in the shape of a cone. You can vary the cone and set a nice, soft edge for the light. Spot lights are useful for all sorts of scenes, from headlights, to flashlights, to recessed lighting in architectural environments.

Figure 12.4 shows the shot of the keys with an area light. Area lights are some of the best lights you can use because they offer very realistic shadows, as well as greater control over intensity. They work this way because area lights simulate the size of a real-world light. In modo, you can press the **y** key and find two handles on an area light that will allow you to scale the area width and height. Area lights can be square, such as a big, soft light in a photography or video studio. They can also be oval in shape, which changes the throw of the light. You'll see this in a project a bit later.

Figure 12.5 shows the keys with a dome light. The look is similar to an area light with soft shadows, but rather than emitting from a directed source, the dome light emits from all over, simulating an environmental lighting situation.

Figure 12.2

The point light, an omnidirectional light, emits light in all directions. Its rotational value does not matter in your scene.

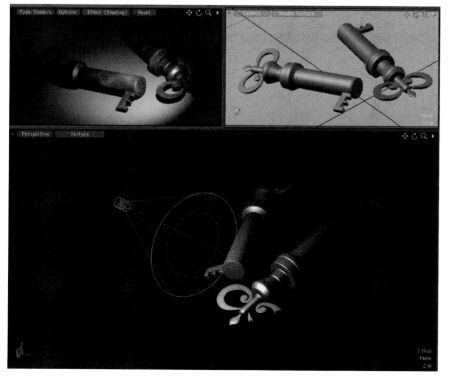

Figure 12.3

The spot light offers you control over position and rotation for maximum flexibility.

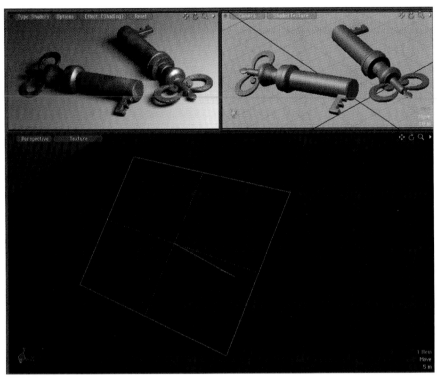

Figure 12.4

An area light allows you to create soft, bright light in a directed fashion. Shadows are accurate and soft.

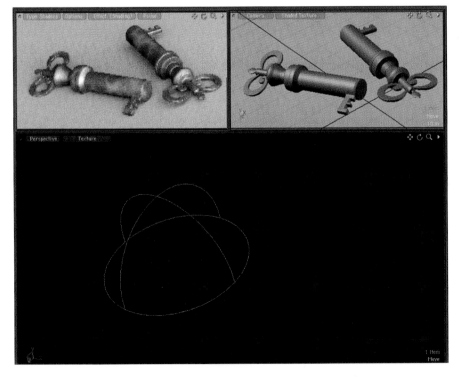

Figure 12.5

A dome light is a great way to light the entire scene, similar to an environmental light.

Figure 12.6 incorporates a cylinder light, something that's very cool to use in your scenes. The cylinder light emits light in a cylindrical fashion and is great for setting concentrated light sources, perhaps in shots of medical imaging. With this light, you can change the length of the cylinder, as well as the radius. Think of this light as a fluorescent tube.

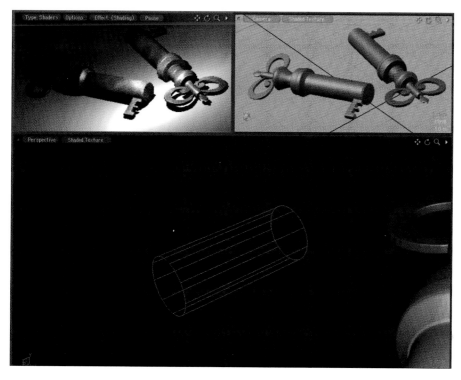

Figure 12.6

A cylinder light allows you to light your scene as if you're using a tube or fluorescent light.

You can use any light type in any way you see fit, but there are some basic principles that can guide you. Lighting in modo is a matter of preference, both in light type and attributes. But it's always a good idea to gain general knowledge of CG lighting principles, which can apply not only to modo, but to any 3D application.

Lighting Concepts

Light is everywhere. Light is everything. Unfortunately, many 3D artists don't consider the light as an equal part of their scene. In fact, calling light an equal part of the scene might be an understatement. Light is part of our everyday world, in everything we do. Although it's important to understand light theory and color, this chapter is geared more toward your working relationship with modo's lighting capabilities. There are tremendous books on lighting in 3D, such as Jeremy Birn's *Digital Lighting & Rendering* (New Riders, 2006), or perhaps *Inspired 3D Lighting and Compositing* by David Parrish (Thomson Course Technology PTR, 2002), which you should definitely read and refer to on a regular basis. But without me taking up too much time talking about all of the intricacies of CG lighting, take a look at Figure 12.7. What you're seeing is the visible spectrum of light we see every day. Here, it's shown curved, in the form of a rainbow. Look familiar?

Electromagnetic energy is all around us, and we perceive this in wavelengths that range from 400 to 700 nm, as visible light. The *nm* stands for wavelength. Taking a look at the rainbow spectrum, on the left side you see blue. Electromagnetic energy in this range is in the form of X-rays and gamma rays. On the right of the spectrum is red, where you'll find radio waves. But how does this all relate to light-

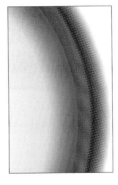

Figure 12.7

The visible spectrum of light we see every day.

ing in modo? This spectrum of colors is represented in the computer world as RGB—red, green, and blue. These three colors are the primarily colors of light, and mixing them is an additive approach that creates white. For example, if you take the RGB values in a color selector on your computer and drag them all up, you'll create the color white, 255 RGB. But why RGB? This has to do with the way our eyes perceive the visual spectrum. The receptors in our retinas respond to these values of the spectrum, but they also respond to the areas between these colors.

Quality of Light

You might not always think about the light in your 3D environment as something that has quality. But a light does have quality, and it is something you need to pay attention to. The quality of light refers to the softness, angle, color, brightness, and throw pattern. The throw pattern is the shape of the light, and a good example of this is the square area light versus the oval area light. This is different from the light angle, which is more important for setting the mood of the scene. For example, a midday sun would be angled from above your 3D elements. Or, an evening sunset would be angled from low and to the side.

With modo, you might find yourself the victim of noise in your renders. Although you might consider this a low-quality issue, it's really more a matter of properly setting the correct values. You'll perform a project that enables you to apply lights, render, and then adjust to see how the various settings change how a light affects the scene.

Other Light Sources

You've seen that you can choose from any of six lights in modo and put any combination of them into your scene. But there is a little bit more you can do to light your scene using other types of light sources.

Figure 12.8 shows the key scene from earlier in the chapter lit without lights. That's right, no lights. The keys are lit by another 3D object.

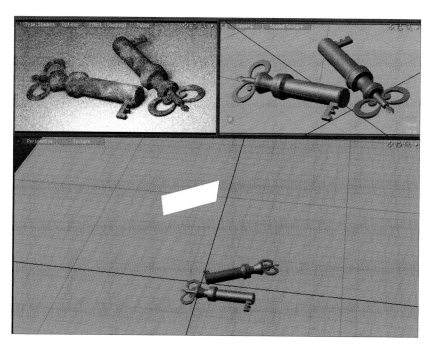

Figure 12.8

The key scene lit with a single polygon and no lights.

You see, modo has the capability of global illumination, or GI. GI is the art and science of calculating the rays as they bounce in the scene. If an object is brighter, it will have a greater effect on the scene with global illumination. You'll set this up for yourself shortly.

You can use any object as a light source. This is great for neon tubes, nighttime windows on a cityscape, or simply as soft light boxes, as shown in Figure 12.8.

Figure 12.9 shows the key scene with the Use Environment as Light option checked on in the Render panel.

Here, your modo environment is used as a light source. So if you have a white background, modo carries those colors into your scene, using it as a light from all directions. Of course, this is all based on the RGB values in the scene.

Finally, modo also allows you to use HDR, or *high dynamic range,* images. Computer screens can't display the full dynamic range of what lighting is like in the real world. The dynamic range is the ratio between the dark and bright regions of an image. But if a series of photos is taken at different exposures, then compiled in something like HDR Shop or Photoshop CS2, a high dynamic range image is created. This type image contains more dynamic data than you might think, enough to light an entire scene. Figure 12.10 shows the same key scene with an HDR image used as a light source.

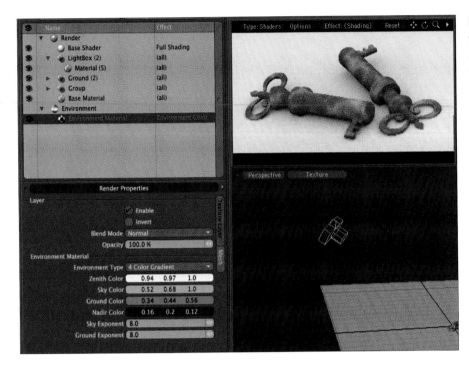

Figure 12.9

You can employ the environment as a light source in modo.

Figure 12.10

Incorporating HDR images into your scenes can produce very realistic lighting conditions.

The intensity of an HDR image allows greater exposure in your 3D scene. For this to work, two things need to happen: The image must be an HDR, and you need to activate global illumination in the Render panel. Later, you'll experiment with your own HDR images and set up a scene using them. For more information on this amazing science and technique, visit http://www.debevec.org. Paul Debevec was the pioneer behind merging high dynamic range imagery and computer graphics. Gregory Ward is credited with being the founder of the HDR format.

Creating a Lit Scene in modo

Perhaps by this point in the book, you've tooled around enough to have created some decent-looking renders. And perhaps you were adventurous and applied some various lighting effects to the scene. Tremendous! Experimentation is key. This next project will take you through how to set up a scene and how to apply different light sources. Along the way, you'll see explanations for various settings that might have eluded you up to this point.

1. Load the sonylcd.lxo scene from the book's disc. It's in the Chapter 12 projects folder.

2. Once the scene is loaded, click over to a Render Tri view. Figure 12.11 shows the scene.

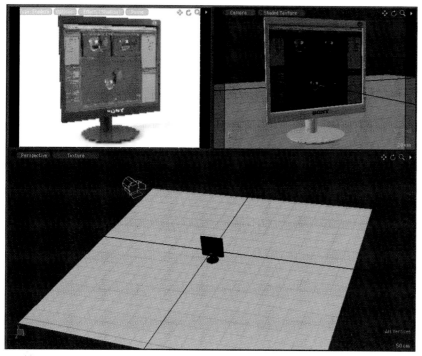

Figure 12.11

Load the LCD monitor from the projects folder on the book's DVD.

3. This nice-looking setup was created and generously donated for use in this book by Mr. Philip Lawson. Thanks, Philip! You can see that you have a nice-looking LCD monitor, image mapped with a screen grab of modo. Also notice that there is just white all around the monitor. How is this scene lit?

4. Take a closer look at the Item List. Mr. Lawson has created three groups—models, textures, and lights. Figure 12.12 shows the lights group expanded.

5. You don't want to save over the original scene, so resave it as a different name.

6. In the Item List, select the three lights in the group, right-click on them, and select Delete. When it asks to delete child items, say yes.

7. Next, in the Render Settings tab on the left side of the screen, click to the Global Illumination tab in the Render Properties panel. Turn off Indirect Illumination, as shown in Figure 12.13.

   For now, you'll work with just modo's practical light types. In the next chapter, you'll work with HDR and indirect (global) illumination.

8. From the Image List, click on the Add Item listing. It's ghosted and just below the last item in the list. Choose Area Light, as shown in Figure 12.14.

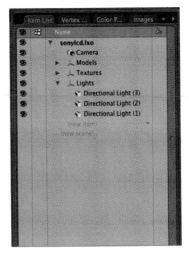

Figure 12.12

This default scene that Philip Lawson has created uses three directional lights. The result is an evenly lit object and a bright white set.

Figure 12.13

Turn off the Indirect Illumination option in the Render Settings tab.

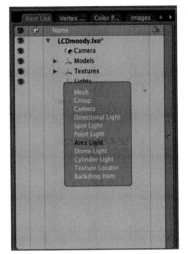

Figure 12.14

Adding a light to the scene is as easy as clicking New Item in the Item List.

9. Once the area light is loaded, it's plopped down right the middle of the scene, as in Figure 12.15.

10. Make sure the new light is selected in the Item List, then press the **y** key on your keyboard. Although you can move the light by pressing the **w** key, the **y** key is ideal for an area light because you can move, rotate, and change the area width and height all in one tool.

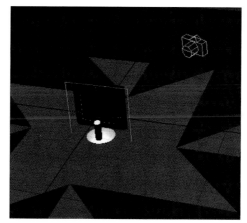

Figure 12.15

When a light is added to a scene, it's dropped to the middle of the viewport, at the 0 XYZ axes.

Note

Action Center should be set to Automatic.

11. Click and drag the green handle to bring the light up on the Y axis about 1m. Remember that you'll see the position on the left side of the interface in the Render Properties panel.

12. Now click the blue handle and drag the light back on the Z axis to –1m. This will place the light in front of the monitor screen.

13. Click the red ring and drag the light about 35 degrees. What happens? Not much! You see, area lights have one direction. And because the light's direction indicator (the orange arrow) is now pointing up with a 35-degree rotation, you're not lighting the object at all. Rotate the light to –35 degrees, and the LCD monitor will now be lit, as shown in Figure 12.16.

14. Do you see the light-blue squares on the edge of the light? They'll appear when the light is selected and you press the **y** key to access the Transform tool. Drag the right side square out to expand the area width to 3m. You can see the amount in the Render Properties panel. Then, drag the top square up to 2m for the height. Figure 12.17 shows the change in light size and brightness.

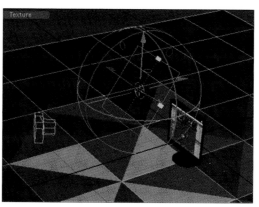

Figure 12.16

Rotate the area light to –35 degrees so the direction of the light faces the object.

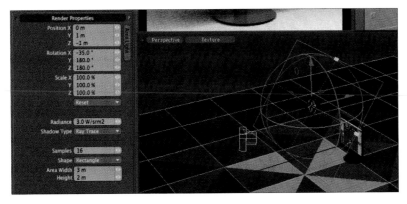

Figure 12.17

Changing the area light's width and height increases its strength.

Notice in Figure 12.17 that the light is soft and well-placed above the monitor. But the backdrop is awful, and the light falls off and doesn't light the set. When lighting your 3D scenes, there's more to it than just placing a light. The environment plays a key role in every scene you build. Here, the environment is just white, so change it.

15. In the Shader Tree, expand the Environment layer and select the Environment Material. In the Render properties for the Environment Material, notice that the Environment Type is set to Constant. This sets one single color, currently white. How about something more dramatic? Change the zenith color from white to black. You can do this quickly by holding the Shift key, then clicking directly on the color values and dragging to the left.

16. Taking a look at the preview window in Figure 12.18, you can see that with the area light falloff and the black background, you've instantly changed the appearance of the render.

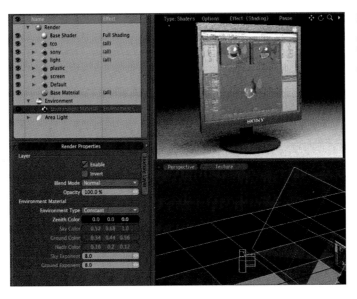

Figure 12.18

Change the Constant background to create a different mood in the scene.

17. Go a step further now to pull the object from the background. Save your work. Then, in the Item List, add a spot light. Do this by clicking New Item.

18. Drag the light to about 4m on the Z axis, as shown in Figure 12.19.

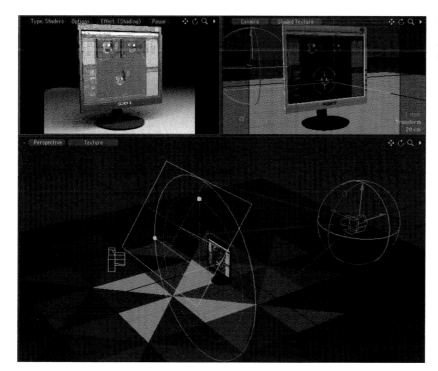

Figure 12.19

A spot light can coexist with an area light, no problem!

Closely look at Figure 12.19. Notice something on the end of the cone? With the **y** Transform tool selected, there are Move and Rotate handles, as well as two small light-blue squares, as there were on the area light. Yet here, these two squares change the cone angle, which is the spread of the light, and the soft edge.

19. Drag the cone angle to 60 and the soft edge to 80. By setting the soft edge higher than the cone angle, you can effectively pull the light away from the center spot. It's a nice effect for a light like this. Because this light is being used behind the subject and not as a main light, a softer edge works well.

20. Bring the spot light up on the Y axis to about 1m. Then, grab the red ring and rotate the light about 24 degrees, so it's pointing at the back of the monitor.

21. In Render Tri view, change the top-right camera view to Perspective. Then, change the main large view from Perspective to Light. This way, you can see exactly what the light sees, making it easier to set up. Note that the selected light is the light you'll be seeing through in the Light view. Figure 12.20 shows the setup.

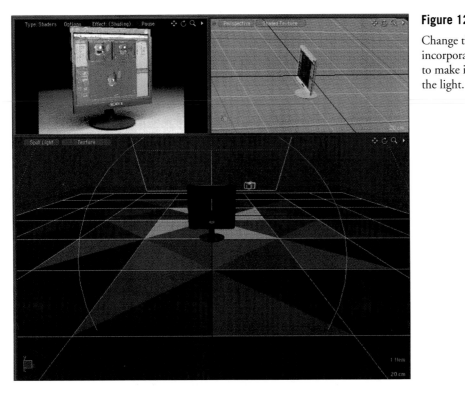

Figure 12.20

Change the views to incorporate a Light view to make it easier to set up the light.

Note

When working in a Light view, you can move the light by holding the Alt/Option key and the Shift key, then clicking and dragging in the viewport. You can rotate the light by holding the Alt/Option key and clicking in the viewport. To zoom the light, hold the Ctrl and Alt/Option keys, then click and drag.

22. Position the light on your own to cast a back light on the monitor, something like you see in Figure 12.21.

23. The position is good, but the light itself doesn't seem to do much for the render, if you take a look at the preview window. So, click over to the Shader Tree and expand the Spot Light layer, and then select the Light material for it. Notice that in the Render Properties panel, the color is white, and the shadow is black. For now the shadow color is fine, but you can change this if you want.

24. Change the color for the light to a bright orange, roughly 1.0, 0.54, 0.56. Press F9 to render the frame. Figure 12.22 shows the render. Notice that there's not a soft, warm color behind the monitor on the floor? The spot light adds a bit of warmth to the scene and helps pull the monitor from the dark background.

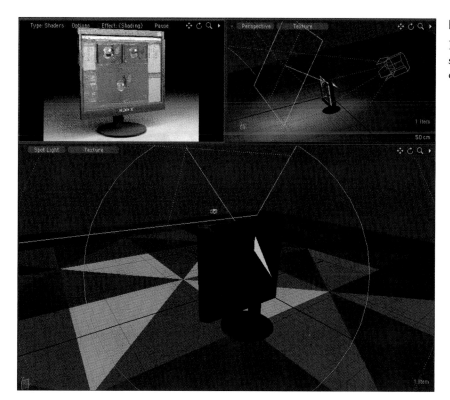

Figure 12.21

Position the light so that it's slightly above and to the side of the monitor.

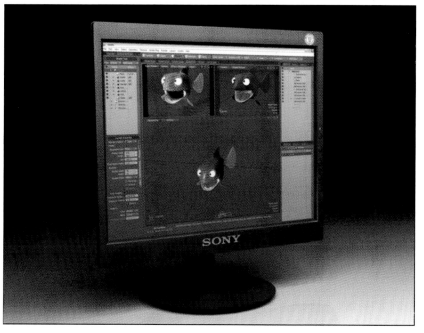

Figure 12.22

Adding colored lights brings warmth to your 3D scene.

25. To take this a step further, change the Action Center to Selection. Press the **y** key, and then you can grab the blue handle to pull the light back on its own axis to fill more of the scene.

    In the Shader Tree, select the Spot Light layer. When this is selected, you'll see the Render Properties appear with Position and Rotation settings. Additionally, you can change the Radiant Intensity. Bring this value to about 21. The W/srm2 is the radiation—remember earlier in the chapter, when wavelengths were discussed? This is how modo calculates light, and the W/srm2 refers to the mathematical function of radiation, both long wave and short wave.

Note

Unlike many 3D programs, modo's non-distant lights have a falloff. Because of this, they perform in a more realistic behavior.

26. You can also change the Shadow Type in the Render properties, but in this case a spot light only has a ray-traced shadow. Figure 12.23 shows the scene with the light moved and set to a bright radiance.

27. Back over in the Item List, add a New Item and choose Point Light.

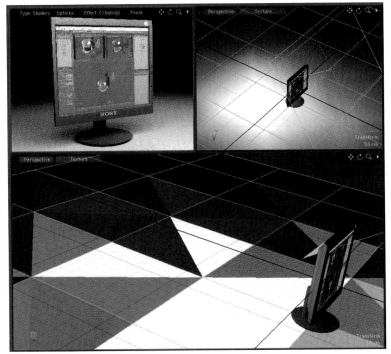

Figure 12.23

With the spot light moved back and at an increased radiance, the backdrop becomes even warmer.

28. Position this light to the back-left of the monitor, similar to what you see in Figure 12.24.

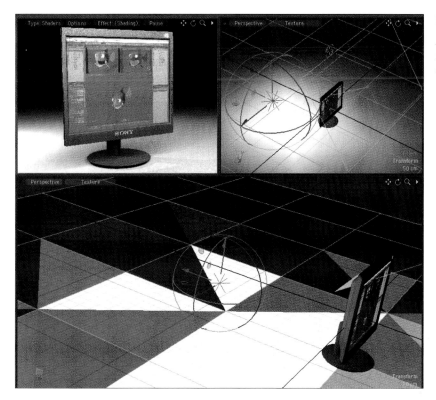

Figure 12.24

Add a point light and move it to the other side of the monitor.

29. In the Shader Tree, change this light's color to a medium blue, about 0.36, 0.47, 0.69.

30. For this light, rather than bringing down the radiance, change the Effect Diffuse setting to about 65%. An object's reception of light is a combination of its material's diffuse value and the strength of the light. By lowering the Effect Diffuse percentage, you are telling the light to have less effect on the material's diffuse value. This makes the material less receptive to the light's energy, in effect darkening the material.

What you've set up here is similar to a basic three-point lighting shoot, with slight variation. A three-point lighting setup requires a main key light (your area light), and then a back light (your spot light) and a fill light to help balance dark shadows or lost edges, such as the left side of the monitor. This is what your point light is doing. In addition to helping light the model, these lights also enhance the overall mood and tone of your scene. So although Philip Lawson's original scene was great and very product shot–like, the setup you've created is richer and takes on a whole different look.

Rendering

If you're from the modo 103 camp and have upgraded to 201/202, then you know that one of the biggest new features in this release is the modo render engine. The incorporation of the render engine allows modo to now have advanced texturing capabilities, lights and shadows, and more. It is the next step in this next-generation program.

modo incorporates a physically based shading model. This allows you to create some pretty stunning results quickly and easily. Figure 12.25 shows a render from the 3D Garage modo Signature Courseware (www.3dgarage.com). Here, you can see that modo has done a great job with shadows, light color, falloffs, and reflections. But how does this all come together?

Take a look at Figure 12.26. What you're looking at are the Render Settings, which are accessed from within the Shader Tree.

Figure 12.25

A teacup. Simple, but nicely rendered.

Figure 12.26

The Render properties for the teacup example.

Let's break down the settings, which will help demystify the myriad tools. When you select the Render listing in the Shader Tree, all of the necessary render parameters appear. Easy enough, right?

Frame

It's important to pay attention to the vertical category listings within the Render Properties panel. They are Frame, Settings, Global Illumination, and Mesh. Figure 12.27 shows the Frame tab and its settings. At the top of the panel is the camera. In modo, you can have multiple cameras, and it's here that you will select which camera you want to use as the render camera.

In the Frame tab, you can set the Resolution Unit. By default, it's set to Pixels, the most common render type in 3D applications. But if you're rendering for print, you can change this to Inches. Beneath this setting is where you'll set the frame width and height. When you render your frame, this is the size of the image. You also have a DPI (*dots per inch*) setting, which defaults to 300. Three-hundred DPI is the typical setting when working in the print world. The Pixel Aspect is important to set properly because it will change the look for your render. By default, it's set to 1.0, square pixels. This should be used for images staying in the computer, such as for image processing in Photoshop, Web sites, and so on. But, if your final render is going to video, the square pixel setting (1.0) won't look right. For video you'll want 0.9, which sets a rec-

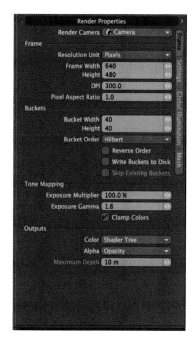

Figure 12.27

The Frame tab within the Render Properties panel.

tangular pixel. Note that a pixel setting of 0.9 is for NTSC and DV video, but not HD. Further changes to the Pixel Aspect can be set for widescreen at 1.2 or 1.5.

In the middle of the Frame tab is the Buckets setting. Modo uses bucket rendering to draw its frames. Basically, bucket rendering is a technology that separates the frame buffer into different regions that are rendered independently. The result is faster rendering and more control over the process.

Another cool thing about bucket rendering is that this technique significantly decreases the use of frame buffer memory, but the size of the buckets makes all the difference. By changing the bucket height and width, you can tell modo to use less memory when rendering. Each scene will vary, and the Luxology team has set the default bucket height and width to 40, a good working size. Using these settings helps you balance memory versus CPU consumption. The end result is that you have the ability with bucket rendering to render billions of polygons. Experiment with these settings and see what results you achieve. The bucket order is also important when rendering with buckets because it determines how the buckets (regions) are rendered.

The Hilbert is a mathematical function that finds a coherent balance for better memory management and speed. However, you can also set Bucket Order to Rows, Columns, Spiral, and Random. Additionally, there is a checkmark to Reverse Order for the buckets. Set to Hilbert and Reverse Order, you can render your frame from the inside out.

Turning on Write Buckets to Disk tells modo to save the bucket data to a temporary space on your hard drive, helping ease the strain on your system's memory.

Under the Tone Mapping settings, you can increase the overall exposure of the scene with the Exposure Multiplier. Changing the Exposure Gamma is primarily useful for global illumination. If you increase the value, you'll pump up the midtones in your image. Every once in a while, a render might come along in which there is an aliasing effect in high-contrast areas. This is mostly prevalent on CRT or LCD monitors. Setting the Clamp Colors option helps blend the high and low values.

Finally in the Frame tab, you have the options to set the output color to Shader Tree (default), Ambient Occlusion, Surface Normal, Surface ID, or Segment ID. With the Shader Tree setting, the standard shading model is used, whereas Ambient Occlusion helps bring out the smaller details of your model. Suppose you have a complex landscape. The areas not hit directly with light—the ambient areas—are boosted with this output method. The Surface ID and Segment ID colors are applied based on either the surface or segments, purely as optimization and scene management. Lastly, there is the Alpha setting, which defaults to Opacity. You also have a Depth setting and Shadow Density. Shadow Density is an excellent choice for the rendered alpha when compositing images. It will allow you to integrate images with alpha channels, rather than just laying one on top of the other in a compositing program.

Settings

Next to the Frame tab is the Settings tab. Figure 12.28 shows the settings.

At the top of the panel, you can tell modo to render in Scanline mode, Automatic, or Ray Trace. Scanline mode will use a scanline-based front end, while the Ray Trace setting employs a full ray-traced render engine throughout your scene. For best results, keep this setting to Automatic and let modo choose the correct render settings for you.

Anti-aliasing in modo works differently than what you might be familiar with. The AA setting *only* affects geometric edges and material boundaries; it does nothing for any texturing, shadows, reflections, refractions, objects behind transparent materials, or basically anything on the interior of a polygon. The combination of shading rate and refinement shading rate is used to sample and AA all the pixels in the scene on the interiors of the polygons. The balance between these two rates is controlled by the refinement threshold. The default shading rate of one sample/pixel results in very fast rendering, but it's not nearly accurate enough for clean renders. The refinement threshold default of 10% will let pixels that are only 25 steps apart in brightness (.1 × 255 = approx 25 steps) pass the threshold and be sampled at the default rate of one sample/pixel. All other pixels that are farther apart in contrast are shaded by the refinement shading rate (which defaults to .25 or 16 samples/pixel).

The other factor here that is limiting the sampling is the anti-aliasing value, which sets the upper limit for the shading samples. So if you leave the setting at eight samples/pixel, then the refinement shading rate of .25 will stop after eight samples (instead of reaching 16). Therefore, if the threshold is set to 0%, then only pixels that are 0 steps apart in brightness will pass—no pixels, resulting in all pixels being shaded at the refinement rate. If the threshold is 100%, then pixels that are up to 255 steps away in brightness will pass—so all pixels.

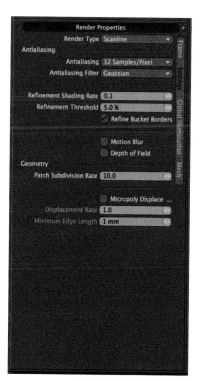

Figure 12.28

The Settings for rendering.

Lastly, in the Settings panel, you can set a Patch Subdivision Rate. When using subdivisional surfaces, this value determines how deep the subdivision is applied at render time. A lower value will subdivide the geometry more. Beneath this setting is the option for micro poly displacement. When this is turned on, you can control the displacement rate, which determines the number of polygons created during the render. It's important to note that lowering the rate always results in finer settings, whether it's shading, displacement, irradiance caching, or subdivision. A lower value will subdivide the geometry more. A value of 10 means modo will pick a subdivision setting for the layer that will result in the longest edge being no more than 10 pixels long. If the subdivision rate is set to 1, for example, then the edges would be subdivided down to one pixel each. A lower rate equals more polygons. This is important because if your polygons were continually refined, the render would never finish!

From this point, it's important to know that these basic lighting principles and render settings can apply to anything in modo. Their usage is the same, from adding, to positioning, to setting the radiance.

But modo is so much more powerful than what you've seen here, so instead of wasting pages with additional setup, you might really enjoy seeing more dramatic lighting examples. These can be achieved with global illumination, a technique employed by most 3D applications today, but performed better in modo.

Turn to Chapter 13, "Rendering with Global Illumination," to perform projects based all around global illumination and advanced rendering.

Part IV

More on Lighting and Rendering

13

Rendering with Global Illumination

A few years ago, the concept of using global illumination was foreign to most everyday 3D artists. With the advances in computing power, memory capabilities, and powerful graphics cards, achieving the high-end render is quite possible.

Global Illumination

Global illumination is composed of algorithms that, when determining the calculation of light, take into account not only the light from a direct source, but the indirect light as well. In modo, when you select the Render layer in the Shader Tree and view the Global Illumination tab within the Render Properties panel, you'll see a section for Indirect Illumination, as shown in Figure 13.1.

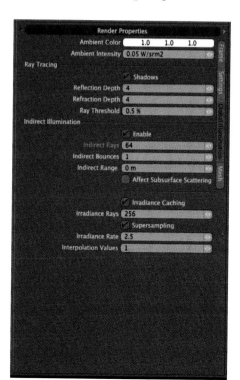

Figure 13.1

The Indirect Illumination category within the Global Illumination tab is found in the Render Properties.

When you render with global illumination (Indirect Illumination enabled), it takes more time, no question. However, the results are more than worth it. Also take into consideration that modo 201 and 202 are not animation programs, so you're only rendering single frames. Figure 13.2 shows a scene with typical lighting. Figure 13.3 shows the same scene lit entirely with the environment, using global illumination.

The funny thing about comparing Figures 13.2 and 13.3 is that both look really good! The render engine in modo performs so well that even what would be a boring, poorly lit scene looks good. But you can see that Figure 13.3 with global illumination active is softer and looks more realistic. This is because the global illumination is lighting the scene from all around, from the entire environment, rather than just from a single source.

Figure 13.2

An array of glasses, lit with a single spot light.

Figure 13.3

The same array of glasses lit with global illumination, using a white environment and a large, white polygon.

To further understand what's happening with global illumination, think of a room in your home. Imagine the morning light coming through the window. The room is lit up, and you can clearly see all around the room, even though the light is only coming in at one location. The reason you can see all over from this single light source is because the light is being diffused throughout the room. Each surface the light hits—the floor, chairs, or cabinets—adds to the overall color and lighting. In the computer with a similar setup, unless global illumination is active with Enable Indirect Illumination active, all you would see is the light coming through the window and hitting the floor or its subject. Light is bouncing off of objects and diffusing throughout the room.

It's important to understand that many things affect a scene using global illumination. Because the algorithm takes into account the brightness of everything in the scene, the environment in which you place your objects makes a big difference in the way a scene renders. Reflection is also another factor in effective global illumination. That's not to say you need reflections, but in the example of the glasses in Figures 13.2 and 13.3, the added realism comes from reflections in the elements. As another example, Figures 13.4 and 13.5 show a simple object lit with global illumination, but Figure 13.4 has no reflections, whereas Figure 13.5 does.

Figure 13.4

Three silver things don't look so silver, even with global illumination active.

Figure 13.5

The same scene with on one change: reflection.

So although many of your scenes might not incorporate reflection—perhaps a dirty-looking wood crate or a soft and plush carpet—global illumination and surface properties all work together.

Ray Tracing

You might have heard the term *radiosity*, and you might even be familiar with it. Radiosity is simply an algorithm used in global illumination. You see, global illumination uses many different algorithms, such as radiosity, ray tracing, beam tracing, cone tracing, path tracing, and photo mapping. Many of these can be combined, and modo certainly uses ray tracing. You've been rendering with ray tracing throughout this entire book. In the mid 1990s, the introduction of ray tracing to 3D applications was a very big deal. Today, it's commonplace.

Ray tracing is when a ray of light travels within the 3D environment and reacts to what it hits. This ray of light is traced in a backward direction, and if it hits an object, a shadow is created. When this happens, a secondary ray is now cast, and then a reflected ray is generated. That ray is then computed against other rays. What this all means is that ray tracing allows you to have accurate, realistic shadows and reflections.

Figure 13.6 shows Philip Lawson's drink glass. It has no ray tracing applied. Figure 13.7 shows the shot with ray tracing.

Figure 13.6

Philip Lawson's drink glass without ray tracing.

Figure 13.7

The same scene with ray tracing.

In Figure 13.6, the Base Shader in the Shader Tree was selected, and in the Texture Layer tab, Cast Shadows was turned off, as well as Receive Shadows. Also, the Visible to Reflection Rays and Visible to Refraction Rays options were turned off. The result is a not-so-good-looking image. The reason this glass rendered black is because it's a transparent object that relies on refraction, the bending of light as it passes through a surface. Ray tracing needs to be active to calculate that data, and by turning it off, you lose the surface. The umbrella, on the other hand, rendered just fine because it's a flat, diffused surface.

Advantages of ray tracing are that you can obtain very realistic situations with it, such as accurate shadows, soft shadows, reflections, and refractions for glass and transparencies. The disadvantage, however, is performance. Isn't this always the case? Even so, computer processors have become much faster, and the coding that goes into programs such as modo has become smarter. The bucket rendering method is one way that modo helps make rendering faster, especially when it comes to ray tracing.

Note

You can also quickly turn shadows on or off by selecting Render in the Shader Tree. Then, from within the Render Properties panel, you'll find the Enable Shadows option.

Ray Tracing and Global Illumination Combined

In this next section, you'll set up a lighting situation that will employ environmental light, traditional light, and global illumination. You'll use ray tracing and render the final shot.

1. From the File menu in modo, select Reset to clear out modo.

2. Load the 8balls.lxo file. This is a scene that will help demonstrate the power of modo's render engine, combining ray tracing and global illumination.

3. Switch to a Render Tri view to see the preview.

4. Over in the Shader Tree, take a look at the variety of materials for the different balls. You have plastic, glass, eggshell, and others. Each has been created based on what you've learned throughout the book, applying different color, variations in reflection and specularity, as well as transparency.

5. In the Render Properties panel, select the material named eggshell. This is one material that was intentionally left blank. Figure 13.8 shows the scene.

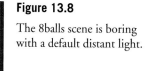

Figure 13.8

The 8balls scene is boring with a default distant light.

6. This scene as it stands has eight spheres set on a flat, textured plane. There is one default directional light in the scene. To begin, in the Material Ref tab of the Render Properties panel, set the eggshell material's diffuse color to white. Hold the Shift key, then click on the color values and drag to the right.

7. Choose Conserve Energy. This helps balance the reflection and color values.

8. Next, click to the Material Trans tab in the Render Properties panel.

9. You don't need this material to be transparent, nor do you need to set up a subsurface scattering value. What you do need is luminous intensity.

10. Set the Luminous Intensity value to 6. The material will be come fully opaque, as shown in Figure 13.9.

11. At this point, the bright white sphere just doesn't blend well in the scene, and perhaps the Luminous Intensity value is set too high. Before you make any changes, you're going to turn off the directional light and use global illumination to light the scene.

Note

Units for the luminous intensity of polygons are the same units you set for lights.

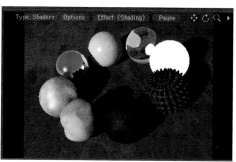

Figure 13.9

A very luminous object, the eggshell material is now overpowering the other balls.

12. In the Item List, select the Directional Light, right-click on it, and choose Delete to remove it from the scene. Figure 13.10 shows the deal.

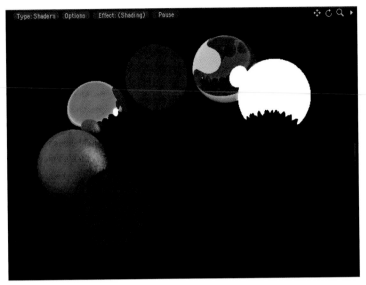

Figure 13.10

Without any light in the scene, various surfaces are still visible, but they lack much more.

13. In the Shader Tree, click the Render listing. Then, in the Render Properties panel, under the Global Illumination tab, enable Indirect Illumination. Let the Preview viewport update, and look what you get. Figure 13.11 shows the scene.

Figure 13.11

When the Indirect Illumination option is active, modo calculates the entire environment as a light source.

14. Because the entire environment is now calculated as a light source, the bright white eggshell material casts light onto the other balls. This gives the appearance of a lightbulb. Imagine now the variations you can make to this, perhaps creating neon tubes!

15. In the Shader Tree, change the eggshell material's diffuse color to yellow, 1.0, 1.0, 0.0. Then, in the Material Trans tab, set the Luminous Intensity value to 4.0. Figure 13.12 shows the result.

Note

If you're trying to make a light source out of geometry, it's a good idea to set all values to 0% except Luminous Intensity and Luminous Color.

Figure 13.12

A slight change to the eggshell surface, and the scene takes on a different look.

16. As you look at Figure 13.12, what do you think of? Perhaps early evening at a beach? Although you can think of the bright yellow sphere as a sort of campfire, with the other spheres gathered around, what really makes this shot feel like it's early evening outdoors is the environment. Click to the Environment Material in the Shader Tree.

17. Looking at Figure 13.13, notice that the Environment Material is set to an environment type of 4 Color Gradient. The zenith color, the color atop the 3D universe, is blue. The sky color is a pale blue, and the ground color is an evening blue. These colors give your scene its ambience. The nadir color, set to a deep green, is the color at the bottom of the 3D universe that encompasses the scene. This color doesn't play too much of a role here because the ground plane object blocks it.

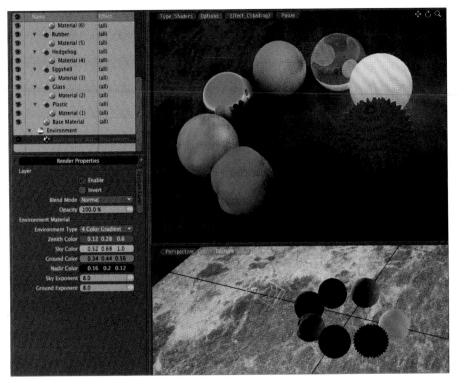

Figure 13.13

A very luminous object, the eggshell material is now overpowering the other balls.

Note

Setting the Environment Type is also setting a background color in modo.

18. You can do a few things to change the environment surrounding the spheres. The Environment Type can be set to Constant, which is one solid color. You can also choose a two-color gradient. Or, simply make changes here to the four-color gradient.

19. Set the zenith color to 1.0, 0.96, 0.94. This creates a soft, warm color. Apply this value to the sky color as well.

20. Set the ground color to a deeper version of the sky color, 0.91, 0.74, 0.42. Then, set the nadir color to a reddish orange, sort of a sunset color, about 0.67, 0.25, 0.13. Figure 13.14 shows the change.

What's more, you can change the sky exponent and ground exponent. This will scale the colors closer together or farther apart. Also notice that the bright eggshell sphere is still luminous and affecting the scene, but with more environment color, brighter environment color, the eggshell sphere appears to have less impact.

Because some of the surfaces on the spheres are reflective, such as the Chrome material, the material reflects the environment colors, as well as the other objects in the scene. This happens because of the ray tracing set within the Base Shader in the Shader Tree. The same goes for shadows.

Figure 13.14
By changing the environment colors, you change the entire look of the scene using global illumination.

Note

The main switch for ray tracing is on the Global Illumination tab of the Render Item. But, modo checks all shaders in the scene to make sure that reflections, refractions, and shadows are enabled before rendering.

But what about combining more elements, such as a light or object? You've seen through various projects in the book that a luminous white plane can act as a light source. The principle is the same as for the luminous sphere you're using here.

21. Add a 1 meter unit plane primitive to the scene. Do this by holding the Shift key and clicking the plane icon in the toolbar within the Basic tab.

22. The plane will be added directly to the middle of the scene, something like you see in Figure 13.15.

23. Select the plane in the Item List. Press **m** to set a material name of LightBox.

24. With the new plane still selected, press the **y** key to activate the Transform tool, and move the plane up and to the left of the spheres, as shown in Figure 13.16.

Note

So things aren't too busy in your scene, press the **o** key on your keyboard for viewport options. For Item Visibility, turn off Show Cameras.

Figure 13.15

Adding a plane to the scene dumps it right in the middle of the spheres.

Figure 13.16

Move the lightbox plane up and to the left of the spheres.

25. Then, rotate the plane so it's facing down toward the spheres, as shown in Figure 13.17. Remember that when the plane was created, the surface normal was facing upward. You'll need to rotate it up and over (about 120 degrees) to have it face toward the object.

Figure 13.17

Rotate the plane so it's pointing toward the spheres.

26. As it is now, this plane isn't doing much to the scene. Not a very good light-box! Select the lightbox material in the Shader Tree and click to the Material Trans tab in the Render Properties panel. Bring the Luminous Intensity value up to about 9. You'll see a light source appear from the front-left, looking at the Preview viewport. Figure 13.18 shows the result.

27. If the eggshell sphere had a Luminous Intensity value of 4 and lit the entire scene, then why would a value of 9 for the plane not show up that much? The reason is that the size of the plane can change its effect. Make sure your Action Center is set to Automatic. Then, with the lightbox plane selected, press the **r** key for scale. Click and drag on the center light-blue handle and scale the object up to about 400%. You can view the scale by clicking the Mesh tab within the Render Properties panel. This works similarly to an area light.

Now the lightbox is too bright and overpowers the scene, as you can see in Figure 13.19.

Figure 13.18

Adding a flat plane to the scene, making it luminous, starts to affect other objects, but not quite enough.

Figure 13.19

A large object creates a larger luminous area.

28. Back in the Material Trans tab, bring the Luminous Intensity value down to 4.

29. In the Shader Tree, select the Environment Material. Change the Environment Type to Constant and set the color to a deep brown that is not quite black, but close. Figure 13.20 shows the change in the scene.

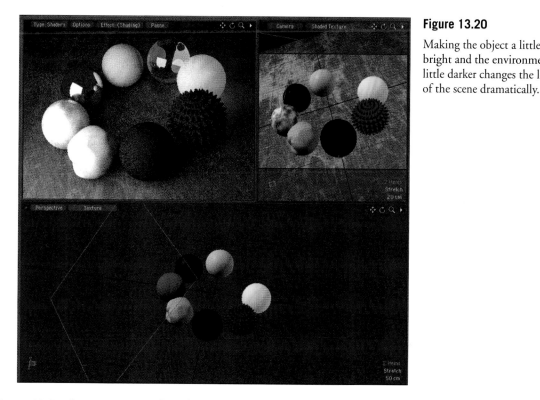

Figure 13.20

Making the object a little less bright and the environment a little darker changes the look of the scene dramatically.

30. Figure 13.21 shows an F9 render of the scene. The spheres on the left are a little hot—too bright. This is easily changed by adjusting their Diffuse values for the specific materials.

Note

If you select the Base Shader for your scene, you have a global intensity control for your scene's global illumination. Using the Indirect Illumination Multiplier, you can increase or decrease the intensity.

Lighting with global illumination in modo is a balance—a balance of color, light, luminosity, reflection values, shadows, and more. It's up to you to control this balance. You do this by studying other people's work. Find what you like, and more particularly, what you don't like. If you feel something is too bright or too dark, change it. Remember, you're the one driving.

Figure 13.21

A full render of the scene, lit with global illumination and ray tracing.

Try setting up one more render. This next project will use the corkboard you textured in Chapter 7.

1. Load the Corkboard_noLight.lxo scene from this chapter's project folder on the book's disc. Figure 13.22 shows the scene.

2. This scene does actually have a light, but it's a basic default directional light. Your goal is to light it so it's softer, like an interior light. To begin, change the current directional light to an area light. Right-click on the light in the Item List and select Change Item Type.

3. With the light changed to an area light, you can immediately notice a difference, as shown in Figure 13.23.

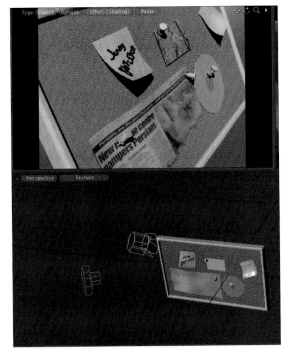

Figure 13.22

The corkboard scene from Chapter 7 loaded, but not lit too well.

4. There is a difference, but not necessarily a good one! First, the background has too much color, so you'll change that in a moment. Second, the light is not bright enough. If you remember the example of increasing the area width and height for an area light in the last chapter, you'll need to do that here. Select the light in the Item List and press the **y** key. Grab the light-blue square on the edge of the light (in a Perspective viewport) and drag it out. In the Render Properties panel, you'll see

Figure 13.23

Changing the directional light to an area light changes the look of the scene.

the Area Width value increase. Bring it to about 5.8m, as shown in Figure 13.24.

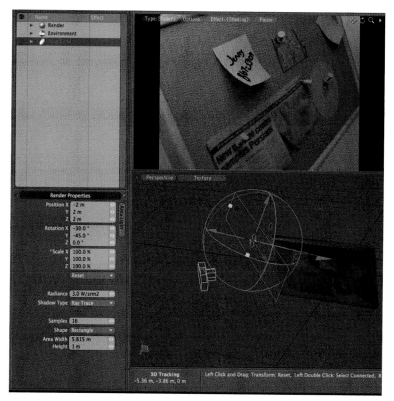

Figure 13.24

Increase the area width for the area light.

5. Increase the Area Height value to about 2.4m or so. Figure 13.25 shows the increase.

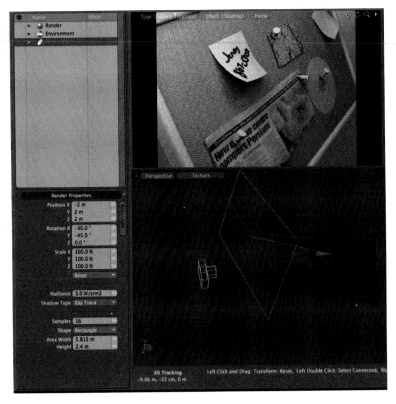

Figure 13.25

Increase the area height for the area light, and the shot is well lit.

6. In the Item List, right-click on the area light and create an instance.

7. Select the instance and move it to the right side of the corkboard, opposite of the original. Figure 13.26 shows the scene.

8. Change the backdrop color by selecting the Environmental Material, just as you did previously for the 8balls scene. Make it a constant and set it to black.

9. With the two area lights in place, you now have a corkboard lighting situation. What's that, you ask? Where do you usually find a corkboard? Perhaps in an office or a hallway at a school. The two area lights help create that effect with a more diffused lighting look and soft shadows.

10. Press F9 to render a frame.

You can experiment with different lighting situations on your own and adjust the global illumination values for different types of looks. The following section contains a few tips when setting up global illumination in modo.

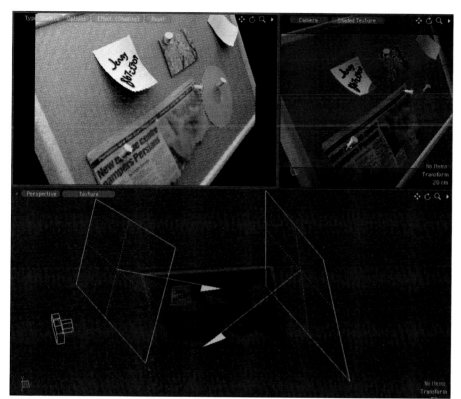

Figure 13.26

A copy of the area light helps light up the other side of the corkboard.

Noise and Render

A common problem users have with global illumination is noise. Some might call it grain, but it's actually noise (or variance). This happens when you try to estimate some sort of shading without enough samples. Using area lights will cause grain, and the larger the light, the more samples you'll need to avoid noise in your render.

In addition, objects in the scene casting shadows can also aid in creating grain, and to avoid this you can increase the number of rays in the light's Properties panel for better quality. If you are using indirect light, as you did throughout this chapter, when you have higher contrast and detail, more rays will be needed. You can control this using the Irradiance Rays setting in the Global Illumination panel. Irradiance caching must be turned on to set this. This setting performs finer or higher-quality evaluations of the scene. The irradiance rays are similar to indirect rays in that rays are fired out from a surface to calculate the indirect illumination. The higher this value, the more rays will be fired, and the more quality you'll achieve.

> **Note**
>
> If you have a more complex scene, you can use modo's limited region render to check how a shadow renders, or a specific portion of your model. Select Render from the Shader Tree. In the Tool properties, click the Region tab. Check on Limited Region, then set the values to render a specific region. Press F9 to render a full preview, then click and draw over a specific region to isolate and render again. Then, you can adjust values, such as increasing the rays, until the shadow is smooth and has less noise. Then, re-render the full frame.

If you are using a high-contrast HDR image, you might find that increasing the minimum spot in the Image Map properties helps eliminate noise. The same goes for using blurry reflections. The more you blur, the more rays you'll need for a cleaner render.

What's Next

As stressed throughout the book, always experiment on your own. But as a recommendation, when rendering, always perform one trick at a time. That is to say, set up your scene, and then set up one light. Render, and then see how you like it. From there, set up another light or an environment variable, render, and see how you like it. If grain appears, increase the rays and render again.

3D is about time. It's about experimentation and trial and error. It's also about your creative talent, so remember to explore your ideas as much as possible.

Now, move on to the final chapter to learn a little bit more about rendering and how you can output your scenes and images.

14

Outputs

It's always interesting to follow the user group forums and read the posts from people about 3D software. For whatever reason, the majority seem to be loyal to one 3D application only. Certainly, there's an investment in 3D, both in cost of the software and time to learn it. However, no single application can do it all. Each 3D application on the market today has its strengths and weaknesses, including Maya, LightWave, XSI, Cinema 4D, Max, and even modo.

Does this mean that one software is more or less superior to another? Absolutely not! To ride the bandwagon of software favoritism is childish, and it's something you shouldn't get wrapped up in. Truly, what is the point of getting a 3D application if you're going to spend all of your time whining on a public forum about which software is better or worse? You're better than that, and the Luxology team thinks so too. This is why modo is so flexible for your 3D pipeline. It is a program designed to work well with other applications. Figure 14.1 shows the Remapping section of the Preferences panel (also discussed earlier in the book). Here, you can see that the Luxology team has graciously made modo work to support other applications. Although it's important to learn modo with its default settings, you can set the input presets to any major 3D application.

The input presets are just one way modo allows you to work well with other 3D applications. However, the input presets are not necessary to play well with others.

Figure 14.1

In the Preferences panel, modo offers a variety of input presets.

Lack of Animation

By now, you've probably figured out that modo lacks the ability to animate. Sure, it's coming, but right now versions 201 and 202 do not animate. Like many, you don't just model, texture, and render for a living; rather, you animate! So how do you do this with modo?

One trick in modo allows you to render your model in motion. Figure 14.2 shows the Render Turntable option, found in the Render drop-down menu.

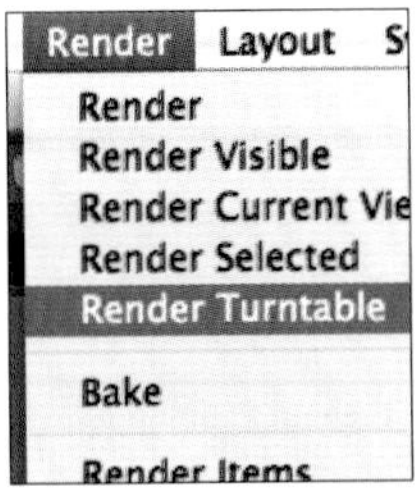

Figure 14.2

The Render Turntable option allows you to create a bit of motion directly out of modo.

This allows you to do a quick turntable render of your model. You can't keyframe, but you can set up a few options. Selecting the Render Turntable option opens a few settings, as shown in Figure 14.3.

Here, you can set the length of the render, as well as the frame rate. Additionally, you can save a movie or render in sequences. Part of the process also allows you to

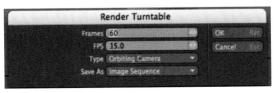

Figure 14.3

The Render Turntable feature offers a few options for saving an animation.

choose an orbiting camera or simply spin your model. And truly, that's the point of the turntable render, to spin your model. You can run this operation to preview your model from all angles and see how it reacts to light, reflections, and so on. This is also an excellent way to present your models to clients. Try it out!

When talking about render outputs, take a closer look at the options available in the Render menu. Figure 14.4 shows the full menu expanded.

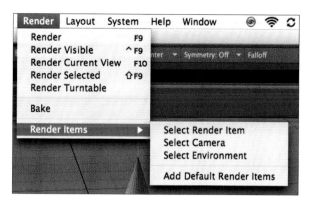

Figure 14.4

There are a few options for outputting your creations in the Render menu.

Render and Render Visible

The first choice in the Render menu is a full frame render, also accessed by pressing F9. You've done this throughout the book, but you can choose Ctrl+F9 to render visible. Suppose you have a large scene and are using auto visibility in the Item List. Pressing F9 will render your entire scene, regardless of what's visible from the Item List. Pressing Ctrl+F9 will render only the visible items from the Item List. Very handy!

Render Current View

The next option in the Render menu is Render Current View. How many times have you wanted to render directly from the Side or Top view? How about rendering your Perspective view? No problem. Just press F10, and the viewport you're using will be the shot you render, rather than a camera render (F9).

Render Selected

Similar to Render Visible, Render Selected allows you to select an item in your scene and, when pressing Shift+F9, render just that selection. This is exceedingly handy because you don't need to worry about auto visibility in the Item List. Just select an object, press Shift+F9, and go. The benefits of this are primarily for testing your render and saving time. Perhaps you're working on a complex scene and adding a new main element. As you continually tweak and update the textures, you don't want to waste time re-rendering everything in the scene just to see how this one element is coming along. And, rather than worry about changing visibility options in the Item List, you can simply use Render Selected.

Bake

There is also the option to Bake. You've probably heard the term *baking* when referring to many 3D programs. This is the process of precomputing texture and lighting information directly to an image map. This image map can then be

Note

To make items visible in the Item List, just click the eyeball icon in the left column next to the item you want to hide. To clarify, this hides visibility; it does not remove the item from the scene.

reimported into the 3D application and applied to the model. So rather than rendering every frame and having the computer calculate shadows, bumps, and reflections, they are already done and mapped onto the model. This is excellent for real-time environments, such as video games. The way this works is that complex shaders and lighting situations are often too complex to render in real time, but by having them precomputed to an image map, you can apply the rendered image to an existing UV texture.

In modo, render baking will render into the currently selected UV texture. Because of this, you need to make sure that you have the correct mesh layer selected, as well as the proper UV map. You can also bake directly to the Shader Tree by right-clicking (Command-clicking on the Mac) and choosing Bake. Baking textures from within the Shader Tree is beneficial for baking an effect, such as diffuse or color, into an image. This differs from the Bake option in the Render menu in that the latter takes into account all lighting and texturing in the image.

Render Items

Lastly in the Render menu, you have the options to choose your render items. You can choose to select Render Item, Camera, and Environment. Typically, you would select your render items from the Shader Tree and choose the appropriate render method, as described previously, such as F9, Ctrl+F9, and so on.

Saving Images

When you press F9, Ctrl+F9, Shift+F9, or otherwise in modo, your frame will render and you'll see the progress, as well as the buckets rendering in the Render Frame panel, as shown in Figure 14.5.

As you can see from Figure 14.5, as you render, the orange squares appear throughout the panel. These are the render buckets, and they will vary based on the settings you've set up for them, such as their size, bucket order, and so on. When your render is complete, the Save Image button is active in the top-right of the Render Frame panel. Click it, and you'll be able to save the rendered image, as shown in Figure 14.6.

modo offers a wide variety of image formats, from TGA, to TIF, to XPM and OpenEXR.

It's very important to know that once you close the Render Frame window, either by choosing Close Window or by pressing the Esc key on your keyboard, your render is still available to you. modo 202 offers nine slots that save your renders. It is a good idea to save your renders by choosing the Save Image button in the render window. However, here's a trick you can use to automatically save an image after rendering, completely unattended.

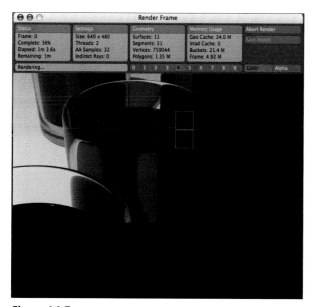

Figure 14.5

The Render Frame panel appears when you choose a render option, such as F9.

Figure 14.6

After you render a frame, you can click Save Image from the Render Frame panel.

Auto Save Render

Like many, you might press the Esc key on your keyboard simply by habit. Or, you might lose your rendered frame, and depending on what you're creating, it could be hours of work. So, use the Render Turntable option as a way to save your frame! Select the Render Turntable option. In the Options panel that appears, instead of the default 60 for Frames, set this value to 1. Tell modo to render just one frame. Then, set the type to Orbiting Camera and choose Image Sequence for the Save As option. Click OK, and you'll be presented with a dialog box asking where to save the image. Give it a name, a place to be saved, and a format such as TGA or JPG, and click OK. modo will then proceed to render the image and save it for you.

Additionally, the Render Frame panel will still appear, and after the render is finished, you can select Save Image and save the image in a different format as a safety precaution.

Outputting Models

When you are talking about working with other 3D applications and modo, it's important to understand how this application allows you to export your models.

From the File menu, you can choose Export As, as shown in Figure 14.7.

When you select this option, modo offers you options to bring your models to other 3D applications. Figure 14.8 shows the choices available to you.

You can choose from a variety of options, including X3D, a new Web 3D standard formally known as VRML. If you're going to animate your model, you might be exporting to LightWave or Maya, and you can choose between .LWO for LightWave and .FBX, .MA, or .OBJ for Maya.

When you import your exported model, depending on what format you chose, you might not be able to export all shading information. modo will tell you this as necessary. From there, open your 3D application and import the model.

This is not to say your model will only export as a default white clay-looking object. It means that depending on what you've assigned in modo, it might not be compatible with your chosen 3D application. Here, it's a matter of testing depending on where you're sending your model. However, you can count on base shading to transfer quite well, including color, diffuse, specular, and so on.

If you've created image maps, either imported or painted, you can simply reapply those in your animation application. The UV data will keep with the model, so any UV maps you've created simply need to be reassigned. Again, each situation is different, and it's up to you to export your model and experiment with what works and what doesn't work based on your applications.

Figure 14.7

Choosing Export As from the File menu allows you to send your model to other 3D applications.

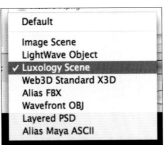

Figure 14.8

Once you select the Export As option, you're presented with various output choices.

There are a few things to know about exporting models beyond color and shading. Certain programs, such as LightWave, might not like how you create your model. For example, modo supports subdivisional surfaces, or n-gons. This means that geometry can be subdivided with three or five or nine vertices. LightWave through version 8.5 could only use subdivisions with three or four vertices. However, LightWave v9 now supports Catmull-Clark subdivisions, allowing you to import models from modo that are subdivided beyond three or four vertices.

Another aspect to know is that any edge weights you apply in modo will not transfer to LightWave. They will, however, stay with your model when exporting to Maya.

Your Next Step

So now we've come to the end of the book. Hopefully the information on these pages, as well the videos on the DVD, have helped you grasp this amazing program. Be aware that modo is constantly evolving, and you should check the Luxology Web site often for updates.

From here, you can experiment on your own and tackle almost any modeling project. The challenge with any 3D application is to forget about the buttons and panels and concentrate on your model. The goal of this book is to help ease your pain in learning a new application so that you're spending more time creating and less time trying to get a tool to work or figuring out what it does. Although there are many technical aspects and intricacies within modo that are spelled out in the modo manual, this book has helped you use the program. The combination of the modo manual and this book makes a great mix, and you should refer to the modo manual often for definitions of terms and concepts. To further enhance your learning, check out the appendixes for links to key Web sites focused around modo and general 3D.

Thank you for supporting this book! Your commitment to 3D and modo is appreciated. Please let us know if you have any questions and suggestions for future publications and training videos. For more information on modo training, visit 3DGarage.com. For book support and errata, visit www.danablan.com. You can also contact the publisher directly with publication questions at www.courseptr.com.

Part V
Appendixes

A

Reference Materials

No matter how complete a software product is, and no matter how thorough a book may be, there's always room for more information. Because of that, I've put together a nice list of resources that not only relate to modo, but relate to 3D as well. It's important to gain as much knowledge of 3D modeling, 3D space, color, light, and cinematography as you can. All of these real-world principles can play a role in your quest for the perfect modo creation.

Web Sites Related to modo for Discussion and Information

- Get your own full working demo of modo! Visit www.modo3d.com today.

- Luxology's own forums: http://forums.luxology.com/discussion

- 3D Garage.com for video training: http://www.3dgarage.com

- Vertex Monkey for scripts and info: http://www.vertexmonkey.com

- CGTalk for discussions: http://forums.cgsociety.org

- modo mode—Japan: http://popover.blogzine.jp/weblog

- Yahoo Groups: http://groups.yahoo.com/group/Luxology

- CGarchitect: http://www.cgarchitect.com/vb/129-modo

- CGFocus: http://cgfocus.com/forums

- Lighting: http://3drender.com

- Animation and effects: http://www.vfxworld.com

- Studies on various topics: http://www.pixelcorps.com

- Paul Debevec: http://www.debevec.org

Reflection Properties

Table A.1 presents a good mix of materials and their basic reflective properties. There are many factors that affect an item's reflectivity, so use these values as a starting point.

Table A.1 Percentage of Incident Light Reflected by Various Materials

Material	%
Aluminum	45
Aluminum Foil	65
Asphalt	14
Brass	40
Brick	30
Bronze	10
Chrome	70
Copper	71
Earth, Moist	08
Gold	84
Graphite	20
Green Leaf	21
Iron	15
Linen	81
Marble, White	53
Mercury	69
Paper, Newsprint	61
Paper, White	71
Pewter	20
Platinum	64
Porcelain, White	72
Quartz	81
Rubber	02
Silicon	28
Silver	90
Slate	06
Stainless Steel	37
Steel	55
Tin Can	40
Vinyl	15
Wood, Pine	40

Refraction Properties

Table A.2 displays an extensive list of items. Certainly you won't use all of these properties, but they're a good reference to have just the same. Indices of refraction for various elements, materials, liquids, and gases at STP (*Standard Temperature and Pressure*) in visible light are listed.

Table A.2 Indices of Refraction

Material	Index	Material	Index
Vacuum	1.000 (Exactly)	Beryl	1.577
Acetone	1.360	Beryllonite	1.553
Actinolite	1.618	Brazilianite	1.603
Agalmatoite	1.550	Bromine (liquid)	1.661
Agate	1.544	Bronze	1.180
Agate, Moss	1.540	Brownite	1.567
Air	1.000	Calcite	1.486
Alcohol	1.329	Calspar1	1.660
Alexandrite	1.745	Calspar2	1.486
Aluminum	1.440	Cancrinite	1.491
Amber	1.546	Carbon Dioxide (gas)	1.000
Amblygonite	1.611	Carbon Dioxide (liquid)	1.200
Amethyst	1.544	Carbon Disulfide	1.628
Amorphous Selenium	2.920	Carbon Tetrachloride	1.460
Anatase	2.490	Cassiterite	1.997
Andalusite	1.641	Celestite	1.622
Anhydrite	1.571	Cerussite	1.804
Apatite	1.632	Ceylanite	1.770
Apophyllite	1.536	Chalcedony	1.530
Aquamarine	1.577	Chalk	1.510
Aragonite	1.530	Chalybite	1.630
Argon	1.000	Chlorine (gas)	1.000
Asphalt	1.635	Chlorine (liquid)	1.385
Augelite	1.574	Chrome Green	2.400
Axinite	1.675	Chrome Red	2.420
Azurite	1.730	Chrome Yellow	2.310
Barite	1.636	Chromium	2.970
Barytocalcite	1.684	Chromium Oxide	2.705
Benitoite	1.757	Chrysoberyl	1.745
Benzene	1.501	Chrysocolla	1.500

Material	Index	Material	Index
Chrysoprase	1.534	Feldspar, Oligoclase	1.539
Citrine	1.550	Feldspar, Orthoclase	1.525
Clinozoisite	1.724	Fluoride	1.560
Cobalt Blue	1.740	Fluorite	1.434
Cobalt Green	1.970	Formica	1.470
Cobalt Violet	1.710	Garnet, Almandine	1.760
Colemanite	1.586	Garnet, Almandite	1.790
Copper	1.100	Garnet, Andradite	1.820
Copper Oxide	2.705	Garnet, Demantoid	1.880
Coral	1.486	Garnet, Grossular	1.738
Material	Index	Garnet, Hessonite	1.745
Cordierite	1.540	Garnet, Rhodolite	1.760
Corundum	1.766	Garnet, Spessartite	1.810
Crocoite	2.310	Gaylussite	1.517
Crown Glass	1.520	Glass	1.517
Crystal	2.000	Glass, Albite	1.489
Cuprite	2.850	Glass, Crown	1.520
Danburite	1.633	Glass, Crown, Zinc	1.517
Diamond	2.417	Glass, Flint, Dense	1.660
Diopside	1.680	Glass, Flint, Heaviest	1.890
Dolomite	1.503	Glass, Flint, Heavy	1.655
Dumortierite	1.686	Glass, Flint, Lanthanum	1.800
Ebonite	1.660	Glass, Flint, Light	1.580
Ekanite	1.600	Glass, Flint, Medium	1.627
Elaeolite	1.532	Glycerine	1.473
Emerald	1.576	Gold	0.470
Emerald, Synth flux	1.561	Hambergite	1.559
Emerald, Synth hydro	1.568	Hauynite	1.502
Enstatite	1.663	Helium	1.000
Epidote	1.733	Hematite	2.940
Ethyl Alcohol (Ethanol)	1.360	Hemimorphite	1.614
Euclase	1.652	Hiddenite	1.655
Fabulite	2.409	Howlite	1.586
Feldspar, Adventurine	1.532	Hydrogen (gas)	1.000
Feldspar, Albite	1.525	Hydrogen (liquid)	1.097
Feldspar, Amazonite	1.525	Hypersthene	1.670
Feldspar, Labradorite	1.565	Ice	1.309
Feldspar, Microcline	1.525	Idocrase	1.713

Material	Index	Material	Index
Iodine Crystal	3.340	Periclase	1.740
Iolite	1.548	Peridot	1.654
Iron	1.510	Peristerite	1.525
Ivory	1.540	Petalite	1.502
Jade, Nephrite	1.610	Phenakite	1.650
Jadeite	1.665	Phosgenite	2.117
Jasper	1.540	Plastic	1.460
Jet	1.660	Plexiglass	1.500
Kornerupine	1.665	Polystyrene	1.550
Kunzite	1.655	Prase	1.540
Kyanite	1.715	Prasiolite	1.540
Lapis Gem	1.500	Prehnite	1.610
Lapis Lazuli	1.610	Proustite	2.790
Lazulite	1.615	Purpurite	1.840
Lead	2.010	Pyrite	1.810
Leucite	1.509	Pyrope	1.740
Material	Index	Quartz	1.544
Magnesite	1.515	Quartz, Fused	1.458
Malachite	1.655	Rhodizite	1.690
Meerschaum	1.530	Rhodochrisite	1.600
Mercury (liquid)	1.620	Rhodonite	1.735
Methanol	1.329	Rock Salt	1.544
Moldavite	1.500	Rubber, Natural	1.519
Moonstone, Adularia	1.525	Ruby	1.760
Moonstone, Albite	1.535	Rutile	2.610
Natrolite	1.480	Sanidine	1.522
Nephrite	1.600	Sapphire	1.760
Nitrogen (gas)	1.000	Scapolite	1.540
Nitrogen (liquid)	1.205	Scapolite, Yellow	1.555
Nylon	1.530	Scheelite	1.920
Obsidian	1.489	Selenium, Amorphous	2.920
Olivine	1.670	Serpentine	1.560
Onyx	1.486	Shell	1.530
Opal	1.450	Silicon	4.240
Oxygen (gas)	1.000	Sillimanite	1.658
Oxygen (liquid)	1.221	Silver	0.180
Painite	1.787	Sinhalite	1.699
Pearl	1.530	Smaragdite	1.608

Material	Index
Smithsonite	1.621
Sodalite	1.483
Sodium Chloride	1.544
Sphalerite	2.368
Sphene	1.885
Spinel	1.712
Spodumene	1.650
Staurolite	1.739
Steatite	1.539
Steel	2.500
Stichtite	1.520
Strontium Titanate	2.410
Styrofoam	1.595
Sugar Solution (30%)	1.380
Sugar Solution (80%)	1.490
Sulphur	1.960
Synthetic Spinel	1.730
Taaffeite	1.720
Tantalite	2.240
Tanzanite	1.691
Teflon	1.350
Thomsonite	1.530
Tiger eye	1.544
Topaz	1.620
Topaz, Blue	1.610
Topaz, Pink	1.620
Topaz, White	1.630
Topaz, Yellow	1.620
Tourmaline	1.624
Tremolite	1.600
Tugtupite	1.496
Turpentine	1.472
Turquoise	1.610
Ulexite	1.490
Uvarovite	1.870
Variscite	1.550
Vivianite	1.580
Wardite	1.590

Material	Index
Water (gas)	1.000
Water 100°C	1.318
Water 20°C	1.333
Water 35°C (room temperature)	1.331
Willemite	1.690
Witherite	1.532
Wulfenite	2.300
Zinc Crown Glass	1.517
Zincite	2.010
Zircon, High	1.960
Zircon, Low	1.800
Zirconia, Cubic	2.170

B

What's on the DVD

The accompanying DVD has been provided as an additional bonus to the book. The following sections contain descriptions of the DVD's contents and how to use the content included for the tutorials in this book. In addition, exclusive video tutorials have been included just for this book, direct from 3D Garage (www.3dgarage.com). These video tutorials will help you get up to speed quickly and easily with modo 201/202.

For specific information about the use of this DVD, please review the ReadMe.txt file in the DVD's root directory. This file includes important disclaimer information, as well as information about installation, system requirements, troubleshooting, and technical support.

DVD Contents

We've literally packed the DVD with hours of video and cool resources to enhance your learning. On the DVD, you'll find:

- Four and a half hours of additional video tutorials to complement the chapters, exclusively from 3D Garage.com Here's a list of the videos:

CH1_QuickStart.mov	15:16
CH2_TheWorkplane.mov	3:36
CH5_LegoBlock.mov	10:44
CH5_ImageSynth.mov	8:34
CH7_ShaderTree.mov	18:16
CH9_RockTexture_1.mov	9:44
CH9_RockTexture_2.mov	8:07
CH9_RockTexture_3.mov	8:00
CH9_RockTexture_4.mov	15:05
CH9_RockTexture_5.mov	14:54
CH10_Stoplight_1.mov	8:10
CH10_Stoplight_2.mov	11:01
CH10_Stoplight_3.mov	22:39
CH10_Stoplight_4.mov	21:10
CH10_Stoplight_5.mov	8:23
CH11_PaintIntro.mov	6:38
CH11_CandleSSS.mov	11:09
CH12_Character.mov	Online at www.3dgarage.com
CH12_ToyGun.mov	Online at www.3dgarage.com
CH13_Morphs.mov	4:32
	203:18 minutes

- You'll also find 3D Garage appendix videos:

A_HelpFiles	1:28
B_CameraBasics	6:20
C_PaintingBumps	3:18
D_ActionCenters	5:44
E_ReferenceCoordinates	1:51
F_BackdropImages	6:14
G_Mac_Preferences	4:09
H_PC_Preferences	6:48
I_SplineStuff	7:03
J_UsingHDR	2:49
Painting	14:39
GradientClouds	12:16

■ One-hundred seventy-five high-resolution, royalty-free textures and backgrounds from Dan Ablan. Use these photos as texture maps, backgrounds, or reference photos. There's quite a few that will work well in Luxology's imageSynth Photoshop tool.

Using the Video Files

To play the 3D Garage video tutorials supplied on the book's DVD, you'll need to install the proper codec. The Appendix videos have been recorded using TechSmith's EnSharpen codec and work on both PC and Mac. To play the video files on a PC or Mac, just install the EnSharpen decoder, which allows the QuickTime movies to play back. You'll need QuickTime, and an install has been provided for you. All other QuickTime movies use the Sorenson3 video codec and should play without issue.

The video tutorials are supplements to the chapters, some of which coincide with the tutorials in the book and some of which stand on their own. Be sure to check out all of them for additional tips and tricks.

For more video training and full modo courseware, visit www.3dgarage.com.

System Requirements

This DVD was configured for use on systems running Windows XP and Macintosh OS X.

Please view the Read-Me text file on the DVD for complete information on the free DVD third-party content.

We've worked hard to make sure the contents of this DVD are just as useful as this book. The combination of the two makes this a tremendous resource. Enjoy!

Index

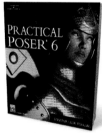

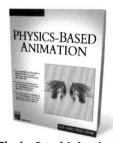

License Agreement/Notice of Limited Warranty

By opening the sealed disc container in this book, you agree to the following terms and conditions. If, upon reading the following license agreement and notice of limited warranty, you cannot agree to the terms and conditions set forth, return the unused book with unopened disc to the place where you purchased it for a refund.

License:

The enclosed software is copyrighted by the copyright holder(s) indicated on the software disc. You are licensed to copy the software onto a single computer for use by a single user and to a backup disc. You may not reproduce, make copies, or distribute copies or rent or lease the software in whole or in part, except with written permission of the copyright holder(s). You may transfer the enclosed disc only together with this license, and only if you destroy all other copies of the software and the transferee agrees to the terms of the license. You may not decompile, reverse assemble, or reverse engineer the software.

Notice of Limited Warranty:

The enclosed disc is warranted by Thomson Course Technology PTR to be free of physical defects in materials and workmanship for a period of sixty (60) days from end user's purchase of the book/disc combination. During the sixty-day term of the limited warranty, Thomson Course Technology PTR will provide a replacement disc upon the return of a defective disc.

Limited Liability:

THE SOLE REMEDY FOR BREACH OF THIS LIMITED WARRANTY SHALL CONSIST ENTIRELY OF REPLACEMENT OF THE DEFECTIVE DISC. IN NO EVENT SHALL THOMSON COURSE TECHNOLOGY PTR OR THE AUTHOR BE LIABLE FOR ANY OTHER DAMAGES, INCLUDING LOSS OR CORRUPTION OF DATA, CHANGES IN THE FUNCTIONAL CHARACTERISTICS OF THE HARDWARE OR OPERATING SYSTEM, DELETERIOUS INTERACTION WITH OTHER SOFTWARE, OR ANY OTHER SPECIAL, INCIDENTAL, OR CONSEQUENTIAL DAMAGES THAT MAY ARISE, EVEN IF THOMSON COURSE TECHNOLOGY PTR AND/OR THE AUTHOR HAS PREVIOUSLY BEEN NOTIFIED THAT THE POSSIBILITY OF SUCH DAMAGES EXISTS.

Disclaimer of Warranties:

THOMSON COURSE TECHNOLOGY PTR AND THE AUTHOR SPECIFICALLY DISCLAIM ANY AND ALL OTHER WARRANTIES, EITHER EXPRESS OR IMPLIED, INCLUDING WARRANTIES OF MERCHANTABILITY, SUITABILITY TO A PARTICULAR TASK OR PURPOSE, OR FREEDOM FROM ERRORS. SOME STATES DO NOT ALLOW FOR EXCLUSION OF IMPLIED WARRANTIES OR LIMITATION OF INCIDENTAL OR CONSEQUENTIAL DAMAGES, SO THESE LIMITATIONS MIGHT NOT APPLY TO YOU.

Other:

This Agreement is governed by the laws of the State of Massachusetts without regard to choice of law principles. The United Convention of Contracts for the International Sale of Goods is specifically disclaimed. This Agreement constitutes the entire agreement between you and Thomson Course Technology PTR regarding use of the software.